Ouida

Pascarel

Only a Story

Ouida

Pascarel
Only a Story

ISBN/EAN: 9783742821843

Manufactured in Europe, USA, Canada, Australia, Japa

Cover: Foto ©Andreas Hilbeck / pixelio.de

Manufactured and distributed by brebook publishing software (www.brebook.com)

Ouida

Pascarel

COLLECTION
OF
BRITISH AUTHORS

TAUCHNITZ EDITION.

VOL. 1316.

PASCARÈL BY OUIDA.

IN TWO VOLUMES.

VOL. I.

TAUCHNITZ EDITION.

By the same Author,

IDALIA	2 vols.
TRICOTRIN	2 vols.
PUCK	2 vols.
CHANDOS	2 vols.
STRATHMORE	2 vols.
UNDER TWO FLAGS	2 vols.
FOLLE-FARINE	2 vols.
A LEAF IN THE STORM	1 vol.
CECIL CASTLEMAINE'S GAGE	1 vol.
MADAME LA MARQUISE	1 vol.
HELD IN BONDAGE	2 vols.
TWO LITTLE WOODEN SHOES	1 vol.
SIGNA	3 vols.
IN A WINTER CITY	1 vol.
ARIADNÊ	2 vols.

PASCARÈL.

ONLY A STORY.

BY

OUIDA,

AUTHOR OF "TRICOTRIN," "CHANDOS," ETC.

COPYRIGHT EDITION.

IN TWO VOLUMES.

VOL. I.

LEIPZIG
BERNHARD TAUCHNITZ
1873.

"Se
Non Ami
Firenze,
Questo Libro
Ti
Noferà."

"LOVE IS ENOUGH; though the World be a waning,
And the woods have no voice but the voice of complaining,
Though the sky be too dark for dim eyes to discover,
The gold-cups and daisies fair blossoming thereunder,
Though the hills be held shadows, and the sea a dark wonder,
And this day draw a veil over all deeds passed over,
Yet their hands shall not tremble, their feet shall not falter;
The void shall not weary, the fear shall not alter,
Those lips and those eyes of the loved and the lover."

TO THE READER.

WITH feminine obstinacy the Donzella sacrifices truth to pictorial effect, and justice to high-coloured contrast, touching Rome.* The love that Rome begets is different to that which Florence inspires; but it is never less strong and is even more reverent; less familiar, and more close on awe; as tender, but more solemn. In Rome, Art and Nature strain together in perpetual conflict for supremacy; a struggle of a Titan with a God that holds mortal onlookers breathless: in Florence, Art and Nature clasp hands and smile on men, and even the Mercury Agoreus, being in Florence, borrows the flowers of Dionysus to deck his scales of barter. But who, with any power of vision or soul of artist in them, can live a day blind to the vast and sublime beauties of the Capital of the World?—who can fail to grow at once the humbler and the greater by dwelling on that sacred soil?—who will not draw nearer to God himself as they see how mighty human genius can be?—who will not yield to Rome a

* Vol. I, p. 165.

homage that is a passion as well as a religion? If any such there be, let them see the sun fall once on the face of the Faun, let them see the moon shine once on the Palace of the Cæsars:—and surely they will repent.

OUIDA.

ROME, *Feb.* 12, 1873.

CONTENTS

OF VOLUME I.

BOOK I.
THE CITY OF CATULLUS.

			Page
CHAPTER I.	King Carnival		13
— II.	The Bird and the Fates		15
— III.	By the Broken Donatello		25
— IV.	With the Popolani		42
— V.	The Peacock's Plumes		60
— VI.	Mater Dolorosa		70
— VII.	A Twilight Tale		73
— VIII.	The Little Red Box		84

BOOK II.
THE CITY OF LILIES.

— I.	The Gifts of Gala		92
— II.	The Veglione Masquer		101
— III.	The Last Sleep		113
— IV.	At Ave Maria		115
— V.	The Feast of Faustino		122
— VI.	Fuori		129
— VII.	Under the Garisenda		140
— VIII.	The Maidenhair		148

		Page
CHAPTER IX. The Snow-flower		156
— X. La Reine du Moyenage		161
— XI. The Midnight Fair		170
— XII. With the Wild Crocus		174
— XIII. The Great Magician		189

BOOK III.

THE DAUGHTER OF HERCULES.

— I. Under the Red Lily		206
— II. The Rose and the Florins		220
— III. The Golden Celandine		242
— IV. Beside Dead Fires		251
— V. Giudentu dell' Anno		263
— VI. The Old Star Tower		264
— VII. Due Amori		268
— VIII. The Lily-queen		279

BOOK IV.

THE WANDERING ARTE.

— I. Il Bianco Aspetto		288
— II. Etoile qui file		294
— III. The Riband and the Mandoline		304
— IV. The Poets' Country		310
— V. Fuma di Gloria		320

PASCARÈL.

BOOK I.

THE CITY OF CATULLUS.

CHAPTER I.
King Carnival.

It was the first day of Carnival.

The populace was out all over the city in a many-coloured and ever-changing swarm of human life. The gay masque reeled madly round the marble iron-bound flanks of the Duomo, and flung its hail of toys and flowers against the frowning masses of the old palaces and prisons; and surged in its foam of mirth and mischief all along the length of the green Adige in the light of the winter noon.

For a month King Carnival would reign supreme in mockery and merriment over the lives of men; his path strewn with violets, his sovereignty shouted over wine, his dynasty proclaimed far and wide—everywhere, by high and low, from the cobbler who pranked himself in the guise of Stenterello to the great lady who laughed through her velvet mask of Venice.

And at the month's end, at nightfall, just as the moon should rise, with music and many a jest and sound of horn and drum, and rioting of Arlecchino and Pulcinello and all their immemorial brotherhood, at nightfall the fickle people would lead the old King out to his funeral pyre in the great square, and there would burn him in all pomp and cruelty until the flames should redden grim Roland standing at his vigil at the cathedral doors, and be seen afar off, where the last outposts of the great Alps kept watch and ward in the quiet of the silence and the chillness of the snow.

Burn him,—a monarch yesterday, to-day a scapegoat, in grimmest ironic symbol of all human histories.

Poor King Carnival!

His rule has lasted longer than any other dynasty; for though his nations burn him one year, he rises from his ashes, and they cry All hail! to him the next.

But the axe is at the root of his throne. The old glad days of his mumming are numbered, and the pomp of his pageant is shorn. The world is old and very weary.

Here "nel aer dolce, che del sol s'allegra," life is brighter and more buoyant than elsewhere.

Here the people still laugh from clear throats, and the hours still reel away, marked with flowers; here they sit in the sun, and still know the priceless pleasures and true uses of leisure; and here the heart of a child still beats in the war-scarred breast of the nation.

Yet even here the world is older, greyer, sadder than of yore; and even here the day is close at hand when King Carnival will ride his last ride round the city walls, and be burned for the last time, in all the panoply of his historic robes, upon a pyre whence his ashes shall never rise again.

'The world is too wise to be foolish—so they say. Or is it too foolish to be wise?

King Carnival might tell us if he would. Perhaps he would answer:—

"In the days when men were so great that they did not fear to stoop, and were so strong that their dignity lost nothing by their mirth, they rode in my train and followed me—Carnivale, the old King—and laughed as children laugh—those men of those days of Dante, of those days of Lionardo, of those days of Shakspeare. Are you wiser than they? or weaker? or only more weary, perhaps? No matter. I have held high feast with the giants, and they were not ashamed to be glad. But you, who blush for your mirth because your mirth is vice, bury me quickly. I am a thing of the Past."

And the old King would speak sadly aright; for his name is almost emptiness, and his earth-swaying orb is but now an empty gourd in which the shrivelled beans of the world's spent pleasures are shaken in fruitless sport and sound.

For in the old days,—when he reigned supreme, over all men's lives, from sovereign's to serf's, for a few weeks' span of full feast and fair folly,—in the old days men lived greatly great lives to great ends.

Their faith was ever present with them—a thing of daily use and hourly sweetness. Their households were wisely ruled and simply ordered. They denuded themselves of their substance to give their gold to the raising of mighty works—*vivis lapidibus*—which to this day do live and speak.

Great artists narrowed not themselves to one meagre phase of art, but filled with all its innumerable powers the splendid plenitude of their majestic years.

And that art was in the hearts of the people who followed it, and adored its power and were nourished by it, so that it was no empty name, but an ever-vivifying presence—a divinity at once of hearth and temple that brooded over the cities with sheltering and stainless love.

Therefore in those days men, giving themselves leave to be glad for a little space, were glad with the same sinewy force and manful singleness of purpose as made them in other times laborious, self-denying, patient, and fruitful of high thoughts and deeds.

Because they laboured for their fellows, therefore they could laugh with them, and because they served God, therefore they dared be glad.

In those grave, dauntless, austere lives the Carnival's jocund revelry was as one golden bead in a pilgrim's rosary of thorn-berries.

They had aimed highly and highly achieved; therefore they could go forth amidst their children and rejoice.

But we—in whom all art is the mere empty Shibboleth of a ruined religion whose priests are all dead; we—whose whole year-long course is one Dance of Death over the putridity of our pleasures; we—whose solitary purpose it is to fly faster and faster from desire to satiety, from satiety to desire, in an endless eddy of fruitless effort; we—whose greatest genius can only raise for us some inarticulate protest of despair against some unknown God;—we have strangled King Carnival and killed him, and buried him in the ashes of our own unutterable weariness and woe.

For the old King is heartsick to hear the manful laughter that he heard in his youth; and we—we cannot laugh; all we can give is a sneer—and a sob.

CHAPTER II.
The Bird and the Fates.

NEVERTHELESS in Verona this first day of Carnival men made believe to be glad.

In the deep wintry gloom of the old sad city the gold of the alien tyranny had been scattered broadcast that the people might wear at least the mask of contentment; and on the whole they wore it, nothing loth, grinning gleefully from ear to ear.

The old stone balconies were draped with amber and rose and silver; the beautiful trecento windows were filled with eager faces; the dusky crypt-like streets were full of colour and tumult; the great marble tombs, looming white in the darkness of their sepulchres, were flecked with the pretty pallor of violets from Rome.

Verona under her taskmasters took holiday.

Under a deep porch, sculptured with vine foliage and the heads of griffins, two children stood looking on the pageantry, and not thinking very much about it; for one of them—the girl,—was full of trouble, and the boy tried his best to solace her.

"Do look at Stenterello!" the little lad murmured. "How nimble he is—look, look! the boys have caught him. No!—he slips through like an eel. Ah, ah! do look! There is Arlecchino angling for a priest's hat with a gilded fishing-hook. Oh, carina mia! to think you have no heart to laugh to-day—"

The tears brimmed over in his companion's eyes.

"How can I laugh? We have nothing—absolutely nothing. We must sell those poor little jewels of my mother's, or Mariuccia will starve. It must not be, you know; she is so old, so old! And yet to sell the jewels! See here, 'Ino. I have a voice, and I am fifteen years old, and I am good to look at, you all say. Why should I not sing in the choruses? You know how often we have laughed at them—the fat ugly women with the crowns that would always tumble off. Now I am as thin as a cane, and am handsome, and could wear a crown as one should be worn. Why might I not sing in the chorus?"

The pretty boy looked perplexed, and his little bare foot traced nervously an arabesque on the stone of the dusty stair.

"That would never do, dear donzella! Your father is too illustrious——"

"But one cannot live on being illustrious. One wants to eat—somehow. And there is nothing to eat. Nothing. We have not heard of my father for more than a year, and Florio even does not send now. Why should I not sing in the chorus? It is quite easy, all that sort of music."

He shook his pretty, curly, golden, Venetian head, in grave concern.

"Oh no, dear donzella; it would never do. Mariuccia would never allow it. It is so late at night, and the women are not fit for you: it would never do."

"Then the jewels must go? And they are all that I have of my mother's—the only, only, little thing!"

The words ended in a sob; and the whirling, many-coloured procession of the Carnival was hidden from the child's sight by a haze of sudden tears.

At home there were an empty cupboard, a cold hearth, and an old woman of eighty years, who had not broken her fast. Such things seem hard to bear when one is very young; and it is the first day of Carnival; and beneath there, in the street, all the mad and merry masque is flaunting on its way.

The boy listened wistfully, with a tender and anxious face.

"See here, dear donzella," he murmured, after a pause. "I have a thought. Sing in the chorus you must not; but why not sing in the streets? The people are all happy and good-tempered to-day. I have got my lute here, and we will sing, and then ask them frankly to help us. Why not? We have made music for them often out of pure love and goodwill. They will certainly give us a little money now, and no harm done."

"Oh, 'Ino! You never sang for money yet, nor I. It is so different——"

"We have not sung for it, because we have not wanted it. But if we do want it, where is the harm——"

"It is shameful!"

"Shameful! How shameful? When the great singer Lillo went through here last spring, do you not remember that the least atom of standing room in the theatre was worth gold, and the people took the horses from his carriage, and drew him through the streets, shouting and smothering him with Easter lilies?"

"That is very different."

"Not at all different. Except that they pay Lillo by millions and we only want a few florins."

"But why, then, will you never take money when you play yourself? You never do."

He crossed himself, and glanced gratefully at an old battered, black-faced Madonna that hung behind an iron grating high up above in the doorway.

"Our Lady has been so good to me, and I have never wanted for anything. And the people who would have paid me have always been so poor—so poor. But I would play for money rather than sell a thing of my mother's. Perhaps your mother up there says to Our Lady,—'Look at my donzella; she is proud: take that sin out of her heart.' And Our Lady says,—'We will prove her: she must love you a little, though she never looked on your face.' And so Our Lady sets this thing in your way. And your mother up there waits, watching and trembling, to see if indeed you do love her, or only care for your pride. For mothers never forget. That I am very sure. No, not though they sit on the right hand of God with His angels."

The boy's voice was very sweet and solemn, and murmured with a strange softness and clearness through the riotous laughter and uproar that rose from the Carnival crowds in the street below. He looked no longer at the antics of Stenterello and the pranks of Arlecchino, but up at the breadth of blue serene sky which stretched above where the gabled roof parted.

His companion listened, with the colour coming and going, fleeting and burning, in her downcast face; then suddenly she caught his hand and sprang down the first stair.

"Let us go, 'Ino—let us go!"

And hand in hand they ran down, and were mingled with the hundreds who were streaming in frolicsome humour, through the narrow tortuous street towards the great Piazza.

A few minutes later they also were standing in the Cathedral square.

They were a picturesque little pair—the girl taller than the boy by full a head.

He was barelegged and barefooted—a child of the populace; he wore the loose shirt and the red waistband of the Venetian gondoliers; and slung round him by another bit of scarlet was an old ebony mandoline. She was clad in quite another guise, so that she looked like some silky-leaved flower growing out of the grey stone pavements; she had a hood of dark velvet over her head, from which great, bright, trustful eyes looked out wonderingly upon the world; her skirts were of heavy amber satin, that seemed to have been fashioned out of some brocaded train; her hands were full of flowers that she had picked up from the ground as the people of the balconies flung them downward.

As they stood together, hand in hand, the contrast of colour and the grace of attitude made a picture against the dusky pile of the Duomo and in the crisp whiteness of the sunny frosty air. Many people passing paused to look at them; the little lad whispered to her, and then unslung his mandoline.

There was a lull in the sports of the day. Some sporting of a band of mummers headed by a scarlet Mefistofelo and a gorgeous Dulcamara was over and done with: the commencement of the traditional Galà was delayed; the crowd was unoccupied and willing to be amused, but not impatient nor out of temper, because it was a crowd of Italy.

The boy judged his time accurately, and touched the cords of his lute. The girl wavered a moment with the colour hot in her face; then with a sudden gesture threw the hood back off her curls, and lifted up her voice and sang.

Her song was an old familiar street-song of the Lombard population.

Far and wide on the clear wintry air, keen with the hard breath of the mountains, the strong pure notes of a voice in its earliest youth rang out like a bell over the muttering and shouting of the people. Those nearest to her listened, and hushed down the noise around them; the silence spread and spread softly like the circles in the water where a stone is thrown; the boisterous gaiety dropped to a quieter key; in a little while all the square was still.

The hood fell back wholly upon her shoulders; the sun shone upon the little group; the amber of her skirts, the violets in her hands, the scarlet wool of the boy's sash, all glowed in the light; above all hum and buzz from the other quarters of the city the song rose on the air clear as only the tones of childhood can be.

"L'Uccello!" the people shouted. "Go on, go on!"

A smile rippled over her face, as at some familiar word of greeting: she sang on at their bidding song after song of the sweet unwritten melodies of the nation. Now and then the boy struck a chord or two from his mandoline, but seldom; her voice was rich enough and strong enough to fill the square without aid, and it leaped aloft in the wintry air with the eager, straight, upward flight of a hawk that is loosed from its holdings.

When at length it ceased, the throng in the great square screamed, laughed, almost cried with delighted applause; the people in the balconies clapped their hands, the loungers at the caffé dashed their hands on the marble tables till their glasses rang, the masquers and merry-makers shrieked a hundred times,—"Viva l'Uccello! Viva l'Uccello!"

The boy marked the propitious hour. He took the red berretta off his curly head, and advanced amongst the multitude, and with the infinite grace of his nation, the grace which is so perfect because so utterly unconscious of itself, stretched out his hand to them for charity.

"Some little thing, signori, for the love of God. There is an old woman at home who wants bread."

He was generous, and he sought to bear all the shame of the alms-seeking for his own portion. But his companion saw his purpose, and sprang to his side. Her cheeks were flushed, the tears were bright on her lashes, the winds blew the heavy gold of her hair and the snow off her courtly skirts; her voice had lost its strength, and trembled a little.

"It is not for him, signori!" she cried. "It is for me. For himself, when he plays and the people would give him coins or cakes or confetti, he will never take payment for his music. He says it is God's gift, not his. The money that he begs now is for me. I am illustrious; oh yes! but I am very poor. I have an old nurse at home who wants bread, and sits by a fireless hearth. She is so old, so old. And we have nothing to sell but a few little jewels, and they were my mother's, who is dead. Will you give me some little thing, if my songs pleased you?"

The answer came from a hundred hands at once —from above and around, on every side.

Paper money fluttered to her feet; loose silver rolled like sugar-plums; here and there a piece of gold flashed like a star through the air; flowers and toys and gilded horns of sweetmeats, and ribboned playthings of the pageantry were all showered upon them from the balconies above and from the throngs around, until their arms ached with stretching for the gifts, he his red berretta, and she her amber skirts.

Great ladies, leaning in the draped galleries of old palaces, cast down money with lavish hands; white-coated soldiers, laughing over their wines at the marble tables, tossed bright florins to swell the store; a child-noble in his gala-costume of white and gold and powder and jewels, ran down some palace steps and shyly thrust a roll of notes into the singer's hand, and hastily lifted his soft smiling mouth to kiss her cheek; the poorest of the people sought in their leathern pouches for some copper pieces to give.

In vain the boy and girl, being honest, protested, laughing and crying both at once—"Basta, basta!— enough, enough!"

In vain; the golden shower did not cease until, in

the distance, as the first of the patrician pageantry appeared on the entrance of the square, there rose a glad shout,—"The Galà! the Galà!"

And the populace, kindly of heart, but fickle of temper, turned to the new pastime, and the little noble ran to his people, and the great ladies looked the other way, and the golden chariots rolled under the historic walls, and the sea of the bright masque surged outward; and the children were forgotten where they stood.

Then to them there came one who had listened and watched all the songs and all the payments where he had leaned in the shadow of the cathedral wall.

He uncovered his head as he approached, and the sun fell full on his face—the dark, poetic, historic face of Florence.

"Ah, cara donzella," he murmured softly with a smile. "Money I have none to give you, until I make some more to-night. I too am an artist; and so—it goes without words—I too am poor. Nevertheless, let me thank you."

He dropped a ring into her amber skirts, amongst the violets of Parma and the daffodils of Tuscany, and turned away and vanished in the throng.

The girl sought for the ring amongst the flowers and toys and money and sweetmeats with which her skirts were full.

It was a very old seal ring—an onyx, cut with the heads of the Fates.

She looked at it long and curiously, with a dreaming look on her face; then thrust it into the bosom of her dress. Then she gathered closely up about her the heavy brocades of her garments, and turned to the boy.

"Let us run, 'Ino. The people are not looking now. We shall lose the Galà, but Mariuccia is so cold at home."

So they turned away from the square, and went back into the old, irregular, gloomy streets where even at mid-day there was no gleam of brightness.

But now they could not run; their fleet feet were powerless to bear them swiftly; they were too heavily laden with the spoils of their prosperous efforts; it was of no avail to try and move quickly; at every step they trod upon a knot of violets, or trampled a bright narcissus under foot.

They were forced at last to go very tranquilly, with bent heads and with cramped limbs, along the cold and dreary passage ways.

"Oh 'Ino!" the girl cried. "When we sang for love and goodwill, we were so light of heart and of foot. But now——"

She sank down upon a flight of steps, her skirts glided from her hands, her treasures rolled to the ground and were scattered. She sobbed as if her heart would break.

"That is ungrateful to the people, cara mia," said the little lad softly. "Is it that stone with the Fates that has chilled you?"

"Nay she is right," said a voice above them. "Count art by gold, and it fetters the feet it once winged."

He who had given the ring spoke the words, passing swiftly in the shadow so as not to be delayed nor questioned.

After him ran a gay and giddy throng of masks, thrashing each other with coloured bladders, and chasing him with tumultuous shouts as of a band of mummers to their chief.

The shouts in their hoarse vibration filled the tunnel of the narrow twilit street as the parti-coloured group of the masquers reeled down it like a score of anemone leaves blown heedlessly upon an autumn wind.

They all cried one word:—Pascarèl.

I,—the child who sat on the stone stair, weeping over my fallen violets and my scattered wealth,— treasured the name in my heart on which the carven Fates were resting.

The masquers reeled on out of sight, a cloud of misty and tangled hues; over the high grim roofs and the sculptured buttresses the name came back flying gaily in glad echo on the air—

"Pascarèllo!—Pascarèll!"

CHAPTER III.
By the broken Donatello.

THE first thing I remember is of how poor we all were; how horribly poor, how terribly poor!

When I went to take my first dancing lesson at four years old, I had holes in my little lace frock, and a pair of faded blue shoes nearly out at the toes. I cried bitterly for very shame sake.

"Never mind, carina," said old Mariuccia, my nurse. "Never mind. If you dance away with a light heart, what does a tatter or two in the dress signify? It is better to have holes in the shoes, little one, than a leaden weight on the feet, believe me."

Oh! and what a fool I thought her! Though she was sixty and I was not six.

But when my father's man Florio came in and lifted me up before the old battered silver mirror, and murmured in his soft tongue, "Ah! what does a shabby frock matter when one has an angel's face like the signorina's? The other little ladies may be all hung with rubies and pearls if they chose; nobody will look at them if the signorina be there"—then, indeed, there seemed some sense in the argument, and Florio appeared to me a person so discerning that I consented to be pacified and to be led away to the vast bare frescoed dancing-hall, where one little shrill fiddle was piping and shrieking to a score of Lombardic babies, all more or less noble, I believe, in descent.

We were at that time in Verona. Poor old Verona! World forgotten, though having given so much to the world.

The city of Lesbia's lover is but a sorry desolation now, despite its hidden treasures, that no man remembers once in a score of years.

Those narrow sun-baked streets, those grim dust-covered fortifications, those little lines of stunted sickly trees, those simooms of lime dust, those bitter piercing mountain winds, those pale grasses, all alive with brown lizards, those lofty desolate houses, palace and prison in one, those straggling vines choking the strangled maples, the dreary weary "waveless plain,"—how miserable it all is now, how miserable it all was then!

Verona never seemed like Italy to me. Perhaps because I saw it always under the dominion of those white-coated stranieri, who pampered its greedy priesthood and bribed its lazy proletariate, and who waltzed themselves into favour with me by swinging me round many and many a time to the gay measures of their regimental bands, and spending on me floods of sweetmeats and pretty phrases, although old Mariuccia, whenever she saw me thus polluted, would snatch me away from the barbarian's arms with fiercest flashes of her still eloquent Tuscan eyes.

Mariuccia told me many a tale of the old grandeurs of the city of Can Grande; and I used to wander about it gazing at its amphitheatre and its acacia hedges, and its green Adige and its two Paladins at the door of the duomo, and dreaming of Marius and Theodoric, of Catullus, and Carolus Magnus, of Romeo, and Ezzelino, of Vitruvius, and Paolo Veronese, in the strangest confusion of fable and truth, in which my little brain floated as on a gorgeous, but misty, sea.

I never loved Verona.

The four first years of my small life had been spent with Mariuccia on a farm on the distant Romagna.

There I had lived in the open air, rolled in the grass, gleaned the gold of the millet, got drunk in my innocent fashion off the grapes at vintage time, and filled my hands with wild wood flowers all the whole year round. There I had owned all a child's delicious riches of freedom and sunlight, of chains of daffodils, of fans of chesnut leaves, of friendships with birds and beasts, of long, happy, heedless days in which the sky seemed always blue, and the angels of God always near.

When at four years old I was taken and cooped up in the dusty duskiness of Juliet's birthplace, I rebelled bitterly, and at first pined constantly, refusing to be comforted. I fretted for the free air and the

glad light, as many a prisoner had done before me in
the days when

"Death and sin played at dice with Eccelin."

Of course after a while my sweet first memories
paled a little, and I grew a little reconciled. But I
never forgot that bright beloved Italy of mine, away
there southward in the blue ocean of the distant
Romagna; I never grew to care for these grim streets,
these filthy courts, these parching heats, these frozen
winters, these masses of frowning stone, these labyrinths of palaces and prisons, which seemed always to
my fancy, as I grew older, to have still upon them
the mark of the scourge of Attila, the grip of the
gauntlet of Scala, the scorch of the crimes of Romano.

At the time when the little shrill fiddle played to
me in my little shabby shoes, we were, I say, in Verona
for no better, or lesser, reason than that having got
in there we had not the means to get out again.

We had the second floor of an old palace; such
a palace as you used to rent for a song in Italy, before Italy changed her proud "Farà da Sè," from a
boast and a dream to a heroism and a truth.

A palace with superb staircases reeking in filth;
courts which would have held a troop of men, armed
and mounted, given over to lizards and centipedes;
chambers with tapestries of Rosts, from the cartoons
of Bronzino, ancle deep in dust and dirt; and walls
that were due to the designs of Fra Giocondo, hung
with the padrona's ragged garments, drying in the sun
after their wash in the Adige.

"Peintures aux plafonds; ordures aux pieds." It
is Georges Sand, if I remember aright, who wrote that

bitter line, or something like it, upon Italy. It is terribly bitter, for it is at times terribly true.

Our palace was no exception to the rule.

It was magnificent as a dream, even still overhead, where some wondrous-eyed woman, worthy almost of Leonardo himself, laughed down from her frescoes of roses, or where some apotheosis or cenacolo by Gentile, or Pisanello, still kept its radiant colours, despite all ravages of time, and neglect, and fire, and dust. It was magnificent too from that beauty of proportion, in which, as by some almost unerring instinct of symmetry, so many Italian buildings have a beauty that cannot perish whilst one stone is left upon another, even as in so many Italian faces there is a perfection which, being born not of hue but of outline, is unharmed by age, and endures even after death itself, as did that golden loveliness of Faustina that was found a century after death unharmed in the dusky depths of Santa Croce.

But it was also unutterably dreary, dirty, ghastly, dismal, comfortless; bats rustled through its passages, and downy owls haunted its roof timbers. The upper rooms were all tenanted by working people, or rather by people who affected to work, and in reality lived on the Austrian doles; and the lower halls were the abode of the padrona and her eight children. She was a stout-built, black-browed, comely soul; the most good-natured creature in existence; and her children lay in the sun, or played boccetta, or fought for the chesnuts on the stove, or did whatever seemed best to them all day long in an endless strife and riot.

The padrona was poor enough; she beat her own linen in the river, and baked, and swept, and cooked unaided, and added to her scanty means by stuffing mattresses with grass and wool, at which she was an adept. But it was owing to the padrona very often, and to nobody else, that Mariuccia had a meal to give her beloved little illustrissimi.

There were four of us; the others were boys; beautiful boys, who might have come out of a Tiziano or Giorgione canvas; gay, kindly, saucy, daring creatures, popular with the people everywhere, and caring nothing how their linen blouses were torn, quite content to sit and eat polenta for their only dinner with the woman below and her dirty children.

My poor brothers! They were so bright and so bold, so mirthful on nothing, so full of goodwill to all the world; and they all died so young; mere children. One of fever in Verona itself; another of a knife-thrust in a street scuffle in Rome; the last in a white squall off Cagliari, that swamped the little felucca within sight of land.

But at the time of which I now write, whilst they were all three around me, they were the pride and torment of Mariuccia's life, the delight of the padrona's, and the wonder of all the town, for the skill with which they—bambini inglesi—poured quips and cranks upon the people in true Veronese tongue and fashion.

The padrona would stand in her great arched doorway, with her arms akimbo, rocking to and fro with laughter at their encounters, whilst her onions frizzled neglected in her frying-pan. They were quite happy teasing the market-women, riding in the bullock waggons, driving the ball at pallone, fishing with the boatmen, dancing the tarantella in the wine shops, playing at dominoes with Pepe and Zoto and Giàn, and all the rest of the padrona's brood. It was only into my soul that the iron of our degradation entered.

With the male children in the market-place, they were still the young signori, whose shabby clothes could not lessen their distinction, so long as they threw the ruzzola unerringly, and had a lightning-like skill in morra: but for me it was otherwise; with the feminine aristocrats in embryo of the dancing-lessons I was only a little detestable forestiera, who had shabby shoes and a torn frock, and who had nevertheless the intolerable insolence not to be ugly in proportion to her poverty, and also to dance very much better than they did themselves.

"Look at the signorina, little ladies, all of you," the old dancing-master would say a dozen times in an hour, suspending the screams of his fiddle to point at me with its bow. "Look at her! only a month in this room, only half the age of most of you, and look at her! What grace, what accuracy, what lightness; the sweep of the swallow, the poise of the sea-gull! And such a baby! It is wonderful. Are you not ashamed to carry yourselves as you do, with such an example as the little Uccello's before you?"

Dear old Fortunato! He taught me, out of pure good will; having met me often in the street, and having at last succeeded in persuading Mariuccia that not to initiate a woman child into the ways and wiles of Terpsichore was to fly in the face of all the designs of Providence. He taught me from sheer love of his art, and some touch of love I think for me; but he did me an ill service with the little Lombard ladies by his praise.

They dared say nothing; for Fortunato could rap both feet and hands sharply enough with his bow, when he was irritated by contumacy or clumsiness; but they eyed me askance very evilly and munched their chocolate chicchi, grouped all together at the top of the room, muttering scornful things of me and mine in an offensive and defensive alliance.

Unhappily, there were few scornful things which could have been said of us that would not have been sufficiently true to hit us hardly. We were all of us handsome; in all times, they say, the race we came from had had the gift of the "fatal face;" but we had very little else.

It was the old, old story; I used to make Mariuccia tell it me as far as she knew it, over and over again, when she used to sit of an evening shelling beans on the great staircase, under a half ruined statue that they said was by Donatello.

I can see her now,—so plainly,—as she used to sit there, with a big round brass basin in her lap; she had a dark red skirt and a yellow kerchief; her costume never varied; she had a huge silver pin in her white hair; she had the noble frank face and the changeful kind eyes of her country people; she was weather-beaten till she was as brown as a chesnut, though she had the broad flap hat of the country spreading its roof over her head to keep her from the blaze that streamed through the vines that hung over the grated casements.

The sunbeams and shadows used to play on the old marble stairs and the old grey statue; a passion flower had somehow thrust itself through the stones

from without and blossomed there at her feet on that
chill bed; the brass bowl used to glitter like gold in
the light; above at a vast height there was a lunette
with frescoes of the labours of Hercules; from below
there rose a smell of garlic, of fried meats, of coriander seeds, of stabled cattle; the crack, crack, crack of
the beans used to sound on the silence regular as the
ticking of a clock; the huge straw hat would shake
itself slowly and sadly as she spoke:

"Do I remember your mother?" she would say.
"You ask me that so often, 'Nella. Surely I remember
her. I was with her at the birth of every one of you.
I was an old woman then. At least as you children
count age. She was beautiful, yes;—else your father
had never looked at her. You are more like him.
Oh, you are handsome enough; I do not deny that;
you have a face like a flower, and you know it, though
you are such a little thing. The people spoil you:
they will turn your head with praise. You will end
just like that wicked Speronella of Padua whom they
sing about to this day in all Romagna. It was a name
of horrid savour, of ill omen, for you; I always said
so; but your poor mother would have it; it had been
her mother's, she said. It is no use teasing me to
tell you more; I have told you all I know a hundred
times, and none of it is any good. When I first went
to your mother she had not been long wedded; she
was happy then; they always are,—for a week! There
were difficulties; that I saw the first hour; but they
did not press much. He had met her in Florence;
she was an opera singer; he was a great signore, in
his own country, so they said; it is always a mistake.
He was double her years; but he was so handsome,—

Milordo Maurice. You only see the wreck of him. But you may see that still——"

"And I am like him!" I cried where I sat at the feet of the mutilated Donatello, shedding my quota of beans into the brazen bowl.

Mariuccia nodded.

"Yes, you are like him," she said gravely. "In more ways than one, signorina. When you get older, take care you do not throw your life away as he has thrown his. A noble in his own country; and I have to beg a meal for his children from the woman below!"

My father was not a nobleman, though Mariuccia, in the common continental incapacity to understand insular titles of courtesy, always called him so. He was only the fourth son of a northern marquis:—God help him!—but even so much as this I scarcely knew at that time.

Now I adored my father with very little reason for it, for I saw him perhaps six days in the year, and each time I saw him received about six careless words. But he was so handsome, so easy and good-humoured, so indifferent to every created thing or any possible fortune, that he seemed to me the very perfection of humanity.

I adored him, at a distance indeed, for it was chiefly when I was eating figs on the stairs or cracking walnuts in the court yard, that I ever saw him at all; but adore him I did, and with the inconsistent ingratitude of human nature, I cared more for a slight or a reproof from him whenever he deigned to notice me by one, than I did for all the untiring goodness of Mariuccia.

She, dear soul, was very wroth against him always, and could not forbear letting out her wrath to me.

Mariuccia did not think very much of filial duties; her own parents had been a travelling cobbler and his paramour, who had rid themselves of her in her babyhood by the simple process of leaving her at the Innocenti; and she considered that she broke no moral canon when she inveighed against the shortcomings of her master to me on the old grey stairs. Indeed, I think she honestly believed she only did her duty in trying to turn me from my unreasonable worship of a false god; a god moreover who provided next to nothing, and left her to puzzle her brains as best she might how to find bread for three hungry, healthy boys, and how to turn my poor mother's costly faded wardrobe into decent attire for my use.

"He broke your mother's heart," she used to say with a sharp crack of a bean; and I used to feel a certain pang, yet also a certain incredulity. My mother was a mere vague name to me; I had not even a portrait of her. "What did he do?" I used to persist, and Mariuccia would respond in anger:

"What did he not do, rather? He did as he does now. He went and amused himself, and threw away the little he had in gambling, and left us for weeks and months to starve in some hole, whilst he feasted in gaming-towns and winter-cities, and spent such gold as he might win on creatures as bad and as useless as himself. Oh, it is no good your curling your lips and getting on fire like that, signorina. It is the truth, as you will know to your cost one day. Why do you ask me of your mother if you do not believe what I say? You are always angry that you are so poor; pray whose fault is it if not your father's, and how should he be worth anything, I would be glad to know, when not a soul of all his own people ever takes notice that he lives, but every one of them leaves him alone as men pass by a trodden fig, or a dead dog on the causeway."

That used to silence me, for I knew it was true; and I could only sit in mute rebellion shelling the beans with a swelling heart, while the bright golden lizards darted to and fro on the stairs, and the radiant sunset lights poured down from the frescoed lunette.

Then Mariuccia, whose temper was as close a mingling of sour and sweet as the core of a ripe pomegranate, would relent, and would suspend her bean-shelling to lay her hand on my head.

"Carina," she would say tenderly, "why will you vex yourself about your father? Little one, he cares as much for that lizard as for you. Do your duty by him; that is proper, of course; but do not make a god of him. Fret yourself for some good love, not for a foolish one. It is all very well for the maple to be choked for the vine's sake; but it is rubbish for the maple to die for the nightshade."

Which hard saying she left for me and the lizard to digest as best we might, whilst she went into the cavernous gloomy little crypt which served her for a kitchen to fry her beans in oil, or set them to stew with a cabbage. That, or something like it, was our daily meal; dainty little birds and tempting little pots of chocolate went in for my father when he was there, procured and prepared by Florio, who was a sort of universal genius; but we children never tasted of such fare. We thought ourselves in wondrous luck if we got a big dish of eggs and macaroni in the Pasquà Week, or could have a handful of sweet ciambelle or a lump or two of pan giallo for the Befana night.

As for envying my father his quails and thrushes and mullets, I should have thought it as blasphemous as Mariuccia would have thought it to envy the Madonnas in the churches their weight of jewelled garments and crowns of beaten gold.

At such times as Florio was with us, which was but seldom, I had more success in my endeavours to hear good of my idol.

Florio, in Italian fashion, had attached himself to us, and having once done so was not to be separated from us by anything that adversity could do to him. Once on the staircase I heard the padrona ask him how he could waste his years in service, so little lucrative, so often indeed, actually only repaying him by privation.

Florio shrugged his shoulders with the most expressive pantomime in the world.

"Eh! what would you?" he replied to her. "I have got to love them,—it is all said."

Florio would acquiesce in all my enthusiasm for his master, though he looked a little grave sometimes. But when I would fain have learned from him how my father spent those innumerable long absences of his, Florio would tell me nothing. He would pretend to laugh and show his white teeth.

"No, no, no," he would cry. "In good time the donzella will see for herself how men live; but she could not understand it yet;—no, no, no."

Once again also I overheard him say to Mariuccia,

"It is almost always such bad luck with him now; sometimes he has a good vein, and then we live like quails in the fattening coops; but it is very seldom now. They are all scared of him. At Nizza this very winter they warned him privately from the Masséna. And to be too bad for the Masséna——!"

Florio threw up his hands in the air with a gesture that concluded his sentence more eloquently than any speech.

Florio was about forty years old at that time; a little plump man, as round as a ball, with merry eyes, and the frank, tender smile of his nation.

He was a charming creature. There was very little he could not do. He could put on a white apron and cook to perfection; he could talk most languages, more or less correctly; he could draw inimitable caricatures; he did not disdain to wax a floor, and skim on it with brushes for skates; on occasion he has woven Machramme as well as any woman lacemaker along the Riviera; he could string a lute and sing on it in a very pretty tenor; and he would go to market with a big basket and bargain for butter and cheese with a terrible acuteness that was feared by the stoutest shrew that ever sat under a green or crimson umbrella on a sunny piazza, with her live hens screeching in her old mule's panniers.

As far as his principles went, looking back to that time, I should say he was absolutely innocent of even knowing the existence of such things.

He would lie with the sweetest smiling serenity in all the world, and he would cheat—in our service at least—with the most exquisite dexterity. Yet in other ways he was as frank as a babe, and if moved to pity

he gave with both hands, withholding nothing from
any thought of self interest. Yes,—Florio was a charming creature; the most perfect mixture of intense
shrewdness and entire simplicity that I have ever met;
and wholly and entirely devoted to a service in which
his multifarious talents were utterly lost and almost
utterly unrequited. And yet even Florio blamed my
father!

It was a terrible perplexity to me. What evil could
my father do?

Night after night I used wearily to wonder over
the problem, lying awake on my truckle bed, in a vast
room painted with the loves of Orpheus and Eurydice,
while the bats beat against the lofty windows and the
beautiful white moon sailed past them backed in
clouds.

To the condemnations upon him I attached no
idea of gambling, despite Mariuccia's invectives.

I saw everybody gamble; the children in the court
below, the people in the streets and at the public
lotteries, the men in the coffee houses and taverns, the
boys in the market-places, the old beggars on the
church steps: they all gambled, with cards, or dice, or
balls, with nuts, or little cheeses, with dominoes on
the pavement, with the gay painted cards at taroc, or
by means of their fingers alone, at morra, if they had
no other method available. That a pastime so universal
in the broad daylight could be in any one criminal
never occurred to me.

And having a strong and entirely reasonless adoration of my father, who fascinated me into love for
him by his mere look and gesture, as he fascinated
Florio into his service by a mere surface kindness and

gracious trick of manner, I came to the conclusion as I watched the clouds and the moon, that my father was a man deeply wronged by his world and his relatives. It was very easy for me to solace myself thus, for I knew nothing of either one or the other.

He was called Milordo, and our name was Tempesta —as the Italians had it—that was all I knew: and I had mingled my ideas of him vaguely and oddly enough with that great Tempesta, who has left his sign on so many frescoes and canvases throughout Italy, and who fled to Isola Bella with his fatal love and all its crime upon his soul, and dwelt there between sea and sky.

Such small obstacles as centuries and probabilities were nothing to me, lying awake under the smile of Eurydice, and watching the bats in the moonlight beat their wings against the painted casements.

One winter in Verona he stayed longer than usual. He was not well in health Florio told us; and he had found some Austrians who amused him. He used to go out every evening and return at dawn; that I knew, for I could tell his step and listened for it. I do not think he rose all day; for Florio was perpetually in and out of his master's rooms, with some frothing cup of chocolate, some sparkling cool drink, or some dish of dainty flavours, compounded by his skill.

One evening I was upon the stairs as he came down them.

Our stairs were very dark. One little poor oil lamp burning under a hapless Madonna who had lost her nose and hands was all that illumined the immense depth of it from hall to dome. I had been to my lesson with Fortunato; it was cold; I was muffled in a little purple-velvet hooded cloak that Mariuccia had made me out of one of my mother's dresses; my cheeks were warm with the run home; I had in my hands a silver laurel-wreath—Fortunato's yearly prize —with which he had just presented me, for the fourth time, in all solemnity and honour.

In the deep shadows I saw my father descending the steps; involuntarily I paused; my heart gave a great bound; if he should notice the laurel-wreath, I thought!

By a miracle he stopped likewise.

"Is it you, 'Nella? Let me look at you."

He drew me up under the lantern which was hung a step or two above, and bent his eyes in studious scrutiny upon my face; I trembled from head to foot; I was a bold child enough, but I was afraid of him because I loved him, and because he was to me such a majestic mystery, unapproachable, and inscrutable.

He looked at me long; my hood had fallen back; my hair was blown about me by the wind; I felt my cheeks changing in colour every second under his gaze.

"Heavens! how like you look to your mother," he murmured. "And yet you are like us too;—how old are you?"

I told him that I was nearly ten years old—at least so Mariuccia said.

"I daresay, I daresay," he said, carelessly. "You have grown very much of late. You will be a beautiful woman, 'Nella. Do they tell you so?"

"Many people do," I murmured; my limbs shook under me; my face was scarlet; my heart beat like a wild bird's:—he had praised me!

He laughed a little, wearily.

"Already? Very well! Good-night, little one."

He slipped a little gold piece into my velvet mufflers, and, for the first time in my life, touched my lips lightly with his. As he went out of sight into the gloom below, I sat down on the filthy marble stair under the Madonna and her poor dull lamp, and burst into tears,—tears of passionate joy.

When Mariuccia found me, she found me sobbing bitterly, the laurel-wreath neglected on the stones.

CHAPTER IV.

With the Popolani.

THAT small gold piece I treasured ever afterwards; piercing it, and hanging it round my neck. I used to be often hungry in those days, but no temptation of coriander cakes, or anchovy pastries, of Neapolitan *confetti*, or Florentine *dolci*, ever allured my little precious five-franc from its hiding-place.

The next day Florio summoned Mariuccia into my father's room; he gave her a sum of money, and bade her get me with it such education as she best could in Verona. She had taught me to read; Fortunato had taught me to dance; Florio had taught me to sing ritornelli to a mandolin; but these were all my acquirements; at ten years old I was barbarously ignorant, and knew nothing, except such quaint old stray pieces of knowledge as I had gleaned from some odd volumes of Vasari and Ammirato, of Villani and Muratori, and the like, which I had found left by some former tenant in our chambers, and which made me conversant with some art-lore and with the heroical histories of

> "Le donne, i cavalieri, le armi, gli amori,
> Le cortesie, le audaci imprese"

of the by-gone centuries.

"It is the Tedeschi's money," grumbled Mariuccia, with her face dark, and full of reluctance and of abhorrence.

Florio showed his white teeth.

"What is that to you?" he responded. "All your business is to spend it. That is enough."

Florio theoretically hated the Tedeschi as much as she did, but practically he thought the best use Tedeschi could be put to was that of spoliation.

"They are foreigners; they are hateful; they are our tyrants and our oppressors; and we will make them fly one day," he would say. "But while they are here, we may as well get what we can out of them. That is the true patriotism."

It was the true philosophy, at all events; and one that served its professor exceedingly well.

As for me, I could not understand how my father's money could be said to be the Austrians' also.

"It is not much, anyhow," I heard Mariuccia say, when she busied herself over her pots and pans while Florio plucked a Piedmontese partridge as plump as himself. "As I had the chance to see the signore, I spoke up the truth a little. When he had given his commands for 'Nella, I said to him, "And the boys, excellenza? What of them? They are growing tall, strong, dauntless lads, and they live with Pepe, and Zoto, and Giàn, and the children of the people; and they are as ignorant as so many young mountain bulls. Will vossignoria deign to say what is to be done about them?"

"He only laughed a little. 'They must do as they can,' he answered me. 'When they are old enough, your Tedeschi friends will give them rank in some regiment, I daresay; and there is very little learning wanted for that.' Did ever you hear such an answer, Florio? As if the blessed children would ever draw a sword against Italy? But he would not say anything better; he bade me begone in that gentle way of his which, as you know, there is no gainsaying. But was it not horrible?" she went on lifting the lid off her stewpan. "The noble lads! I am sure they would be cut in a thousand pieces before they would wear the white, and help to enslave Italy, who has been a foster-mother to them from the very days of their birth."

Florio smiled, as having plucked, he proceeded to truss his partridge.

"To be sure; to be sure. Of course we none of us would. Nevertheless, the Vienna beer tastes very light and good in the caffès, they say; especially when it costs nothing; and I have seen a good many of our people with their noses buried in the tankards."

Mariuccia poured her stew into a dish with a charitable wish that an "*accidente*" might strangle forever all Italians who so far forgot themselves as ever to drink the horrible barley brew of the accursed stranieri; it was to be as vile a traitor as Judas, she averred, when God himself had given the Italians the juice of the vine.

So it came to pass that I had such teaching as Verona could afford, whilst my brothers ran wild like young colts.

Mariuccia locked the sum my father had given her

away in a stout bronze coffer, and eked it out, with religious fidelity, as long and to as good purpose as she was able. Every atom of it she spent loyally, as she had been bidden; and shrewdly as became her Florentine citizenship.

She wanted many things direfully, for he and Florio went away with the first months of spring, and left her but a miserable pittance for all household purposes. But to take the smallest note from that money to procure rice, or wood, or onions, or flour, or oil for her daily needs, would have been a falseness to the trust of her stewardship which I am certain never even tempted in imagination that good, sturdy, honest soul of hers.

She laid it out to the last in the culture of my worthless little brain; if I did not profit by it as I might have done, it was no fault of hers. It was the fault of the saucy impatience of restraint, and the indolent love of basking in the sun, doing nothing, which the country and its habits had fostered in me. For I was decidedly a naughty child; I loved my own way and generally took it; and my sins of omission and commission were so many and various that with every Eve of Epiphany I listened in fear for the tinkling bell in the streets, and dreaded the bag of ashes and the long cane with which the black-faced Befana punishes the wilful.

Mariuccia went very wisely to work; she would have nothing to do with women teachers or schools; there were many old professors, old scholars, in the town whom she knew were terribly poor, and yet full of erudition, and not too grand to take something for imparting it. To these men she went, and so she secured me the means of getting a knowledge much more worth the having than the convent-culture which the children of my sex ordinarily obtain; that I profited too little by it was, as I say, no fault of my dear old nurse.

For the only teacher amongst them all to whom I really gave attention and obedience was my singing-master.

I adored music; it is impossible, I think, not to care for it, if you are reared in Italy. Everything seems to sing, from the cicale upwards. All that unwritten music of the populace whose scores no hands have ever penned, is exquisite; and every now and then in the streets, or from some high casement in the roof, you hear the notes of a divine voice, and you seek it out through filthy courts, up cut-throat stairways, into dark, dismal, foul-smelling chambers, and you find that it is only Pasqua the washerwoman singing at her tub, or Gillo the facchino amusing himself as he carries up the wood.

I had my mother's voice—so Mariuccia said. It seems that she had been of infinite promise as a singer when my father, desperately enamoured of her for the moment, bore her off from the stage in the second season of her public appearance, and the first of her performances at the Pergola. What my voice was to others, I do not know; I only know that all my life long song has been as natural to me as to any thrush or bullfinch.

The Veronese used to call me L'Uccello, the bird; and where there were so many uccelli, all more or less musically-throated, the name was in itself a distinction. Many and many a time, in Verona, when I have been out alone, I have found myself the centre of an eager little crowd, which followed me because I was singing aloud as I went; and to pacify them, I have vaulted on a parapet or a ledge, or anything that was convenient, and repeated the stornelli to an enthusiastic circle of blacksmiths, and horse-boys, and porters, and fruit-sellers, and beggars;—Mariuccia knowing nothing.

And then they would escort me homeward, humming the choruses of the songs themselves, delighting in me with that mingling of charming familiarity, and yet perfect respect, of which the Latin nations alone seem to know the secret; and saying nothing to me, that a little princess might not have heard, but waving their caps to me, and tendering me, by the hands of some old butcher, or some young ostler, a knot of china roses, or a plume of lilies and verbena, with the prettiest grace, and the sweetest smiles in all the world.

Ah! dear people, dear people! when I think of you, I repent me that I have said I hated your ugly town; for of a truth I loved you, and you me.

My music-master was an old man, by name Ambrogiò Rufi; he was most wretchedly poor; he lived in a little square den in the roof of a tumble-down house; he was very dirty, very shabby, very ugly; the world had never heard of him, and he got a bare living as first violinist at the theatre. In his youth he had created things that the world would never listen to; and he had become instead the interpreter of other men's creations.

He was inexorable as a master; but he was also admirable. His severity had an enthusiasm, and even a tenderness, underlying it which made it endurable. One knew that he was only harsh, because he would allow of nothing slight, or mean, or slurred, to be put forward in the guise of his art. Himself, he was a great master;—yes;—though he had never made a name, and had barely wherewithal to get a daily meal. I have seen the sums of a princely fortune, and the homage of a fastidious society, poured out upon artists who were not fit to hold a candle to my old master for him to read his score.

Circumstance is so odd and so cruel a thing. It is wholly apart from talent.

Genius will do so little for a man if he do not know how to seize or seduce opportunity. No doubt, in his youth, Ambrogiò had been shy, silent, out of his art timid, and in his person ungraceful and unlovely. So the world had passed by him turning a deaf ear to his melodies, and he had let it pass, because he had not that splendid audacity to grasp it perforce, and hold it until it blessed him, without which no genius will ever gain the benediction of the Angel of Fame.

Which is a fallen Angel, no doubt; but still, perhaps, the spirit most worth wrestling with after all; since wrestle we must in this world, if we do not care to lie down and form a pavement for other men's cars of triumph, as the Assyrians of old stretched themselves on their faces before the coming of the chariots of their kings.

Ambrogiò had a few pupils—not many. Most of them were young choristers of promise, whom he had sought on hearing them at some office in the S. Zanone; and whom he taught for pure devotion to his art, as Fortunato had taught me to dance. His method of instruction was wonderful, strict, and inexorable, as I have said, and giving infinite labour, infinite repetition to the scholar, but it was of an unapproachable excellence, and sifted the grain from the chaff amongst his aspirants with unerring accuracy.

There was—there is—an academy of music in the old city of Catullus, but such was the blindness of its direction, or such the rabid envy of its professors, that no effort was ever made to secure for it the inestimable value of Ambrogiò's lessons. Mariuccia's payments for myself were, I verily believe, almost all the remuneration that he ever received. All the rest were so poor; the children of coppersmiths, and coopers, and vine-dressers, and pottery-painters; boys and girls who had fair voices, and who sang in the choirs of the churches.

We used to stand in a semi-circle before him, a dozen children or so, and sing the scale simply hour by hour. You had to be far advanced before he would permit you to leave that first arduous exercise.

It used to be bitterly cold in winter in that little den of his, with its cold stove and its brick floor; and stiflingly hot in summer there amongst the red and grey roofs, the cupolas, and the towers. There was nothing picturesque or poetic in it; it was all hard work in a wretched little place before an ugly old man who flashed fury upon you through his spectacles if you dared to torture his ear with a false note. And yet we all went to him faithfully; and seldom or never rebelled.

There were in him the sincerity and the excellence which impress themselves upon children long before those children are old enough to reason on what they are awed by and admire. I tormented my other masters sadly enough: but I am thankful to think that I never added to the many pains and the infinite disappointments of Ambrogio's life.

I was a favoured pupil with him—I and Raffael Baptista.

Raffaello was the son of a coppersmith in the town, who lived hard by the cathedral, in a quaint old vaulted place filled with coppers of all sorts and sizes, which used to blaze quite red in the sunset.

It was the workshop as well as the dwelling-house, and was full all day of the clash of hammers on metal as well as the discordant noises of the church bells and the people's cries.

Yet amidst all that clangour and uproar, the child had been born with the most subtle and perfect instinct for melody. One would have thought that all that clanging and clashing of copper and iron all the livelong day, from the time he had cried in his cradle, would have deadened his ears to all perceptions of harmony; but it seemed as though it had produced the contrary effect, for he detected an incorrect note, and shivered under it as quickly and as painfully as the Maestro himself.

Raffaelino as we called him, when I met him first at our music lessons, was just eight years old when I was ten; his mother came of a Venetian race, and he had the Venetian look and accent; he was a small, slender lad, with eyes full of dreams and a mouth full of smiles; his fair hair clustered thickly round his head; he had dark, straight brows and a curious half-shy vivacity of expression that changed twenty times in an hour. He was the most picturesque figure in all our little group, with his brown legs bare, and his shirt loose about his throat, and a scarlet woollen sash girt in Venice fashion round his loins.

It was not in song that the little Baptista excelled. His voice was pure and true, but of no great compass. It was for the violin that he showed the extraordinary talent which won old Ambrogiò's heart to him, and one day when he had played on his own little viol a charming little *capriccio* full of life and grace, and I asked him whence it came, he hung his head and coloured, and confessed at last that it was of his own invention.

He implored me not to tell the Maestro; he was quite sure that Ambrogiò would look up with that frown through his terrible spectacles which we all dreaded, and bid him in tones of thunder go back to his scale practice, and not tempt the wrath of dead Cimarosa and Palestrina, and all the immortal brotherhood with such impious audacities. I thought differently; but Raffael had a right to his own secret, so I did not betray him. Which was unfeminine I suppose; but the only two women I had ever had aught to do with had been the padrona and Mariuccia, both simple people as the world went.

I liked Raffaello the best of all the children in Verona; he had an infinite tenderness for his mother, who was blind and whom he tended with untiring patience; and he had a profound homage for myself,—the donzella as he called me,—and would never meet me without some spray of roses, some bough of lemon, some knot of violets, or some cluster of chesnuts, for which he had rifled the hedges or had begged some neighbour.

In my way I was very proud; Mariuccia continually reproached me for it; but I was not the least beset by that sort of pride, which would have made me regret Raffael Baptista's companionship, because his father was a coppersmith, and he ran about the streets without shoes. I had lived too much amongst the people; and I had too much of the bohemian in me for that.

Indeed I enjoyed vastly, when I left Ambrogiò's attic, drawing my little velvet hood over my curls and running home hand in hand with Raffaelino, past the dancing hall, at the hour when Fortunato's pupils, of whom I no longer needed to be one, were coming forth from his lessons.

The little feminine respectabilities,—my born foes,—glorious in starch and ribbons, and coral and silk stockings, would recognise me by a solemn stare and a general drawing together of themselves for mutual protection, and I would laugh in their faces and flash by them holding 'Ino's hand the tighter, and shaking the rose petals all over my little weather-stained purples, which like all purples fared ill when brought down into the streets.

Mariuccia never objected to my complaisance for Raffael. There was much of the old genuine, sturdy Florentine democrat in her. His mother, too, was a gossip of her own.

"It is a rare good lad," she used to say; and that he ran the streets with bare feet was no social sin in her eyes.

At such rare times as Mariuccia allowed herself a

spare hour from her incessant baking and washing, spinning and sewing, she used to cross the piazza to the coppersmith's workshop, under the sign of the Spiked Mace, and drink a cup of black coffee with the blind woman, not losing her time, but whilst she gossipped going on with her weaving of rough linen garments for us from the little distaff which in true old Tuscan fashion was seldom absent from her, being hung round the waist with its hank of flax in readiness for any unfilled moment of her rare leisure.

I used to go with her, and Raffaelino and I used to sit on the threshold and play dominoes on the bottom of some big copper turned downwards to serve us as a table; or at other times he would bring out from its corner his little old quattrocentiste viol, which he had found amongst some lumber, and we would play and sing stornelli whilst the white moonlight was flooding the pavement, and the marbles of the buildings turned to silver in its lustre: Mariuccia beating time with her spindle, and his blind mother nodding her head to the measures.

One of the young painters then in Verona made a little picture of Raffael and of me, playing and singing thus in the moonlight, with the background of the huge arched doors and the innumerable coppers with just the glimmer of a brass oil-lamp behind us where Mariuccia sat and span.

It was a pretty little bit of *genre;* he was delighted to sell it for twelve gulden notes to a German Jew dealer. I have seen it since in a great collector's galleries; and the holder of it told me he had given for it some fifteen thousand francs.

One of the saddest things perhaps in all the sadness of this world is the frightful loss at which so much of the best and strongest work of a man's life has to be thrown away at the onset. If you desire a name amongst men, you must buy the crown of it at such a costly price!

True, the price will in the end be paid back to you no doubt when you are worn out, and what you do is as worthless as the rustling canes that blow together in autumn by dull river sides: then you scrawl your signature across your soulless work, and it fetches thrice its weight in gold.

But though you thus have your turn, and can laugh at your will at the world that you fool, what can that compensate you for all those dear dead darlings; those bright first fruits, those precious earliest nestlings of your genius, which had to be sold into bondage for a broken crust, which have drifted away from you never to be found again, which you know well were a million fold better, fresher, stronger, higher, better than anything you have begotten since then; and yet in which none could be found to believe, only because you had not won that magic spell which lies in—being known?

I was great friends with all those youthful artists who lived in nooks and corners all over the town, and who got their living by copying or by counterfeiting the old masters.

From the time that I had been old enough to climb up their steep stairs unaided, they had made a pet of me always, and often a model. I liked nothing better than to be perched on a table in any one of their big barns, arrayed in peacock's plumes, or old laces, or ancient brocades, or any other of the picturesque useless dusty lumber: and I think the dealers and buyers in the old town must have got very tired of my dark-eyed, golden fringed little face, which these students were wont to use for every allegory or childish subject that was ordered of them.

But painters, if one chance to please them at all, always see so many types in one's face, all more or less contradictory of each other, that one comes to the irresistible conclusion that it must after all only be typical of the poor human nature which makes us all akin,—when it does not set us all at strife.

They were very good to me all those poor lads; though they quarrelled often enough amongst themselves, and not seldom got into trouble for fierce wrangle with the invader. They all of them lived high up in the air, amongst the open rafters of the unceiled roofs; with wondrous lights streaming in through the vast bare garrets and magnificent views of limitless horizons, southward to the plains and northward to the mountains.

They used to be very good to me. They would dance with me unweariedly at the open air balls; they would take me to laugh my heart out over the dear delicious rheumatic burattini; they would play me all sorts of sweet little mad *cansoni*, rippling all over with a very phrenzy of mirth; and when I sat to them they would run out at noonday down six pairs of stairs into the street to fetch me a noonday meal of coffee, simmering in its brass pipkin, and little patties crisp in their white papers. I fear they must often have spent on me the only coins they had for their own dinners, for they lived on about three soldi a day, two of which would go for the theatre and the nightly smoke at their clubs.

To my coming and going with them, Mariuccia having once satisfied herself that they were honest lads, offered seldom any opposition. The Italians are not a people who think evil of every trifle, and Mariuccia had a good deal in her of the stanch, uncompromising republicanism of old Florence.

We amused ourselves; that seemed to Mariuccia the right and proper thing for childhood and youth; and moreover, as she used to say, with a laugh and a frown together, the "signorina is proud enough for six; how she queens it over them, the little imperious thing."

No doubt a nurse duly reared to a sense of her duties would have thought the judgment of heaven would have fallen on her had she allowed a little "illustrissima" of ten years old to clamber up into the roof of houses to sing stornelli amongst paints and pots, and cans and lumber, with a circle of bearded bohemians, or clamber down again in company with some stout-limbed peasant in gold ear-rings and scarlet kirtle, with a grand head like the Donatello Judith's, and a profession which was frankly and undesignedly that of a model.

But the songs had never a line in them for which I could have been the worse, and the model was a good gentle soul who had babies at home that she loved, and whose only care was to get broth and polenta enough for them. And dear old Mariuccia was too straight and simple a soul to be on the watch for evil; besides, as she sometimes mumbled to herself as she unlaced her bodice at night before coming to her small straw bed in my chamber, she thought it might be well if I should take to the people altogether, and be happy and marry amidst them in due time, for of a surety money there would be none for me, and my father's people made no sign.

But when I heard her breathe these wishes for me, she standing over me perhaps with her dull oil lamp and fancying me asleep, I used to laugh her to scorn in silence under the rough hempen sheet.

"Never, never, never!" I used to say in my heart.

Mariuccia used to close her soliloquies by kneeling down to a picture of the Mother of Many Sorrows, and praying to her for my future; but I, silent beneath the sheets, used impiously to think, "what use is it to be handsome if one cannot do for oneself without the Madonna?"

The Madonna was all very well no doubt, for these poor lean old folks who had not a friend in the world, or those pale foolish lovesick girls who could not keep their lovers, but could only kneel down and pray for them in the chapels; it was very well to have a Madonna, no doubt, when one was ugly or old, and when with one's life all was finished: but for me! —there was a little triangular mirror hung in the corner of my room to which I am afraid I said many more orisons than I ever offered to Mary.

I loved the people: who would not in Italy?—the dear, graceful, sunny-natured people, whose very selfishness is more engaging than other nations' virtues.

Where else but in Italy, when you give a franc for an armful of roses will the seller cast to you in free gift of pure good will his choicest magnolia flower?

Where else will the old porter to whom you offer

two sous for his trouble in hobbling up and down the stairs for you, limp off to his snuggery and bring you thence a bough from his lemon tree with a courtesy and a smile that courtiers might envy?

Where else will the facchino who has toiled after you on a summer's day with a heavy load, put his hands behind his back and shake his curly head, and steadily refuse reward, crying:—

"No, no, no! it is pleasure enough just to see the signora!"

Where else, if you pause at a little music shop in a bye street, will the master of the shop come out and hum you the songs that you seek harmoniously in a mezza-voce, whilst your coachman turns round to correct a change to the minor, and the baker-boy pauses to join in the refrain, and a girl, mending her shoe at a window, chaunts her share in the measure, and every mortal leaves off his or her occupation to loiter out and join the chorus with sweet singing rhythm, till the whole narrow street is filled with the melody?

Where else, indeed!

True, if you fail to buy roses next day, the seller may petulantly wish you an accidente. True, the porter next week may keep you languishing for your letters while he gossips over your affairs in the street, and allots you more lovers than there are days in the year. True, the facchino may expect you to nod and smile and be *buon amico* with him all the rest of your life. True, the music-seller may feel not the smallest scruple in giving you imperfect copies at six times their due value.

But all the same how genuine were the grace and

the courtesy and the vivacity and the kindliness! how genuine they will be again a million times over! how they smooth and illumine the rough and dark pathways of life! how easy they render the cordial intercourse between far-sundered classes! how pleasantly they make melody amidst our rude human nature, like the singing flower-sown brooks amidst the hillside stones!

"Italians cheat one as much as other nations do," said a shrewd Frenchman to me, the other day. "Oh, yes, no doubt; some say they cheat one a little more. But then they alone know how to do it amiably; they alone save one's self-respect."

Such was his verdict (a very superficial one, for, except Stendahl, where is the Frenchman who ever could understand the Italian?); but myself I would go farther than he did.

I would much sooner say, and surely more justly, that the Italian, to the fine subtleties of civilisation and the keen astuteness of his natural intelligence, unites a rare simplicity and a joyous frankness which he alone of all people has retained amidst the artifice of modern life.

No, I loved the people; I had enough soul in me for that; but all the same, even in my happiest hours, I never dreamed for an instant, as Mariuccia dreamed for me, of being content to dwell amidst them for ever.

And happy hours I had; though my brothers and I sat at night reading Vasari, or old Pulci, or the Chronicles of Compagni, or Ferreto, or the wonderful stories of Croce, that Bolognese "Homer of Children," by the light of one poor little miserable lamp; and though in the winter sometimes we had barely charcoal enough to heat the small brown jars, and though even on most summer days we had little else to eat than a roll of bread and a broth of herbs, a few ripe figs from the old tree in the court, or a slice of the padrona's polenta.

CHAPTER V.

The Peacock's Plumes.

WE were happiest when we were alone with Mariuccia.

We were children, and strong and well, and there was the bright, broad, living sunlight about us, and all things were possible for us in the future. But when my father came and Florio it was different. We did not reason on it, but we were vaguely affected by their presence, vaguely depressed by it. Some breath from a world we knew nothing of blew in on us, and chilled us in our bare old home in the mellow Lombardic heats.

"Oh, Dio mio! but it is terrible!" Florio would say, lifting his hands as he peered into the faggotless cupboard, the empty stewpans, the ill-furnished bread pot, and then we became sensible of the privations which we had scarcely perceived before, and alive to that vital truth of the old Condottieri, that *"Senza soldi non possono fare."*

"It is terrible," Florio would say, cooking a couple of little larks and some toadstools out of the woods in such magical fashion that they would have deceived any epicure in the country into belief in them as ortolans and mushrooms. "It gets worse, you see, every year; of course it gets worse. He wins less often; and he takes more brandy when he loses. It is always the way. It is a puzzle to live at all, and half the cities are shut to us. Debt—debt—debt. It slaps the gates in our faces. There is hardly anywhere that they will trust him now. It will end in that,—some day,—and soon."

With "that" he gave a gesture as though he drew a knife across his bare throat. Mariuccia shook her head.

"End in that! End!" she echoed. "And, say you, Florio, what pray will then begin for them? For the dear little ones? It is very well to say 'end,' as if he were the only one concerned in the matter. Four of them: and not a farthing except the few notes he leaves with me when he comes and goes, which the Holy Mother knows would be hardly enough to feed up a goose for San Giovanni's day, let alone feeding four big hungry children from one Lent on to another."

Such discourse as this we used to hear between them in stray fragments; and they left on us a subtle, indistinct sense of some impending evil; and even I, despite the innumerable illusions and indestructible faiths in which the name of my father was involved for me, grew by degrees dimly sensible that he only returned to us at such times and seasons as it had become impossible for him to live elsewhere.

The old barren dusky palace was the cheapest roof that we could have found all the world over to cover our heads, and when he came thither for a temporary refuge, the fidelity of his two servants still contrived to sustain around him some show of ceremonial and some sense of comfort. How they did it I cannot tell, nor even at this day can I imagine; but do it they did; with surpassing patience and with unwavering self-sacrifice.

An Italian can subsist on almost as little as an Arab; and if he only offer you but a couple of dates he can serve them on a majolica plate with a few lentiscus leaves and a little myrtle in such fashion that they will lack nothing in grace of service that any king could desire at his banquet.

Such a man as my father was could not be anywhere wholly without companions.

The native nobility and gentry never came nigh him; but the Austrians used to flash their white uniforms on our dark staircase many and many a night. They used to pass within the doors of his room and remain till daylight; and all night long Florio used to be gliding to and fro with glass jars of chartreuse, or fresh flasks of brandy.

They were my old Tedesco acquaintances who had waltzed me round a hundred times to the swell of their military bands; but as I grew older my father sternly bade Mariuccia take heed that I was never about upon the stairs at evening, and she kept me imprisoned by her side under the lamp, weaving the lace, which I hated, or studying the scores of Ambrogió Rufi, which I loved.

Other of my pleasures came to an end too about this time.

It was a lovely spring in Lombardy, mild even as though amidst the Sorrentine orange woods.

Everywhere the meadows were white and hyacinthine-hued with a million crocuses. The violets followed them in countless hordes amongst the grass tufts underneath the vines. The maple and mulberry trees were pushing forth their tender leaflets, and in the dark old city there were soft blushes of colour where the yellow daffodils and the home-reared carnations blossomed in the casements and the balconies.

And away to the northward was the silvery cloud of the Alps, and the students would go outward thither and come back with the fresh winds blowing in their hair, and with their hands full of blue gentian flowers.

In the spring, even, our level plain of the Adige, which had not the beauty either of the mountain or the valley, had a certain charm of its own under the budding vine boughs and amongst the delicate acacias; I used to be in the fields all the day long, with my brothers and Raffaelino, playing till we were tired, and then, lying down to rest, watching the blue sea, of those immeasurable distances beyond which lay the world.

One day when I had filled my arms with masses of wood violets, I clambered up the stairs to the bottega of one of the students. He was very fond of flowers, and introduced them in all his sketches, and I was accustomed to take him a share of my field-spoils. He was a swarthy, large-limbed, tender-hearted creature; a son of peasants of an Aquillian village, whom we always called Cecco.

One day, when I was about twelve years old, I went my round as usual amongst my friends the painters. It was a fine bright day in February; I had been out in the woods by daybreak with my brothers and the padrona's boys gathering violets; the great odorous purple violets that, like so many other flowers, smell surely sweeter in Italy than ever they do elsewhere.

We came home by noon laden with them; the padrona's lads went out to stand with their share of the forest plunder at the corners of the streets, and see if they could get a penny to play with at boccette; I filled Mariuccia's pots and jugs with some of mine, and took the rest to my friend Cecco, who loved flowers, as I say, and so often introduced them in his pictures that the students nicknamed him Il Squarcionino, or the Little Squarcione, from that old Padovan who was the first of the Early Masters to paint flowers and fruits in arabesque.

He lived at the top of a lofty old house in a gloomy bye-street.

I climbed the hundred and odd stairs with labour, for they were rotten, twisting, and slippery from over much dirt; and, with my arms full of violets, purple and white, darted into his painting room, that was as bare as a barn, and not half as cleanly.

With Cecco there were three or four other lads, smoking and laughing, and talking as they worked. He had an admirable light in his great, ugly work-room; and those comrades of his who were not so fortunate in that respect were wont to set up their easels beside his, and labour together all in their various manners.

They welcomed me with enthusiasm, went on their knees to me and my violets, and abandoned their work that they might sketch me.

"Just as you are, signorina!" they called to me. "No! do not touch a thing; it is perfect. Look at her now, with the light on all that ruffled hair, and the little gay skirt full of the violets, and the colour all hot in her face from the wind: ah, bellina, bellina!"

So they cried around me in twenty different forms of admiration—the artists' admiration, which is so curiously compounded of fancy and of fact, and which they were accustomed to pour out on me as unthinkingly as though I had been a porcelain figure.

I was so accustomed to it, that it hardly hurt me more than it would have done the china; I knew Nature had made me good to look upon and picturesque. Altro! I used to shrug my shoulders and think no more about it except to give a passing pity to the unfortunate ones who were not similarly gifted.

So that day they hoisted me up upon the wooden dais where their models were accustomed to stand, and, with their four easels in the four corners of the room, set to work to paint me as I was, with my load of violets, and my hair all blown from the rough mountain breezes.

In a couple of hours they had all contented themselves more or less thoroughly with a first sketch, and simultaneously laid down their brushes.

"I have made her the Genius of Spring," said Bernardino Scalchi, surveying his workmanship with his head on one side, like a robin's.

"And I have made her 'La Primavera della Vita, La Gioventù dell' Anno,'" said Beppo Lavo, who wrote very pretty verses, and could sing them, too, not ill.

"And I have made her the Renaissance of Italy; the type of the Dawn of Freedom, the Symbol of the

Future," said Neri Castagno, who was a patriot and a red republican.

Old, swart, clumsy Cecco laughed a little as he turned round to them:

"I am very prosaic after you. I have only made her what she is—a child."

And yet, when all the sketches stood side by side, in the dying light of the late afternoon, it was Cecco's, they frankly admitted, which had the true poetry in it, after all.

A child with a skirt full of violets, with a rough wintry sky behind her, with a fresh wind tossing her hair, and with her feet gaily flying over the wet earth already green with the coming of spring: that was all that Cecco had made of it; but beside his picture the others looked false in sentiment, strained in fancy, and garish in grandiloquence.

Their work over, they made me jump from my throne; they thrust the violets in a bowl of water; they insisted that I should stay and have a little feast with them. Cecco had been in luck that day; a small panel of his, a girl's face in a garland of roses, had sold for the enormous sum of twenty florins; he was a millionaire, at least, for a day, in his own estimation.

He ran downstairs into the street, and in a few minutes came back in gay triumph with a couple of flasks of chiante, with a pan of steaming chesnuts, with a round sweet-almond cake, and a big bundle of cigars.

Then he thrust me in an old oak chair draped with dusky tapestries; he cast over me a magnificent old brocaded robe that the Jews would have bought

of him to cast in the fire for its gold to melt out of
the threads, but which he would never part with, because it had belonged to his father, who had been an
artist before him; he gave me a sceptre of peacock's
plumes, and a diadem of silvered paper with which
models were crowned when they had to sit for Madonnas; and then our feast began.

How we enjoyed ourselves! how we chattered! how
we laughed! how rich the wine tasted! how crisp were
the chesnuts! how we shouted the "Fuori gli stranieri!"
how we sang every song that occurred to us, from
motives of Rossini's and Bellini's to the last chorus of
the newest street song!

We were merry at heart, and full of zest, in the
deepening twilight and the clouds of smoke, while a
ruddy light from the setting sun glanced on the swarthy
face and kindling eyes of Cecco, and lit up the peacock's plumes of my thyrsus and the gold stitches in
the brocade: so merry, indeed, and so full of zest, that
we never heard the door unclose or perceived that
anyone besides ourselves had entered the painting-room.

Only at the sound of a strange voice did Cecco
tumble hurriedly up from the floor where he was
stretched, and, with eager apologies and bewildered
haste, strike light to a lamp and welcome three strangers,
who, going the round of the ateliers, had come in its
turn to his.

I, seated on my brocaded throne, with my Madonna's crown on my tumbled hair, and my pewter
plate of chesnuts on my lap, paused in my singing,
and looked up; two of the strangers were Austrians,
the third was my father.

Trembling, I slid down and stood like a little culprit, with the folds of the brocade curled like many-coloured serpents round my feet: it was not that I had any sense of doing what was wrong, it was only that he was to me a mystery so full of awe, and wonder, and attraction, that to see him suddenly there appalled me.

It was the first time in my life that I had ever met him in Verona out of our own old home.

His eyes glanced across me and he knew me in a moment; that I saw; but he gave me no recognition.

As chance would, however, have it, one of the Austriaci looked at me by the flickering lights of the lamp and the sunset.

"A charming little figure!" he cried. "Fantastic but very charming. A model, of course, in all that tinsel and brocade."

Dumb and perplexed, and glancing at my father in a vague terror, I stood still, with the silver crown upon my curls, and wished to sink into the depths of the old brocades; but he, hearing his friend speak, came forward and looked at me coldly.

"A pretty little beggar," he said, with a cold, swift glance of his eyes. I knew his meaning in a moment: he chose to affect to avoid all recognition of me.

My face burned, my heart rose, my fear of him was forgotten. I threw off my silver diadem and the old robes, and stood up straight before him, the poor neglected peacock sceptre trailing on the bricks.

"If I be a beggar, it is not my fault, nor yet Mariuccia's," I said, boldly, with a scorn for him that thrilled me with a horrible sense of guilt and of humiliation. "We are very hungry and very cold—all of us—very often. They do not dare to tell you. But it is true. And if I can forget it a little while laughing here, where is the harm? I am not ashamed."

My father's face, haggard and cold though it was, flushed deeply, whether with anger or any more tender sense of shame, I cannot tell. He thrust me from the room.

"Whatever else you be, you are too young to rant so glibly," he said, as he closed the door upon me.

I ran down the street to fling my woes at Mariuccia's feet, and sobbed as I ran, the poor bedraggled peacock's plumes still trailing from my hand, and gathering in their course the dust and ordure of the uneven and uncleanly stones.

I fled along under the darkling shadows of the grim fortresses which overhung the pavement, burning all over with a sense of outrage and of indignant scorn.

My father was not ashamed to starve me, but he was ashamed to acknowledge me because I sat and laughed and sang, and was glad in a garret, in a paper diadem, over a horn of cheap wine, and a handful of chesnuts, and a bowl of wood-violets.

I had a passion of scorn for such shame: and yet the weight of it was heavy on my child's heart, for I had a vague, shapeless, unreasoned-on sense of foreboding that, as my father had judged, so would the world judge likewise.

Mariuccia comforted me in her tender, homely fashion, and washed clean the peacock's plumes, and set them up over the stove with a palm-sheaf blessed for good luck in Holy Week.

But at evening-time she told me sadly that my father had forbidden her to allow me ever again to visit any of the students.

The loss of that cheery, good-natured, chivalrous, riotous companionship of theirs cost me many and many an hour of rebellious tears, and from that moment I ceased to be loyal to my father.

I would look at the peacock sceptre again and again, and think to myself—

"If you had been of gold and ivory, he would have praised you."

And I loved my feather-thyrsus all the more tenderly for other's neglect of it; and for my father a settled scorn fired itself in me, and killed love.

CHAPTER VI.
Mater Dolorosa.

So things went on, until I reached my fifteenth year. I was tall, but I was still,—for I had the open-air life which develops the limb and strengthens the body,—I was still in my ways and my tastes quite a child.

Raffaelino grew apace, too, and his people talked of his entering the priesthood; they did not know what to do with him; he had no taste for any hand trade; he was for ever haunting the churches; and to his mother, who was a religious soul, there seemed no life more beautiful or blessed than life amidst the silent marble cloisters, and the perpetual calm of Certosa or Camaldoli.

One of my brothers long before had died of fever in one of the hot, nauseous, pestilential summers of the uncleanly town; another had gone of his own will off with a Genoese sea-captain, whom he had met by chance, and who had dazzled him with stories of the sea, and he had been drowned on his first voyage; a third had kissed us, and clung round Mariuccia's neck, and confessed, shamefacedly, that his heart was breaking with monotony and inaction, and so had also gone his way to see the outer world with some other young students, as poor and hopeful as himself, who talked of immortality and starved upon a dream; and of him, also, we had heard that autumn that a knife-thrust in a students' scuffle had ended his short life just as it had opened into manhood.

She and I were left alone in the old home.

We closed the great rooms, and lived through a dreary winter in one little chamber abutting on her kitchen, and looking down into the stone court where the fountain that year was frozen, and the cold killed even the hardy bitter-orange-trees.

We had not heard of my father since the previous Easter-term.

Twice or thrice, Mariuccia had gone to the little dark den on the piazza, where the letter-writer of the poor people sat, ready to indite an amorous effusion or a summons for rent, a proposal of marriage or a butcher's bill, according to his clients' requirements; and thence she sent a letter each time to Florio or to her master.

I suppose she did not care for me to know of it, since she did not avail herself of my aid to pen them. Twice or thrice, in answer, Florio sent a little money, as from my father; but I have had many doubts since that Florio had contrived to gain it by some one of his innumerable talents, and robbed himself for our sakes. From my father, directly, we received no word.

The winter was terribly dull.

Mariuccia was getting very old, and wept sadly and often for the loss of her boys.

They had been as the very apple of her eye; she had toiled for them from the very days of their births; she had spent many a sleepless night and weary day beside their sick-beds in their wayward infancy; she had gone without her morsel of meat many a time to feed better with it the young lion cubs she loved; and now—one was dead, and the other two had thrown their arms about her neck, and laughed, and talked of the future, and gone gaily away, thinking only of the worlds they had never seen, and of the dreams they were sure would come true.

That was all her reward: it was hard.

I saw those firm-shut lips of hers quiver often as she sat and spun by the dull lamplight; and I heard her many a night murmur on her knees to the Mater Dolorosa, "Do not forget them, thou Blessed One. They will forget thee—children will—but mothers are not angered for that."

"What has made you stay with us, Mariuccia?" I asked her once, smitten suddenly with some remorseful consciousness of the enormous debt we owed to her. "Why have you stayed with us? It has been a hard life always; and we have been only a trouble to you and no reward?"

She looked at me with a steady look that had a certain pathetic sadness in it.

"One must love something," she said, simply.

I pondered darkly on the saying.

CHAPTER VII.
A Twilight Tale.

The winter was very dull. My father's forbiddance had taken from me many of my old pleasures; and the failure of funds had arrested all continuance of my education. There was only Ambrogiò Rufi to whom I still went, and in whose attic I was solaced by the strains of Cherubini and the melodies of Gluck.

It was bitterly cold there.

The snow was thick on the roof, and the wind from the mountains poured through and through the unprotected place. The old man could afford no such luxury as a stove; and the bare brick floor was like ice to the feet. I used to shiver as I sang.

And yet when I think of the sweet sigh of the violin melodies through the white winter silence; of Raffaelino's eager, dreamy eyes, misty with the student's unutterable sadness and delight; of old Ambrogiò, with his semicircle of children round him, lifting their fresh voices at his word; of the little robin that came every day upon the water-pipe, and listened, and trilled in harmony, and ate joyfully the crumbs which the old maestro daily spared to it from his scanty meal—when I think of those hours, it seems to me that they must have been happiness too.

"Could we but know when we are happy!" sighs some poet. As well might he write "Could we but set the dewdrop with our diamonds! could we but stay the rainbow in our skies!"

During this sad time of privation, I saw a little way into the closed past of my old music-master.

Verona perceived nothing in him but a meagre old man, who took his toilsome way noon and night to the theatre; who chaffered in the market for a pinch of charcoal and a bit of goat's-milk cheese; who wore his clothes so long that they fairly dropped asunder; and who made their boys and girls cry bitterly at many a sharp word and blow of his fiddle-bow when they sung not to his liking.

But I had always felt or fancied—fancy is so much feeling with every child—that there was something sadder, wiser, nobler in Ambrogiò than the townsfolk credited.

Perhaps he liked me better than he did the others, or he liked my voice better; all human creatures were only counted as so many voices by him; at any rate he now and then let fall, in my hearing only, brief sentences which seemed to me born of a mind higher than most of those with which I came in daily contact.

Mariuccia would not listen to any idea of the kind. She was a little jealous of my regard for him.

"Those music-mad people," she would say, "are just like that big sea-shell the dear lads brought me from Genoa. The sea-shell sings all day long if you put it to your ear. Why does it sing? Just because it is empty. Just because the heart that used to beat in it is dead and gone. It is just so with them. They are all melody because everything else born in them is withered up—che-e-e!"

One night, as it grew dark, I ventured, contrary to usage, to go and see my old maestro.

I was dissatisfied with my tiresome fate; I was ill at ease and impatient; I wanted I knew not very well what.

I climbed up his dark staircase, and found him in his chamber.

It was a night when there was no performance at the theatre of which he was one of the orchestra. He sat alone in the cheerless, fireless attic scanning some old scores by the light of a miserable little oil lamp.

He looked up as I entered; I think that he was always glad to see me, though he said nothing in welcome at any time.

"It is late for you to be out," was all his greeting.

I told him the Ave Maria had only just then rung; and asked him to explain again some obscure instruction in counterpoint which had been hard for me at his last lesson.

He went through and through the passage lucidly with me; he was always willing to smooth difficulties to a patient student, and in music I had patience, though in nothing else.

When the point was so clear to me that I had no longer excuse to linger over it, I still loitered by him, sitting there at the old bare table, leaning my elbows on it, and my face on my hands, and gazing at the red, dull wick of the ill-fed lamp.

"Talk to me a little, maestro!" I said, suddenly.

Ambrogiò took off his spectacles slowly, and gazed at me in stupefaction.

"Talk!" he echoed: it never happened to him to be asked for words; such things as he had it in him to say he said through the strings of his violin.

"Yes! Talk," I repeated, with the insistance of a spoilt child,—for poor Mariuccia had spoiled me sadly, despite all her warnings. "You must have seen the world sometime. Tell me a little about it."

"The world!"

He said the words with a startled, heavy breath. He looked like one who hears the long, unuttered name of some dead thing.

"Yes. The world," I said again. "What is it like?"

"Go in a convent, and never know," he answered, with a bitter brevity.

"Is it so bad, then?"

He looked at me across the deal table in the dull, yellow lamplight; a dreary, grey, shrunken figure, very old, very poor, very hopeless, with his great hollow eyes burning bright with the fires of awakening memories.

"Bad? Good? Pshaw! Those are phrases. No one uses them but fools. You have seen the monkeys' cage in the beast-garden here. That is the world. It is not strength, or merit, or talent, or reason that is of any use there; it is just which monkey has the skill to squeeze to the front and jabber through the bars, and make his teeth meet in his neighbours' tails till they shriek and leave him free passage—it is that monkey which gets all the cakes and the nuts of the folk on a feast-day. The monkey is not bad; it is only a little quicker and more cunning than the rest; that is all."

I sat silent; it seemed to me but a dreary prospect, this monkeys' cage which I should be doomed to enter when once I should be across the mountains.

"Tell me a little more," I urged to him. "You must have seen so much when you were young."

"No," he answered me. "I never saw very much. The man who is poor can only look out of a garret window. He sees the skies, and the sun, and the moon, and the changes of the clouds, better than anyone else; but it is all he does see."

"But he can walk abroad?"

"Can he? Shoeleather costs money; and though bare feet might safely tread the sands of deserts in the days of saints, they go but ill upon the flints of the king's highways—now."

This I felt was true; indeed I knew it by many a painful moment when my little worn-out shoes had click-clacked sorrowfully over the scorching stones of Verona in midsummer.

I grew cold with a sort of sickly fear of this new world into which a second earlier I had been all eagerness to plunge.

"But you must have seen so much to what I have seen," I urged, after a pause, again with a child's persistency. "Do tell me something—some story I mean—of your old life?"

His eyes were full of pain beneath his shaggy brows as they met mine across the dim light.

"Child, you should never open dead men's graves," he said, drearily, with a sort of shudder. "I tell you

I was always poor. It is a kind of blindness—poverty. We can only grope through life when we are poor, hitting and maiming ourselves against every angle."

"But you had genius?——"

He shrugged his shoulders in a pathetic, hopeless gesture of resignation that went to my heart through all my thoughtless selfishness.

"I have been most unhappy," he answered simply. "Yes; you are right."

I felt that I knew his meaning, vaguely though his words shadowed it.

"And how then," I said under my breath, "how then—not great?"

He smiled a little, very wearily.

"How? Well, I loved Art, and not the world, and, in my way, was honest. Time was, when I was young, that I dreamed a little of being, as you call it, great. At twenty-five, I was—yes, even I—was happy.

"I was poor indeed; in winter I had to keep my bed lest I should die of cold, and in summer I was glad to dispute the acorns with the swine. But I was happy. I had my Art, and I had a friend closer than a brother.

"He was a German, Karl Rothwald; together we studied music at Milano. He had no strong talent, only a graceful taste. I—well, I had genius, God help me, and of the most arduous study I was never tired.

"At twenty-five I trusted myself to commence my first great work—an opera upon the theme of Alkestis. I was two years engaged upon it. They were the two happy years of my life.

"Rothwald and I dwelt in the same chambers together; we walked abroad in the daybreak and the evening times, and we sat up late into the nights, I all the while dreaming of Alkestis, and giving shape to the creations that haunted me, and calling on his sympathy and joy each time when my composition was good on my own ear and satisfied my own desire. He never was fatigued, nor ever failed to rejoice with me.

"Often and often as we went through the millet-fields at sunrise, or sat in our garret through the long moonless nights, and the power of song that was in me broke forth and arose triumphant, and filled me with its own exultant strength, he—my friend—would laugh and weep in his boyish fashion and fling his arms about my shoulders and cry out how beautiful and strong my music was, and prophesy I should rank with Bach and Gluck and Palestrina.

"Those two years I was quite happy,—quite,—though I was but a starving scholar, and had often to go without bread to be able to buy paper for my scores.

"All the world was full of hope and of beauty to me; everywhere I heard delicious melodies in leaves, and waters, and bells, and winds, and all the things that moved, and my friend was with me,—close as a brother,—dear almost as a mistress. I wanted nothing more, and was sure of fame.

"My opera was barely finished when Rothwald was summoned from my side; some illness in his northern home, he said.

"I begged him to return swiftly; I pledged my word to him not to submit my opera to the direction of La Scala until he should return. 'My triumph would be robbed of half its joy if thou wert not with me to rejoice in it;' so I spoke to him as we bade each other our farewell. It was then autumn.

"The delay was sad for me, for I had hoped to have seen the Alkestis produced that winter; but I never thought of putting it forward in his absence. I loved him only second to my work; and I had pledged him my word that he should be present whenever it should be given to the public.

"The first months of winter are bitter in Milano; they were very cheerless and desolate to me; but I had many tender letters from him to keep warm my heart, and I occupied myself fondly in touching and refining the creation on which all my future hung.

"No one had ever heard a chord of it, except himself, but I had not much fear that it would not be accepted. At the great Scala, they knew me; and the conductor of orchestra, who was powerful with the direction, had a liking for me, because of my execution upon the violin.

"Rothwald had been gone four months; there were snow and ice in Milan; one day I sat shivering in my garret, yet with my heart warm still, because so much hope abode in it. The chief of orchestra paid me a visit; he was, as I say, good to me; I could not have maintained my life at all without the place he gave me amongst his musicians.

"He spoke to me of myself this day. 'Ambrogiò,' he said, 'it seems to me that you have too much genius to sit behind my bâton all your life. I hear that you have attempted original composition. Is it true? Then let me see your score. It should be something great. You are a master of counterpoint.' He argued with me so kindly and so long, that in the end he prevailed, and I drew out my Alkestis, and bade him judge of it.

"'Alkestis! Alkestis!' he murmured, as he heard the name. 'Is that your theme? It is unfortunate. There is a new opera this very week produced in Vienna on that same old story.'

"I was pained to hear that I had been forestalled; I asked him by whom it was composed.

"'Nay, that I forget, and am not sure if I have heard,' he answered me. 'But, anyway, you had best go thither and judge of it for yourself. If it be poor and fail, you can still produce yours; but if a triumph, as I am told, we must needs fit your music to some other narrative. Ah! I know how you love your first thought—your first poem,—but still we might manage to alter the libretto without much injury. Well, go you to Vienna—nay, nay, do not be so proud. Take my gold for the journey, and we will leave the matter as a debt to be paid me when La Scala first brings out your opera. Nay, do not argue. Go. You must, of necessity, judge your rival for yourself.'

"So I took his gold and went through the bleak white winter over the mountains at peril of my life.

"It was night when I reached Vienna.

"The gay city was all ablaze with light. I had travelled far and fast; I was exhausted. Nevertheless, before I changed my clothes, or broke my fast, I made my way to the opera-house. There they played Alkestis.

"I paid my entrance-money, and went into the heat and glare and stood and listened. The house was shaking with thunders of applause. When the clamour ceased, the music rose again—it was my own.

"Phrase after phrase, chorus on chorus, solo and septuor, and recitative, I heard them all like one made stupid by a blow. They were all mine.

"The curtain fell; the rapture of the people cried aloud, 'Rothwald!' 'Rothwald!' 'Rothwald!'

"Then I understood;

"I fell like a stone; so they say; they took me up as dead.

"He had stolen it all—all—all: stored up in his notes and his copied score.

"It made him a great name. You may hear of him now in the world. He has done nothing great since; the world wonders; but it is possible to stretch one triumph over a lifetime so that it covers every after failure. To make a name is hard; but once made, to live on it is easy.

"As for me—I say—I was dead. My heart, my brain, my genius were all killed. It is only my body that has dragged on life ever since.

"I never denounced him—no. For I had loved him. And if I had denounced him, where had been my proof? None would have been found to believe."

As the last words died on his lips, his head sunk on his chest; a film overspread the weariness of his hollow eyes; the silence of the innumerable years that he had passed, mute and alone, amidst his kind, stole afresh over him.

In vain I knelt before him; in vain I caressed his withered hands; in vain I spoke to him, begging his forgiveness for my thoughtless cruelty which had thus torn open rudely this deadly wound so long concealed from every human glance.

In vain: he answered nothing; he heard nothing; his dulled eyes only gazed at the gleam of the lamp; his hands only moved vaguely as though straying over the chords of some half-remembered music; his lips only muttered now and then under their breath:

"He betrayed me; yes; he stole all,—all,—all. But could I denounce him? He had been my friend."

And this he said again, and again, and again, many times; not knowing rightly what he said; and murmuring between whiles softly to himself sweet broken snatches of sad melodies—the melodies, doubtless, of his lost Alkestis.

I stole away, awed and afraid, for I was but a child, and went out into the flood of moonlight, into the bath of cold and luminous air, and there in the streets I sat down and wept bitterly for a woe not my own—for a life that was ended.

On the morrow he did not seem to remember the confession he had poured out to me, nor ever again did any allusion to it pass his lips, or mine. But he had become sacred to me; every time that I stood before him I could have kissed his hands for very love, and reverence, and pity.

From that hour I loved and honoured, and never dared be wayward with him.

He was only an old withered man, very bent and broken and poor, ill clad, and taking snuff with trembling hands in the bitter cold of his fireless attic, but to me from that night onward he was a hero and a martyr, and whilst he lived I never told to anyone what he had told to me, not even to Raffaelino.

When a man's eyes meet yours, and his faith trusts you and his heart upon a vague impulse is laid bare to you, it always has seemed to me the basest treachery the world can hold to pass the gold of confidence which he pours out to you from hand to hand as common coin for common circulation.

It was Mariuccia who had reared me in that manner of thinking.

"Child," she used to say, "if they gave a diamond in trust to your safe keeping, would you run with it to the goldsmith's shops in the public streets? Well, is not human faith of more sanctity than diamonds?"

She thought so; being an old stanch republican of Florence and a woman very poor always, who knew little of the world or of its ways.

CHAPTER VIII.
The little red Box.

AT this time the winter set in with an almost unexampled severity.

All over Italy it was cold; so they said; and poor Verona lying in her open plain receiving full upon her defencelessness the strokes of the alpine storm winds, seemed to crouch and perish under the driving of the hurricanes; her huge old houses were riven through and through with cold, and her high leaning walls whose shadow was so precious in the summer noons, seemed now like barriers of ice.

That winter was a very terrible one to Mariuccia and to me.

Poor we had always been, but that winter we had absolutely nothing. Of my father we had not heard for nearly twelve months, and the last of Florio's letters was already half a year old.

Mariuccia earned a little, a very little, by spinning and by selling the work, but this was all. We lived on the very barest food that could keep life in any human creatures.

Of clothing there was no absolute need, for my poor mother's wardrobe had been costly and almost indestructible. But even in this we had come to the very last, and I was forced either to wear rustling silks and lustrous velvets, which made me look like a figure out of a masked ball, or else go without covering in the bitter alpine blasts.

Happily it did not matter so much in Italy as it would have mattered any where else; yet I used to feel absurdly and cruelly out of keeping with my fate as I wove lace to get a pennyworth of bread to stand between me and starvation, whilst all the time my brocaded skirts swept the brick floor, and a boddice sown with gold thread and seed pearls imprisoned my aching and hungry heart.

I was fifteen; and old enough to know that it was very terrible to be without friends or money in the world; and very bitter to sit endlessly crossing and knotting the threads of my lace all the while wholly powerless to untwist one of the threads of fate.

If I could only escape from Verona, I used to think—it seemed to me it would all be quite simple then, once beyond the gates:—just once.

The Christmas week came, and kept the bells of all the churches ringing all day and night.

The dark, black-faced Befana had her feast day, and the people rejoiced and ate and drank and sang at the midnight mass, and exchanged compliments and confetti, good will and generous wines.

And all this time Mariuccia and I had not so much as a log of wood for the hearth, or a slice of meat for the soup pot; we were cold, poor, alone.

We went to mass all the same; and no one looking at her in her ruddy serge kirtle and her great Tuscan hat, and at me in my satin skirts and my velvet hood, would ever have dreamed we were in want of anything. For Mariuccia in her way was very proud; and so was I in mine. Nevertheless, so utterly did we want that we besought the Madonna humbly to send us a crust of bread.

But no doubt the Madonna hears this cry of "bread, bread, only a little bread," so very often that she has got deaf to it.

Be that how it may she sent us nothing; and in a little while it came to pass that for one whole day we did not even break our fast, and must have gone supperless to our chill beds, had not the padrona, from whom we could never quite conceal our dire needs, toiled up the stairs in the dark with a smoking pan of maccaroni lentil flavoured, and besought us to partake of it for the love of God.

Mariuccia accepted it with tears in her fearless old eyes, which for more than eighty years had never failed to open at dawn to the day's labour. Mariuccia would take a gift as frankly as she would give one; yet to eat the meal of charity was very bitter to her; she had done her best so long to live without alms; it seemed to her, I think, hard not to have died a little earlier, so as to have escaped this degradation.

That night she prayed very long to her Mother of Many Sorrows; I sobbed myself to sleep shivering and without a prayer.

In the morning, when we rose, there was not a thing in the house for our hunger; not a drop of milk for our thirst. Mariuccia set out the cups and plates by sheer habit, but they remained empty; there was not so much as a dust of charcoal with which to heat any water.

It was a very cold day, but very bright. The sun was shining. The bells were ringing. Already in the streets below there was a crowd of quickly moving feet and of laughing voices. The Carnival had come. It was the first day of the corso di gala.

Mariuccia and I looked at one another with the dry eyes of an absolute despair.

After a little space she went to a drawer in an old walnut-wood press, and took out a little red box. She brought it to me where I sat with the pillow of my work lying idle in my lap. She took out of it a few trinkets; corals and mosaics.

"These were your mother's," she said tenderly. "She had a great mass of jewels when I went to her first. After her death your father took them away, and sold them all no doubt. I have never seen them again. He kept these few little things; they are not of much value, though they are good of their kind. I have kept them for you. I could not think it right to sell them. But now it is a question whether they go or you starve. You are old enough to choose;—say."

I held them in my hand whilst she spoke; there

were earrings and lockets and a bracelet, all—in mosaic.

My poor young mother! I had never felt such pity for her, such nearness to her as I felt then.

My eyes grew wet with a rush of tears. I threw my arms about Mariuccia's throat.

"Keep them to-day," I murmured. "Dear, dear Mariuccia!—just to-day. I have thought of something. I am going to Ambrogiò."

I had flung my velvet hood over my head, and was out of the chamber and down the stairs into the street before she had time to question me; moreover she had no fear; I went every other day to Ambrogiò.

The sun was shining radiantly upon the frosty pavements as I went out upon them. It was the fourteenth day of the new year and the first of the carnival.

In the teeth of the cold people were all astir; hugging close their charcoal braziers, and wrapping their faces to the eyes in their cloaks; and although it was scarcely noon, in many a dark doorway there flashed some gay mummer's disguise.

The chimes of all the churches were ringing madly; there were bursts of music here and there; a set of the Tedeschi flashed by me, driving in the Tirol fashion; muffled with scarlet rugs and brown sables, their horses in belled harness stretched like greyhounds; from a balcony above, there fell on them as they galloped by a shower of house-reared violets and roses, a woman laughed gaily as she cast the flowers; their Tirolean postilions roused the echoes of the old gateways with a tarantarratara upon their tasselled bugles—how pretty and bright it all was!

It was the first gala of Carnival, and although the procession had scarcely commenced, all the city was out in holiday attire, and in holiday humour.

There was a wonderful glow everywhere of many various colours.

In the great multitudes that thronged every square and street and passage-way, and shelved upward like banks of flowers against the huge stones of the palaces and prisons, there were beautiful half tones of crimsons and greys and ambers, with here and there a broad flash of white from a woman's coif, or a glisten of golden spangles from a mummer's gear.

Here and there about in the throngs ran Stenterello or Arlecchino, or some other of their quaint, gay, bespangled and beribboned brotherhood.

Now and again the ranks of the people parted with shouts to let through some group of masks in all the colours of the rainbow, or some conjuror all aglow in scarlet, striking at 'them with his magic rod.

Through the swarming masses there began to sweep the gorgeous equipages of the patriciate, ushered forth in all the old-world pomp of Carnival; with the child-nobles clad in the costumes of their ancestors, powdered and jewelled with their rapiers at their side.

The draped balconies and the deep embrasures of the casements were filled with bright-eyed children, dark browed women, and old men with grey and noble heads, like a painter's studies for Prospero or Bellincion Berti.

Sometimes there was a burst of music, sometimes some glittering troop of cavalry clanged and clattered through the press, sometimes there rose the blare of trumpets, the tinkling of mandolines, the cries of the vendors of confetti, the shouts of little lads baiting the pantomime; and above it all, the laughter of the populace was always murmuring like an unresting sea.

I ran eagerly through the twisting passages to Ambrogiò's. I had an idea that he might get me some employment in the chorus of the opera house. I found his attic empty; the people of the place told me he was gone to a rehearsal at the theatre of Don Pacheco.

I ran then not less quickly to the coppersmith's under the Spiked Mace; I thought I would ask Raffaelo's mother to take a little coffee and bread for pity's sake to her poor old gossip and friend. But there was not a living creature in the workshop: even the blind woman had gone forth with her children to hear the echoes of the festivities she could not see.

I thought of poor Cecco, who would I know share his last soldi with me, but he and all his heedless tribe would be I knew as surely out in the town, busily helping or hindering the preparations of the mumming and the harlequinade, and all the gay street shows with which the Carnival would be welcomed in its royal pomp.

Broken-hearted and hungry, and with my cheeks wet with tears, I wandered carelessly about the streets, unwilling to return; the time stole on, the people began to pour out in throngs that grew merrier and larger with every moment; even the very cripples and beggars looked glad and triumphant, and had garlanded their crutches or adorned their rags with wreaths of leaves or knots of ribbons.

I only was all alone and most unhappy.

All at once a flute-like voice called out to me:

"Oh, dear donzella, come up here, come up here. I have looked for you everywhere. My mother is gone with my big brothers, and I have been to the house to look for you, and you had been out quite an hour and more, so the padrona said. Come up here; it is such a good place. One sees everything, and the crowd is getting large."

It was little Raffaelino who called to me, standing on the topmost edge of a flight of marble steps in one of the arched doorways of an old palace.

I joined him where he stood; and so it came to pass, that day, that I sang to the people in the great Piazza in my violet hood and my amber skirts, and that I heard the band of the maskers and scaramouches running down the street, with their coloured bladders, crying, in eager chase:

"Pascarèllo!—Pascarèll!"

BOOK II.

THE CITY OF LILIES.

CHAPTER I.

The Gifts of Gala.

"What is Pascarèl?" I asked of Raffaelino as they passed away, and I gathered my fallen treasures and rose to go homeward to poor Mariuccia.

The little lad did not know; he said that he would ask his brothers. He thought that it must be the name of some new-fashioned game of the Carnival.

At the entrance of my dwelling, 'Ino poured all his own spoils into my arms, and before I could refuse them or arrest him, he had fled off down the street again as fast as his fleet, brown, bare limbs could carry him.

He wanted to avoid being pressed to take a share; and, moreover, altogether to lose seeing the gala would have been a trial too bitter for his pleasure-loving Italian temper to endure to contemplate. He loved me, and had sacrificed himself to serve me; but now that he could no longer benefit me, the gala resumed all its supremacy.

The tears were still wet upon my cheeks, but my heart bounded joyously against the grim, graven stone of the Fates as I crossed the courtyard and flew up the staircase.

The house was quite empty; everyone was gone to see the Corso; there was no sound but the drip, drip, drip of the water in the stone fountain, and the wailing of little Zoto and Tito, the padrona's youngest children, who being too small to go out by themselves without being trampled on, and too troublesome for their mother to spoil her festa by looking after them, had been locked in, in the lower part of the house, and left to console themselves as they could with a few chestnuts and some curls of wood shavings for playthings.

I ran like a greyhound up the stairs and across the bare chambers to the little inner den where Mariuccia always sat and span under the high turret window that was stained in many colours with the life and miracles of S. Bruno.

I was covered with violets and confetti; they had lodged everywhere, in my hood and my curls, in my skirts, in my gathered-up dress which held, like a great yellow pannier, the heaps of rosettes and bouquets, and crisp bank-notes, and florins, gold and silver, and sweetmeat-papers, and knots of carnations.

My old nurse glanced up, startled, as I appeared before her like the very genius of the Carnival incarnated and filled with gifts, for, as I threw open the door, a flood of high noonday sunlight streamed in with me, and danced upon the yellow daffodils and the rosy knots of the other flowers, and the bright bands of the ribbons that streamed away from me in all directions.

Breathless and wordless, I poured my gleanings into her lap before she had fully seen that I stood before her.

"Here is enough for weeks and weeks and weeks!" I cried to her. "You need never be cold any more, and the stew-pots shall always be full. Just a few minutes in the square, and it is done! We shall never want to sell the mosaics!"

Mariuccia looked, stupefied, down upon the confused heap of gold and of silver, of bank-notes and of cakes, of fruits, and of sugared dainties. I dropped down on my knees before her and laughed in her face with delight; a delight to which tears lay close.

"Are you so astonished, Mariuccia? You never thought the people would care so much? It was Ino's thought, not mine. He would not take a thing for himself, not so much as a candied chesnut. But are you not glad, Mariuccia? Only think how we can live now! Just a song or two in the streets, and we are rich!"

Mariuccia's strong old frame shook with a sudden emotion that vaguely awed me; a glance that was stern and yet piteous flashed on me from her dark eyes; a quick sad-stricken cry escaped her:—

"In the streets!" she echoed; "in the streets? for money? And for me? O child, O carina! What shame!——"

"Shame?"

I rose to my feet chilled, silenced, mortified. I had used the one little gift with which Nature had dowered me, and the people had only given me what they would in return for the song that I gave them. Where was the harm? It was simple and fair, and honest; how could it, then, bring any shame?

So I pondered, being but a child.

Meanwhile Mariuccia covered her face with the

hem of her garment, and, rocking herself to and fro, wept bitterly.

"In the streets? for money?" she murmured again and again. "Oh, carina! the shame of it, the shame!"

I said nothing; I felt the tears swell to my eyes, but I would not let them fall.

I took up my poor treasures from the floor, on to which they had fallen in a disordered heap, and carried them to the head of the stairs and sorted them.

The notes and money I put away in the little old oak coffer that always held our riches when we earned any: then I leaned over the deep well of the staircase and called the names of Zoto and Tito.

The poor little lonely babies came tumbling and tottering to me at the summons from their old play-ground in the snow-filled court; I filled their little dirty eager hands with all the ribbons and roses, and sweetmeats, and pretty painted toys, which no longer had any beauty in my sight, or flavour to my mouth.

"Take them—all, all, all!" I cried to the astonished children who stood before me open-eyed at my sudden wealth and their good fortunes: they wanted no second permission to seize on all they saw; in another moment I had nothing left, and they, rapturous and shouting loudly in over glee, toddled down again in the court below, keeping high carnival amidst the snow.

As for me, I sat cold and still and sorrowful exceedingly beside the broken Donatello. Against my heart I still held the Fates.

I was wrong when I was proud, so they said; and now, when I had conquered pride for honesty's sake, I was wrong too;—the perplexity was a knot I could not unravel.

Mariuccia, the dear tender soul, soon found me sitting there, and came to me, and laid her hand upon my shoulder and kissed me between the eyes.

"'Nella mia, I was wrong to be so quick with you," she said, whilst her voice still shook. "You did for the best, dear, and it was good of you to think of me at all. But, all the same, it must not be; you must never go out in the streets again — never, never."

I sat silent upon the marble stairs; I was pained, angered, mortified, perplexed. She spoke to me, I thought, as if I had robbed in the streets instead of simply using the gifts with which Nature had dowered me, and taking nothing but what the goodwill of the people had joyously cast to me.

Mariuccia kept her hand on my shoulders where she stood before me, trying to see down into my dropped veiled eyes.

"Promise me you will never do such a thing again, 'Nella!" she said, anxiously; "I love you for it, carina; dearly, dearly. But it is so shameful!"

I shook her hands off me, and rose. I felt my face burn with anger; anger that was not perhaps so very unjust after all, for I had tried honestly to do right.

"Shameful!" I echoed. "I see nothing shameful in it. You speak to me as though I were a thief. I think it is much more shameful to sit still and see you starve of cold and hunger, and live myself on the padrona's charities. Sell the mosaics, if you like, if you think that better. But they will not last long, and what shall we do then? Altro! I am not a baby now. I know we have no money at all, and that you cannot tell where to write to my father. Are we to die of famine like caged rats, then, because you will not let the people pay me of their own goodwill for pleasing them? I am fifteen now, Mariuccia; and something or other I will do with my life; I will not mope and moulder for ever in this old prison-house. I will go away, as my brothers have gone."

My heart smote me as soon as the words had passed my lips. I saw her sturdy old frame shrink as if I had struck her a blow.

No doubt it was hard—harder than in my thoughtless youth I realized—to have given so many years, so much patience, such long unchanging care to the rearing of us motherless things, only to have us all as we reached our strength and stature impatient to escape her hold and pass from out her sight.

She was silent, and so was I; down in the courtyard the children played with their spoils in riotous glee; a sound of trumpets and of laughter came, deadened, through the closed casements from the distant streets.

"Do you hear them?" I cried to her at last in impotent impetuous pain. "Everywhere there are mirth and riches, and ease and pleasure; why am I not to have my share? I am handsome, so you all say; I have a voice; I am not a fool; I could do something in the world, I think. Anyway, can one do worse than die of cold and of want of food here?

Let me go, as my brothers have gone. Whatever the worst may be, it cannot be worse than this."

Mariuccia grew very pale, with that strange terrible pallor of age when the emotions come and go so slowly and with so much pain.

She looked down into my eyes which now met hers speaking, no doubt, the longing that possessed me with more eloquence than my words could hold.

Her strong withered hands shook where they still rested, on my shoulders.

"Wait a little," she said, at length, "wait, and let me think. The boys, at the worst, can only die; but you——"

She left the phrase unended and went from me, and passed away into the gloom of the passages.

Where I sat, under the broken Donatello, a shiver, that did not come from the chillness of the marble solitudes, or from the winds that blew from over the mountains and the snow, ran through and froze the bright current of my warm young blood.

What was this calamity, worse than death, which could not come to my brothers, but to me alone?

The rest of that day Mariuccia and I spoke not at all to one another; we sat silently as two strangers in the little square dark room with its smell of dried rose leaves and of the onions that keep off the evil eye.

She sat and span on at the distaff at her girdle, for she came of the class that cannot lay aside its daily work however much it may endure or may lament; but I sat aimlessly doing nothing, leaning my forehead against the grated window and watching the

Carnival throngs far down beneath me in the white piazza.

Once as the twilight closed in, Mariuccia called me to her; her voice sounded a little feeble. I could not see her very plainly, the shadows were so dark.

I bent to her to hear what she would say; her hand went up to my forehead, and passed over my hair in her old familiar gesture.

"Bambina mia," she said, eagerly, quite in a whisper, as she held me there; "promise me you will not sing in the streets again. Promise me! What should I say to your mother in heaven?"

"I will promise," I answered her, for there was an accent in the words that vaguely awed me, and almost vanquished the angry rebellion that was astir in my heart.

"Our Lady be with you ever," she muttered, softly and wearily, like one who is half asleep from fatigue, and speaks but on unconscious instinct. I went back to my place by the grated casement and fretted my soul in mute repining.

Now and then people flung up at me crowns of evergreens or showers of sweetmeats, but these all struck against the barred panes and fell back again into the street below.

I did not care to reach my hand and open the lattice so that they might enter.

The day went dully on its course; the duller in that little room of ours because of the mirth and mischief in the town below. It was the first day of the first Carnival in which Mariuccia and I had not clothed ourselves in the best and brightest apparel that we could and gone down to wander through the crowded ways laughing at every step, giving gay greetings, and lingering until with the grey of night the lamps had glittered by their tens of thousands all over the lines and domes of the green old city.

It was the first day in which we sat within and let the rejoicing throng flash by without us.

The hours were very slow, very cold, very dreary; there was no charcoal in the stove; there was no bread in the pot; the padrona and all her flock had gone forth to the popular mirth-making; in the old house all was dark, and still, and melancholy.

The twilight came early; there was no oil for our lamp; no food for our hunger; it was night very soon; we sat quiet in the darkness, which was only broken when some torch-lit procession or some blaze of fireworks flashed a fitful reflection into the chamber from the streets and squares of Verona.

We should go, cold to the bone and supperless, to our chill beds; yet neither she nor I stirred to take the money I had gained in the morning from its place in the oak coffer.

I looked at Mariuccia. She was still asleep.

At length, the rebellion and the weariness in me vanquished every other feeling. Why should I not go and enjoy with the rest? Why should I sit and mope here like an owl in the market-place, because a foolish old woman had quibbles and foibles about the good blood in my veins and the dangers of girlhood?

So I reasoned in the wickedness of my heart until the revolt in me ripened.

I stole again a glance at Mariuccia. She did not stir nor seem to hear. I stole noiselessly across the room, trimmed the lamp afresh, reached down my hood, and went out on to the stairs.

There was no one to say me nay. Every soul in the house was out that night, except the two bambini, who were fast asleep curled together on a heap of pine shavings, the emptied sugarplum-horns and the broken toys strewn all around them.

I was soon in the streets and squares, that were all alive with throngs of people, bent hither and thither, laughing and talking, some singing, others dancing down the gloom of the solemn passage ways.

It was quite late.

Time had glided away unperceived as I had sat in that monotonous vexation and quietude. They were setting fireworks in the cathedral square, and the great bells were ringing the tenth hour of the night.

CHAPTER II.

The Veglione Masquer.

LONG familiarity with the Veronese ways had made me quite able to take care of myself in a crowd; and the Italian crowds, though often riotously mirthful, are never rough or rude.

I got in a coign of vantage just under the grim old stone Roland, and seated myself comfortably and carelessly to see the girandola.

The fireworks were very fine, and shot upward in streams and clouds of glory on the frosty night air, shedding their many colours on the sea of upturned faces, and flashing over the darkness of the Duomo pile. I yielded myself eagerly and with utter zest to the enjoyment of them.

I was very hungry, to be sure, and cold still; but it was much better to be hungry and cold but well amused than to suffer the same thing in loneliness and gloom. I had not been born in Italy without being born to as much philosophy as lay in this simple reasoning.

So I gave myself up to the girandola sitting aloft under the paladins, laughing, and shouting "Bellissima!" and "Brava!" with the throng around me, and for the time utterly oblivious that I had wept such bitter tears under the Donatello, and, alas, equally forgetful, I shame to say, that Mariuccia sat at home alone in her sadness and her patience.

The bands of the Austrian regiments were playing in the piazza, to keep the Veronese in good humour; and the music, the fireworks, the picturesque chiaroscuro of the thronged square, as the various fires illumined it, all combined to make me forget my woes, and to rouse me into an exhilaration which was all the more excited and unreal because I had fasted for so many hours.

I was in no mood to go home and creep to bed in the cold supperless. It was now midnight, I knew, but I was indifferent. Mariuccia would scold; but then— had she not done so when I had tried to please and help her in the forenoon?

So I hardened my heart; and when the last sheaf of coloured flames had died out, and the streams of people began to pour outward, this way and that, I strolled on also, looking to see if by any chance there might be other amusements still forthcoming.

The Stranieri spent their gold lavishly in diversions for the populace; and the Veronese Carnival at the time of that foreign dominance, if its mirth were hollow, was, at least, as brilliant in festivity as any in Italy.

Mariuccia would scold, of course, when I went home, but what of that? Words break no bones.

So I said to myself, in my wilfulness and revolt. Alas! that hour has been a remorse to me ever since.

As I have said before, I was never very good and often very bad in those days, so far as waywardness and daring went. As a child—and I was still no more than a child—I was affectionate always; and courageous, when my imagination was not affected by fear; I told the truth, and I would give anything I possessed, however much I might want it myself.

But there my virtues ended. I was disobedient to a headlong rashness; and I was in a mood to be so to-night.

As I went out of the piazza, there was a little laughing group of sightseers, cloaked and hooded in an odd fashion. They looked like monks, but they were waltzing down the pavement, and singing a tavern song very popular then in Verona.

"Pascarèllo! Pascarèll!" they screamed at the top of their voices, as a flash of red went by under an old archway; and they set off running swiftly, their monkish robes showing beneath them women's little feet with rosetted ribbons flying.

This mystical name fascinated me; the desire to know its meaning grew stronger and stronger.

I flew in their wake, and ran too. The gleam of scarlet had vanished into the gloom of the arch.

Soon I came upon a throng of people standing before some columned steps and some wide entrance doors. Above, many lamps glittered, and against the wall there fluttered on a scroll, in great white letters on a scarlet ground, the word of Veglione.

From the belfries of the city midnight was sounding. The stream of people was passing within the building; they looked very strange to me; they made me think of an old painting that hung in our old palace entrance-hall, and that was called the "Gates of Hell."

But I pressed on to enter with them; I was not afraid; it was the Veglione by the writing on the wall.

I had heard strange and wonderful things of that saturnalia, and I imagined many more; moreover, here had entered those veiled figures who had been seeking Pascarèl.

I ran eagerly up the steps, and was carried by the press of the pleasure-seekers into the body of the hall. There was a barrier at which they stopped me for payment.

I stood helpless, with the rushing sound of the many footsteps on my ears; a man's hand, stretched over my shoulder, cast down the money for me, and a man's voice laughed in my ear, "So handsome, and not masked? Pass in, pass in, carina."

The pressure of the onward moving throngs swept me through the barrier, and away from my deliverer. I was borne into the very midst of the strange torrent of colour and tumult, of laughter and of music.

I stood still and looked, the blaze of the light half blinding me; my face was uncovered; my hood fell back; my feet were bare; my yellow skirts were stained with many a crushed fruit and bruised flower, in the old glad days of my wanderings; my little hot hands held between them the onyx ring against my breast.

There was a broad piece of mirror before me in the entrance-hall; I saw my reflection in it, and was charmed and yet ashamed.

My cheeks burned like wild poppies; my hair was in a lustrous tangle: my eyes looked like great burning lamps in the thinness of my hunger-worn, small face; my mouth was scarlet and parched with excitement; and yet I knew so well I looked handsome—so well that the people would look at me and cry, "Bellina!"

I was frightened, and yet I was fascinated. There seemed some horrible evil about me, and yet it was so vivacious, and so gay, and so full of pictures, that I could not help being allured by it.

Pascarèl I did not discover, and, truth to tell, I forgot all about that mystery.

I was too absorbed in it all to be conscious that I was singular in going thus bareheaded and unmasked amongst the dominoes.

It was a pageantry to me, nothing else; and I moved on as I should have done in the streets; the people supping at their little snowy tables in their boxes; the quaint, glittering costumes that leaned over the panels; the stir and colour of it all, the headlong flight of the mad waltzers, the white mousquetaires wringing the champagne from their long moustaches; the gorgeous eighteenth-century dresses crowned with powdered hair; the crowd of black monk-like figures that served only to intensify the gaiety of colour—all these were so many pictures to me.

I wandered on enchanted, and unheeding the observation that I gathered in my course; the only thing that I noticed was the intentness with which I was followed by the eyes of a Florentine Florindo, who wore that traditional dress with an easy grace that was in a manner familiar to me. But the Florindo did not approach me, and I soon ceased to think about him in the midst of the masquers.

For me, I never doubted that it was pandemonium itself; and yet the fantastic charm, and the lurid brilliancy of it bewitched me. It was horrible, and yet it was beautiful.

The women's eyes, as they glittered like snakes' eyes through the blackness of the masks; the cloud, and flutter, and tumult of colour; the furious speed of the dancers whirling, stamping, shouting, reeling in all the maddest ecstasies of folly; the sombre darkness of the gliding dominoes passing silently with little low, sneering laughs, as the arrows of their whispered speech hit some blot or some wound in men's strength or women's weakness; the intoxication of the loud, gay music crossed every second by the wild war-whoop of the revellers; the dazzle of innumerable hues and shine of countless jewels in the great semicircle full from floor to roof, whilst here and there some masquer, ablaze with diamonds, flung her flowers from above, and some noble, powdered and jewelled, leaned down to pledge a dishevelled, panting dancer, in rosy, foaming wine; the wonder, and chaos, and glow, and tumult of the scene bewitched me as I gazed on it.

It was only the masked ball of the Carnival; but to me it was beautiful as paradise and horrible as hell.

It all swam giddily before my sight, and the music rolled like thunder above my head.

As I stood, a dancer, in the dress of the Louis Treize musketeers, flung his arms about me, and swept me into the circle of the waltzers with a force that bore me off my feet.

"Cara mia," he cried in my ear, "you are in strange guise for the Veglione, but what matter that? I paid for you at the doors. You shall reward me up yonder."

He never ended his phrase. I struck him on the mouth blindly with both hands on the mere instinct for freedom, and broke from his hold, and ran through the maze of the dancers without sense or sight of what I did.

Shrill cries rose round me; the people parted hastily to let me through, and many fled from me in terror; a shout arose that I was mad, and had broken loose from the hospital. The sense of the outcry came to me dully as voices ring over water from a far shore to a drifting boat.

Suddenly I stopped, and flung my head upward like a beaten stag, and looked across the blinding blaze of colour, vaguely seeking help.

Fronting me was the red glow of drooping curtains, a great knot of carnival camellias, a little group of men and women, like a picture from the Decamerone, a medley of violet and gold, and scarlet and black, and diamonds and pearls; it was an opera-box, in which five dominoes leaned and laughed, and drank and jested.

The central figure of them all stood erect, with a red plume tossing in the light; he was in a flash of ruby colour and of white; he wore the dress of the Florentine Florindo, and had a dark oval face like that of an old picture; his hand was on his sword-hilt; he laughed gaily with the masked and mirthful women.

I do not clearly remember what ensued.

A band of debardeurs surrounded me; a hideous cock crowed at me; a clown grinned and gabbered; a set of black masks hooted and threw their limbs hither and thither in wild contortion.

The Mousquetaire seized me afresh; lifted me from the ground, and plunged into the wild gallopade that was rushing down the boards like a troop of riderless horses on San Giovanni's day in Florence.

I shrieked for help and release.

My tormentor, screaming with laughter, held me the tighter. There was a moment's pause; then a crash of sound, a loud outcry, a tumult of the masquers, and the Florindo with the scarlet plume had sprung from the box above, had struck or tossed the arms away that held me, and had hurried me through the maze of the dancers out of the heat and the glare into the cool white moonlight that was streaming through the darkness of Verona.

"Pascarèllo—Pascarèl!" the people had shouted as he came; and there was no pursuit, and no offence taken against him.

He stood and looked at me in the silvery light; a bright and many coloured figure, flashing with the grace and glitter of the old dead centuries under the gloom of the walls of the Scala.

"Well, my singing bird," he said, with a smile in his eyes, "what were you doing there, may I ask?

It is a place for kites and hawks, and all manner of evil birds; but not for nightingales. You did not seem as if you liked the air?"

The voice was the voice of the giver of the onyx. I burst into tears, and told him what had drawn me thither.

He heard me with a gentle amusement in his eyes; dark eyes, tender and poetic, such as Sordello's might have been here in this very same Verona.

"The best thing I can do for you is to take you homeward quickly," he said, moving onward, and bidding me show him the way to my home. "To be abroad on a Veglione night is not the best thing for you, donzella. Courage is very admirable, but a little prudence is needful too in this world.

"It is to make your cake all of coriander-seeds— to make life up of rashness only.

"Tell me—why were you singing in the streets this morning? You look like a little princess, Signorina Uccello. Nay; never mind. You shall tell me to-morrow. You will let me come and see you to-morrow.

"You want to get out of Verona? Oh, fie, for shame. That is not poetic at all. To get away from the Stranieri is always good, I admit, but surely Verona has a charm of her own still, if only you will look for it.

"She is not like my Florence, indeed; it is not given to every city to be born out of fields of lilies, and keep their sweetness with her for ever, as Florence does; a woodland fragrance always amidst the marble and the gold.

"But Verona,—oh, yes,—Sordello's song is here,

if only you listen, and it is the same moon that Giulietta saw from the balcony, and those great Scali —they seem to daunt and to awe the place still,— and do you not see Adelaïda ever bending her terrible brows in the shadows?

"Nor Cunizza, the faithless, with her 'strong, cruel star,' that ruled her life so ill, and her lovely eyes burning with the madness of the Romano, and at her side her gentle Troubadour, Ser Folco? Do you never see them? They lived and loved here in this old Verona that you despise because you are so ignorant of all its beauties.

"And then, far away,—so far away in the dawn of the poets—the pretty Lesbia twisting the roses in her lover's locks in their gardens yonder, while at a bow-shot in the circus the citizens shouted, 'Ad leones!' Oh, you should not hate Verona. It is so ancient, and it was so mighty once, though it never used its might for any very good purpose."

He talked on thus merely of course for the purpose of banishing my fear, and reconciling me to the strangeness of my position, in wandering the streets thus at night, with an unknown masquer in the dress of Florindo. There was that true and kindly delicacy in him which would not to prolong his own amusement, and gratify his own curiosity, increase my embarrassment, or cause me pain.

His voice was so beguiling, his eyes so frank and tender, his whole bearing so full of a certain gentleness and carelessness, that I was attracted into an irresistible sense of confidence in him.

He was an utter stranger; he was one of those mad carnival mummers who had imbued me with a vague sense of unspeakable, intangible evil; he was only a Veglione masquer, gay and grotesque in his vari-coloured disguise in the white Veronese moonlight; and yet I trusted him, and felt a sense of security in his presence, and spoke to him as simply and as naturally as I could have done into the ear of little Raffaelino.

"But this was very naughty of you," he said, still with the smile in his eyes, as he heard my sins.

"I am never good!" I confessed very piteously. "I am like that wicked Speronella of Padova, whose namesake I am—so my nurse says, at the least."

He laughed indulgently.

"Oh come! not quite so bad as that, I trust. And you will grow wiser in time. Let us hope rather that you will end like that good Nella whom her husband, even in a better world than this, if poets may be credited, quoted as a priceless perfection. But what possessed you to go to that place to-night? A freak of mischief no doubt, but what promoted it?"

"I wanted to see what Pascarèl was! That was all. That was all indeed!"

He paused a moment in the silent street, and laughed outright.

"Well," he asked, "did you find out?"

"No! Do you know? Pray tell me."

"I have tried to find out too," he said, with the laugh on his lips. "Tried all my life, and never succeeded yet."

"Is it something so wonderful?"

"Oh, dear, no. No wonder of any sort in it."

"Is it an enigma then?"

"Well—yes—a little. Probably the answer lies

in nothing deeper than in the one word with which
Œdipus answered the Sphinx. Do not trouble your
head after it. It is not worth your while."

"Why? The people seem to care."

A tender and saddened shade swept over his face.

"Ay! the people, perhaps, a little."

"What is it then? Do tell me."

In my eagerness I paused midway in the street;
the snow lay lightly on all the roofs and stones and
balconies; the icy Alpine air had frozen it into all
sorts of lovely and fantastic shapes.

The masquer broke off one of the pretty snow
flowers off an iron scroll, and held it in his hand.

It slowly melted and vanished.

"That is what Pascarèl is; nothing more!" he
said, lightly. "Do not talk of it; tell me about yourself."

I had not space to tell him much, for the old
palace was at a stone's throw from the opera-house,
and he and I stood in a few moments' time before
our huge, cavernous, arched portals, whose nail-studded
ancient doors stood forever wide open, night and
day, for we were all too poor there to have fears of
theft, having naught amongst us all to lose.

At the entrance he paused and uncovered his
head.

"I will bid you good-night, donzella, and go back
to my pranks and my follies. To-morrow, if you will
let me, I will come and see you. Gratitude? Oh,
altro! you have no cause for that. It is I rather who
am grateful to the Fates. By-the-way, I wish that I
had had something brighter and fairer to give you
than the old grim onyx; they are an ugly portent I

am afraid, those stern sisters. Never mind, I will try
and get you some roses to-morrow. They will be
very much fitter for you. Nightingales and roses have
belonged to one another ever since the days of paradise. Addiò!"

He kissed my hand with easy grace, and turned
away down the deep shadows of the street; in the
moonlight the red and white of his dress—colours of
Florence—glistened as the moon-rays caught them; he
went singing, half aloud, the catalogue of the Loves
from the Giovanni.

I watched him until he was lost to sight in the
darkness that fell from the lofty palaces, half fortress
and half prison, the twisted galleries, the marble balconies, the frowning stones of Romeo's city; it was a
little scene from the Tre Cento, from the Decamerone,
from Goldoni; the old dead amorous poetic life
seemed suddenly to breathe and move again amidst
the decay and the despair of old Verona.

I went slowly up the staircase, past the ruined
Donatello, and fancied that the broken, dust-strewn
stairs were the steps of the Capulet palace, and that
I was Giulietta in that tender daybreak, when the lark
sang all too soon.

CHAPTER III.
The Last Sleep.

As I entered the chamber where I had left Mariuccia,
and groping for a match lit the little lamp, I saw that
she was still in her oak chair by the fireless hearth.
Her hands were folded, and her chin had sunk upon
her breast. I knew that she was used to allow herself

a little rest and slumber after her long day of toil, and I imagined that she had dozed on and on, not noticing my absence, nor the flight of time.

I slid down quietly upon the floor at her feet, and did not speak lest I should waken her.

I was glad that she could in sleep forget the hunger and the cold. I was glad, too, to have escaped the reproaches and rebukes that my conduct merited.

I leaned my head against her knee as I had done so often in my babyhood, and sat there, very quiet, with her hands resting heavily against my shoulder.

It was deadly cold; my limbs were frozen; my brain swam a little from long fasting and excitement; it was quite dark; from the streets below there came the hum and outcry of a city in its holiday; Mariuccia did not waken.

I think that I also must have slept a little or at the least lost consciousness of time, for I started as one starts when suddenly roused from a bad dream, as the last fireworks of the night's pageantry rose with a rushing sound above the roof, against the moonless sky.

A great girandola shot its fountain of many-coloured fires up above the black outline of the Duomo, fired most likely by the last revellers of the Veglione, and the reflection from it fell, golden and reddened, through the little grilled window into the chamber; its light fell upon Mariuccia's face.

Something in the look of its closed eyes and silent mouth made my heart tighten with a breathless fear.

"Mariuccia!" I cried to her. "Mariuccia! You frighten me! dear Mariuccia—are you still asleep?"

She was indeed asleep.

The brief and fitful fires of the girandola died away, and left behind it the blank of an utter darkness; the dense impenetrable darkness that precedes a winter's dawn.

Upon the old quiet patient face there was a look of rest, and the withered hands on which I rained my kisses were yet warm. Yet I, who never before had looked on death, knew well that death was here, and that whilst Verona laughed on her first night of Carnival, I sat in the silence of the old palace, alone with the dead body of the sole friend I had on earth.

CHAPTER IV.

At Ave-Maria.

THREE days from that time Mariuccia had gone to her last home.

The wooden shell had been jostled in the common hearse and buried in the common resting-place where the poor lie. The padrona and Raffaello and his blind mother and I had toiled after it through the driving cold of the early morning, and heard the heavy clods fall on it one by one.

It was all over—all over: the strong, pure, honest, tireless life had gone, spent in obscurity and toil, unrecognised and unrecompensed to the last.

I was but a thoughtless, wayward, and selfish child. I had been heedless always, cruel often. I had taken the countless sacrifices that she made to me with all a child's reckless, tyrannous, unconscious egotism. I scarcely even now knew the immeasurable debt I had owed to her.

Yet a vague heavy pain, that was almost remorse, weighed on me, and on some insufficient yet pregnant sense.

I realised all that this one lost life, old as it was, and humble and poor, had yet been to me from my birth, with its buckler of stanch fidelity held ever between me and the evils of the world.

The dreary weeks went by; to all the rest of Verona they were gay with all the zest of Carnival.

Night after night the fireworks would blaze against the skies, and the music would roll through the sad old streets, and the mad and merry maskers would scamper and frolic under the shadow of prison and fortress and monastery.

The echoes and the reflections of the noise and the lights would come to me where I sat in my dismal little chamber, but that was all the share I had in them.

The padrona, though so poor, would have some friends to laugh with her in her dim old kitchen, and would find some copper pieces to give her a sight of the puppets and the shows that enlivened for Verona those long and chilly days when the winds swept down like dragons whose breath was ice from the deep Tirol valleys and the desolate Dolomite range.

But I was all alone, except when Raffaellino came and tried to while away my sorrow by his innocent fanciful talk and the tender strains of his viol.

With the sad morrow my Romeo of the Veglione never returned.

Even in my passionate remorse and grief I could not but think often of him that day.

When we returned from our dreary errand in the snow, there was awaiting me a great cluster of roses, red and white, that must have come from Tuscany or Rome.

Little Giàn, who had been upon the stairs when they arrived, said that a boy about his own age had brought them, saying nothing whence they came.

I knew..

I set the beautiful things before me against the dismal grated window, and wept my heart out over them. The grief was most for the loss of dear dead Mariuccia; but a little also for the broken faith of the Florence masquer.

What could I do?

I knew no more whither my father was gone than whither the crows flew when they passed in a black cloud over the Adige; and though the good padrona served for me, cooked for me, and bade me be as welcome under her roof as were the rains in summer, I was too proud to think a moment that such dependence on another could ever long endure.

The desire to escape from Verona grew stronger on me with every hour. I had no notion of what I should do elsewhere: but all good things seemed possible to me if once only I could cross the dreary plain and seek the sunrise of the south.

I said nothing; for I knew that Raffaello would weep and protest and the padrona take fright, and the priests would be spoken with, and some means perhaps be found to detain me, if ever they knew that I wished to take wing.

But all those winter days, when the Corso was at its gayest and the streets were full of masks and mummers, I sat in my dull little stone chamber and revolved again and again a thousand schemes for my freedom.

As the first step towards liberty, I went out one day at the close of the Carnival to see the scrivere whom Mariuccia had been wont to employ for her communications to Florio.

A certain sense of reluctance to trench on anything that seemed like a secret of the dead had held me back from asking this letter-writer any questions; but as the weeks of silence succeeded one another, I argued that not to try and find my father would be a folly and a fault, and in the last hours of one wintry day I crossed the square to where Maso Sasso held his councils at his little worm-eaten desk.

I thought sadly as I went of the homely old figure that had always been at my side spinning and talking as she hobbled over the stones; I thought a little too of that gay red and white masker whose eloquent eyes had smiled on me in the moonlight of Juliet's city.

Why had he not followed his roses?

He was not a man to me, nor a stranger; he was a poem, a picture, a thing of grace, a shape of the cinque cento; Sordello, only not so sad; Romeo, only not so boyish; Ariosto, perhaps, that gayest of lovers and poets; or one of those patrician improvisatori who spent half their lives in a court and the other half in the marketplace.

I was thinking of him still as I crossed the piazza to the hole in the wall where Maso Sasso sat.

When the Ave-Maria was rung he used to close

his office by a bronze wicket and his day's work was done. Then he would pass methodically across the piazza to his favourite trattoriâ; and in front of it, taking his frugal repast, would make himself amends for the long silence of the day by detailing to an interested audience such of the sayings and doings of his clintela as he deemed it proper to reveal.

He was known to be a miracle of propriety and discretion; nevertheless he was a good companion when the sun was set.

Indeed, they were used to say if you brewed him a bibita to his liking, there was very little that you might not hear concerning your neighbour in Verona. But a public that has to recount its joys and sorrows aloud to its penman cannot be very scrupulous about secresy, and the popularity of Maso Sasso never waned on that account.

He had his office in a little dark stone loggia; curiously black and still in the midst of the changeful life of the piazza.

He was a little meagre, yellow, shrivelled old man, who sat all day long in his den and heard all the comical comedies and tearful tragedies of the city, and never seemed to be touched at all by any one of the innumerable idyls and the pathetic obscure heroisms which came hourly before him, as the citizens and the contadini flocked around his stall eager to have had some good tidings sent to some absent one, or to unfold some stiff and blotted scrawl from over the mountains and the sea.

There was a crowd of people around the loggia in which his desk was placed when I drew near it; it was nearly four, and it was known that no press of public necessities would ever make him prolong his sittings after the Ave-Maria.

I had to wait patiently my turn.

A broad-shouldered crimson-kertled contadina wanted a love-letter sent to a soldier away in Piedmont; she did not care what was said so that it was all as sweet as sugar.

A poor wife held out a dirty miserable scrawl, and fell down in a loose lifeless heap upon the stones, as she heard that her husband had been drowned off Ischia.

A jager of the Tirol, with his green plumes dangling in his saucy black eyes, dictated an offer of marriage, giggling and grinning as the pen flew.

An old meek, timid creature tendered a paper with a trembling hand, and turned away with a heart-stricken moan as the slow changeless tones of the scrivere read aloud to her that her only son was sentenced for life to the galleys far away in the Regno.

What an epitome was Maso Sasso's den of human nature and of human fate!

I stood and listened with my hood drawn over my face: when my turn came I had forgotten my own sorrows.

"Oh how can you bear it—every day and all day long—like this?" I cried to the wizen, immovable, indifferent old man.

He spread his palms outward over his desk in a gesture of silent contempt.

"Signorina—it is life!"

"But the sorrow—the joy—one against the other—the comedy—the tragedy—it is horrible!"

The old man smiled grimly.

"What does that matter to me?—joy or sorrow—tragedy or comedy—I get my scudo for my trouble."

"But how can you bear it?" I cried again, "day after day, year after year—always those terrible things, side by side with all this laughter."

The old man shrugged his shoulders and took off his horn spectacles to wipe them free of dust.

"Signorina—whether it is woe or laughter, what does it matter to me? I get my scudo, and have something to gossip about. That is all that concerns me."

In later years I have found that the world is very much of opinion with the scrivere. It scans the mass of human life through its spectacles, and whether it reads a fiat of death or dishonour, or a jest-story of love and of lightness, it cares nothing so that only it can take out of both its scudo's worth of scandal.

He asked me for the third time what I needed; I was keeping more profitable customers from his stall. I inquired of him whether Mariuccia had addressed her letters to my father. Maso Sasso shrugged his shoulders again, and sought in the full stores of his memories.

"The letters were to be left at the post, anywhere," he said at last. "Sometimes Nice—Paris—Vienna—the last time, I think, Florence. Yes; Florence. But always the post-office. Nothing more."

"You are sure it was Florence the last time?" I cried, entreating him tremblingly.

"Yes, quite sure. But the last time was eight months ago. Will the Signorina please to move aside? People are waiting, and the sun will soon set."

I moved aside mechanically, and walked dreamily

across the square and sat down on the steps of a great church, where the beggars were wont to sit.

Florence seemed a long way off; and the chance but a very slight one. Nevertheless, it was all I had.

The evening was cold still, but bright and windless.

It was at the end of February; there were lovely roseate lights in the sky, and all fresh mountain scents on the air. Women went by with large baskets full of crocuses and daffodils.

In the beautiful pearly hues of the late day the old gaunt city was transfigured.

Its roofs and domes gained a spiritual light, and vast dream-like shadows swept its plains. It was for once possible to believe in Giulietta and to muse on Catullus.

At least, so it seemed to me; but perhaps it was only lovelier that night because I knew that so soon I should look my last on it,—perchance for ever.

CHAPTER V.

The Feast of Faustino.

An hour passed away with me sitting there, dreamily watching Verona.

I could see my old home; the dark gruesome stone pile of it rose sheer as a rock against the blueness of the sky, unchanged since the days when Henry the Seventh had slept beneath its roof, and the bright Conraddin ridden forth from its court yard.

I had never loved the place. Indeed, it had been as a prison to me all my years. And yet my heart ached now to leave it. We are so bitterly ungrateful to the present, so blindly grateful to the past,—always.

The Ave-Maria slowly swung from all the bells of all the churches; the bronze gate of the loggia was shut with a clang, the scrivere hobbled across the square to his place of gossipry; lamps were set one by one in the doorways; the oil wicks were lighted in the iron sconces of the streets; the little charcoal stoves of the chesnut sellers began to glow ruddily in the coming gloom.

As I turned away from the sunset to go homeward, whilst those colours of glory faded over the silent city, a hand touched me, a voice startled me.

"Pregiatissima Signorina! have the Veronese no eyes that you are left to stray their streets alone?"

It was the voice of the Mousquetaire, from whom the Florentine Florindo had rescued me at the Veglione; a voice with a strong and harsh foreign accent. The shudder of disgust and dismay with which I recognised him made an impatient and displeased shadow sweep across his face.

"Wait. Hear me a little," he said eagerly as I turned my back on him and went with quicker steps out of the piazza. "I am a friend of your father's. I have spent many an hour with him. You have nothing to fear. I have pitied you many a time, poverina, sitting up there, all alone, at that grated window; so fair a singing bird in so dark a cage."

I twitched my purple mantle from his grasp.

"I do not want your pity. Let me be."

But he kept step with me.

"Nay, why do you bear me such ill will?" he said,

with a petulance in his laugh that served ill to reassure me.

"Listen, carina mia; you are a beautiful child. Did no one ever tell you so before? I have seen your golden head at that grating many a day, and been sorely tempted to enter your door; only that direful dragon whom you have happily buried for good and all, sat on guard so very grimly."

I shook him off as best I could.

"Respect the dead at least, and leave me!" I cried to him; I hated the sound of his voice, the look of his eyes, and the street into which we had passed was so empty, and now that the after-glow had faded the city was so dark.

He laughed lightly and pursued his way.

"Oh no, cara mia! I let you go that night because I liked you too well to raise a scene around you. But I mean soon or late to have all that I there surrendered out of chivalry to you. See here, my pretty signorina, you were out on a freak, and no one knew, of course, and it was I who passed you in to the Veglione. Well, that is very harmless if you trust in me; I shall be silent, that you may be sure. But otherwise, if you provoke me—if you carry that handsome sunny head of yours aloft in that fashion, why then——"

I paused and faced him.

"Well?—What then?"

"What then? Why then—every one will know that the little Tempesta stole at midnight to the opera ball with me, and she will be very glad to give me whatever I please to take—"

He threw his arms about me, and bent his face to

mine; but with all the strength I had I struck him on the mouth, poured on him all the epithets of injury and of disgust with which my knowledge of the Veronese streets supplied me, and shaking myself free of him, ran as swiftly as a hare through the twisting passages to my home.

The insult of this stranger had decided me. I did not dare to stay another day longer in Verona; I was pursued with the dread of him, and the disgust that he inspired was the last touch of impulsion needed to make me take wing into the unknown lands—into the unknown world.

I reached my own room unobserved; and put together the few clothes I possessed and counted my little store of money. I had changed all that I had gained on the day of Galà into gold with a childish idea that notes were of little comparative value; and so liberal had been the people to me, that when Mariuccia's funeral and my own expenses for the last weeks had been paid, I had left me sixteen broad gold Austrian florins.

I put the money with my mother's mosaics into a leathern bag, and strapped it about my waist. The onyx Fates were round my throat. I had a fancy that they would bring me fair fortune.

I took too a little dead rosebud from the great clusters that the Florentine masquer had sent me; and tied it with the onyx close about me. I had a fancy that it would propitiate the Fates.

My purple and amber costume was an absurd one for travel, but I had no other that had any warmth against the mountain winds, and I was forced to wear it.

I looked longingly around the long, familiar chambers, dusky and grim, with grated windows and deep vaulted roofs and floors of marble; desolate and prison-like though they had been, they were yet all I knew of Home.

With sobs that choked me I kneeled and prayed to the Mother of Many Sorrows, where her picture hung above Mariuccia's bed, then with a last look of farewell I drew the velvet hood over my head and stole down the stairs.

I met little Zoto and Tito, and kissed them.

I could see the padrona in her kitchen wringing out washed linen by the light of a little oil lamp, under a picture of S. Sulpitia. A contadina from the plains sat chatting with her and plaiting straw as they talked.

My eyes filled with tears, and shut out the little picture. In another moment I had crossed the threshold, and was running hard and fast towards the south gate in the twilight.

On my way, I passed of necessity the coppersmith's workshop under the Spiked Mace. I glanced wistfully through the open entrance.

The light of a large wood fire was leaping about all the brazen and copper vessels. The blind woman sat in its warmth. The coppersmith moved to and fro with bare sinewy arms. Little Raffaellino sat reading a score, with his lithe limbs twisted under him, and his lute by his side on the bricks. I dared not let him know that I was going away, lest he should raise, far and near, opposing clamour.

I prayed mutely, in my heart, to the Madonna for

them, then went on my way to the dull crooked passage in which Ambrogiò Rufi dwelt.

I dared not bid anyone farewell, lest they should find means to stop me in my course. I knew well that they would all say I was too young to stray alone over Italy. I dared not speak to anyone else, but I could not bring my heart to quit the city without some word, some look upon the face of my old master.

I stole upward to the desolate garret, and entered it unheard by him.

He was sitting leaning over the little brazier, which was all that he could afford to warm him in the bitterest weather.

It was the feast of the Martyr Faustino, and all the churches were calling to vespers.

The attic was quite dark.

The moon had not yet risen. It was so high in the air, that all the metallic clash and clangour of the bells seemed to beat through its silence like the clamour of a thousand hammers on a thousand anvils.

I went and kneeled down by him without his hearing me. I ventured to touch him gently.

"Dear master, does not the noise of all these bells tire you sometimes?"

He did not lift his head from his chest.

"I am always tired," he muttered. "What of that?"

"But if you lived where it is quieter?—here it is so close to all the belfries."

"It does not matter," he answered me, absently. "They drown the music in my brain. I am glad of them—sometimes."

"But if you wrote the music down?"

He shivered a little where he leaned over the brazier.

"To feed the stove? Not I—not I."

I dared not urge him farther. The utter hopelessness, the terrible apathy of this lost genius, which all its life long had woven beautiful things to which the world was forever deaf. What could I say to these? —I, a child, to whom every sun that rose was as a promise and a smile from God?

I waited a little while, kneeling before the brazier at his side. My heart was very sore to leave him, though he so seldom seemed to note my presence.

"Maestro," I murmured, at the last, "speak to me a little. I am going away."

"Ay, ay!" he echoed, drearily. "To be sure—to be sure. You all go away. Why not?"

I was silent.

How many hundreds of us he must have seen pass away, bright-eyed, flute-voiced children, who stood around him for a little space, and then drifted out of sight, out of knowledge, into the darkness of the unknown world; while he, the old man, changed in nothing, but remained always by his cheerless hearth under his lonely roof.

I pressed a little closer to his side, timidly.

"Maestro," I murmured again, "I have no one in the world, and I am going away. Will you bless me once—just once, for fear I never see your face again?"

He roused himself from his lethargy with a strong shudder. He looked at me a moment with a startled, awakened look in his dim eyes. He laid his hand upon my head, and, as it rested there, it trembled greatly.

"I dare not bless you—I have doubted God; but I wish you well, poor child. That is—I wish you without a heart, without a soul, without a conscience, so that you may deal unto men as surely they will deal unto you."

His hand sunk from my head; his chin dropped again upon his chest. He had fallen once more into his old dreaming stupor over the charcoal fumes under the roar of the bells.

I rose to my feet sorely afraid. It was a dread benediction with which to commence my pilgrimage.

In another moment I was again on my way to the south gate of the city. I looked back once. The old palace was black and full of gloom against the clearness of the skies. I shivered a little, and set my face again to the south-east.

Who could say how the sun might rise for me there!

CHAPTER VI.

Fuori.

HALF-AN-HOUR later I was rolling underneath the stone vault of the gate which faced towards Tuscany, in the old heavy, cumbrous, leathern-curtained diligenza, which thrice in every week droned on its way to Padova and Bologna.

Rich people travelled otherwise, I knew; but I had only sixteen florins in the world.

The soldiers at the gates looked hard at me, but

said nothing. The man with the horn, on the step of the clumsy vehicle, took my money and asked no questions. I was safe on the road to Florence. It seemed a terribly long way off, across those unknown mountains; but the name of the City of Lilies allured me with a strong sweet spell.

Mariuccia had told me many glories of the place of her birth; and my young mother I knew had there won her bright brief fame. And with what love my Florentine masker had spoken of it,—he whose tenderest little rose I had saved when dead with the rest, and had brought away with me where the stone Fates were hidden.

It was a queer, capacious, ill-scented old waggon —this conveyance, which was dignified by the name of diligenza.

There were three peasant women, smelling strongly of garlic, and hugging great baskets of woollen stuffs, of pizzicheria goods, and of live hens that they had purchased in the town. There were two old priests, a burly fattore, and a young Tirolese in the picturesque garb of the Unterinnthal.

The vehicle was as full as it could hold, and no one looked with much favour on me as I entered, except the young mountaineer.

No doubt I had appeared to them, starting up in the heavy gloom of the night, strange enough as they had thundered slowly over the stones in the gateway; all alone at my age, and dressed as I was in my mufflings of velvet, and my most absurd yellow skirts of rich brocaded satin fit for the wearing of any queen.

They made place for me, however, with pleasant good-humour.

The old waggon settled heavily on its way over the plains.

It was a dark, moonless night. An oil-lamp hung in the roof, which gave us very little light. We rolled on with a creaking droning noise, only varied by the crack of the whip.

The contadina and the priests went to sleep; the fattore took out his accounts and reperused them; the good-looking Unterinnthaler and I were alone wide awake, being young, and on a journey that was strange to us.

They had told me that it would be day and night again before we reached Bologna; and to Bologna, as the farthest stage of all, I had said that I would go. The others were to be set down midway at Padova and other places on the route.

I had never been out of Verona since our residence had begun there in my fourth year.

My head was in a tumult, my brain was in a whirl, with the strange movement, the throbbing noise, and that odd sense of jumbling on into the darkness of the night which was but too true an emblem of the obscurity of my fate.

I could with difficulty keep my sobs quite silent as I thought of the old deserted, familiar chambers, of the old bronze lamp swinging by the broken Donatello, of the little quiet, nameless grave in the cemetery of the poor; of the homelike nook amongst the coppersmith's huge, shining vessels, where Raffaellino would still be sitting with his blind mother, scanning some ancient score by the dim light of his bronze lucernata.

It was all gone—all gone forever, never to come back.

Yet I felt with it all a curious sense of liberation and of exultation. If I had been alone I would have laughed and cried aloud.

The pit-a-pat, pit-a-pat of the horses' feet on the hard road seemed to me to beat out an everlasting trisyllable,—"Fuori, fuori, fuori!" Yes, I was "fuori" now,—fairly out of the gates and away. So I told myself again and again, and took an odd, unsatisfactory, remorseful and yet intoxicating pleasure in the freedom of it all.

I must have looked very strange, doubtless, as I sat there with my cheeks changing to red and white in my excitement, and my lips twitching in my longing to cry, and my hair all ruffled by the haste with which I had run, and the ridiculous yellow skirts crushed up between the tattered black robe of a priest and the grey woollen petticoat of a contadina.

We thundered on in perfect silence for a time, with a little light flashing in upon us now and then from some village post-house or some lamplit wayside Calvary.

The nights were still cold, being so early in the spring. Sitting there, I grew very stiff and chilly. The priest was stout and so was the contadina. Both were soundly sleeping, and sometimes swayed heavily against me.

My heart began to sink. The sense of the "fuori" to be more pain than glory. I thought wistfully of the little bed where I had slept for so many years under the sheltering shadows of Mariuccia's Mater Dolorosa.

I was roused by a sheepskin being placed about my knees, and by the gentle rustic voice of the young Tirolese, who prayed me to accept its covering. He was sure, he said, the signorina was very cold.

I looked up and thanked him. In the dull light of the lamp I saw his gentle honest eyes fixed on me, whilst he blushed hotly at his own temerity.

I took his sheepskin. It was roughly dressed, but warm; and emboldened, he asked me if I was all alone.

"Yes," I told him, glad to hear his voice in that horrible gloom and that unceasing gallop. "And you too?"

"I too, signorina? Yes—but then for a man it is nothing," he answered. "Besides, I go to people I know in Este—an uncle of mine married and settled there. But the signorina, does she go to friends too?"

"Oh, yes," I assured him, being too proud to say otherwise. But my heart rose in my throat at the little lie. I knew how far, far away was the only hope to which I clung.

The young Unterinnthaler looked at me wistfully. I think he knew that what I said was not very true.

"It is cold to-night, signorina," he said, gently.

"Yes—very."

"And you go far?"

"To Bologna."

"Your friends meet you there?"

"No."

"Then you go farther still?"

"I am not sure."

Do what I would the great tears brimmed over

in my eyes; his questions made me realise my desolation.

With kindly courtesy he busied himself with rubbing off the mist of our breaths from the glass window nearest him, so that we might see the dark maple-trees fly by us in the shadows of the night.

"Do you know my country, signorina?" he asked me, to divert my thoughts, no doubt. "My country, across the mountains. I am a farmer in the Unterinnthal. No? Ah, that is such a pity!"

"Is it so beautiful, then?"

"Beautiful? Ay, God knows it is beautiful. Not flat like this, with nothing but these weary olives; but all so great, so superb, so wonderful; all pine forest and endless alps, and then the waters that flash like so much light, and the snows that lie so high; and then the clouds that are always about the mountains, and the rich green woods and the yellow maize-fields all below—beautiful? Ah, indeed!"

"You would not leave it, then?"

"To live in Este? The holy saints forbid. I should be a dead man in a year, signorina. Away from the mountains? I will tell you who did that. It was Andrea Zafùr; he was older than I, but I knew him. He was kapellmeister in our burgh. When he led the choir it was enough to make one weep; it was like the singing of the angels in heaven. Well, some day some people came who persuaded him that his voice might be a mine of gold to him if he would only leave the mountains and go into the world along with them. In an evil hour Andrea listened. He was poor, you see, and they told him fine things; so he went. Whether the world cared much for him or not I never heard; but

I know that they shut him up in cities over there, German cities and French. And one day, two years later, they came for his old mother, and told her that Andrea was dying and prayed to see her. She went at once; but even then she was too late. She found him in Paris, but he was out of his mind; he did not know her at all; and all he kept saying forever was 'Take me back to the mountains! take me back! take me back!' He had made a great deal of gold; the old mother was rich when she returned; but he died, crying aloud to see the mountains once more. Nothing had been any joy to him; he had always been cramped and stifled, and sick to death away from the mountains. It must always be so. Love them once, you can never leave them—and live."

His voice was very hushed and quiet as he spoke, and there came a dreamy look into his eyes—the faraway look that men always get who dwell amidst the heights.

I hardly understood him well; for, though he spoke Italian it was not our Italian; yet there was something so gentle and simple in him that it pleased me to hear him talk.

I was glad to have him to speak to in that oppressive endless gloom, with the surging noise of the horses' gallop always on my ears, and only now and then some break in it when a lantern flashed its red glare in upon us, and hoarse, shrill voices piped discordant orders at the doors of some roadside posting house.

Finding that I listened to him, he went on to tell me all about himself—how his name was Marco Rosas; how he was of Italian race; how he was left fatherless in infancy; how his twin-brother and himself lived together on the little farm on the green slope of the Berg; how he was twenty-two years old, and well-to-do in his own way, and indeed quite rich for a farmer of the Tirol.

He described all his treasures to me; his châlet of pinewood, shingle-roofed against the hurricane and avalanche, in autumn hung over with the great yellow ears of the millet; the herds of small dun cattle, with their antelope-like eyes, and flocks of silvery hill goats; his stout little horse, with its peal of musical bells; his vines, that yielded such sweet huge purple grapes as were never ripened save in that clear, lustrous, buoyant air; the painting of the Holy Trinity that was fastened in his wall, over his house door, in an iron grating, to be a blessing on the place; his orchard, and his pastures that stretched in such perfect vivid green up the hillside, whilst above all the great snow slopes towered.

Most of all he talked of his mother—a woman whom, if all he said were true, must have been one of those who are far above rubies. A tender, homely, noble soul as this mountaineer sketched her, such, indeed, as those great silent hills produce not seldom—a woman with the life of a saint and the heart of a hero, though she neither read nor wrote, but span her own linen, milked her own herds, and had had the sweet strong breath of her own mountain air upon her all her years.

So we journeyed on our way, and, like Conraddin before us, passed "per Lombardia e per la viâ di Pavia," into the Romagna country.

The day was one long bright flood of sunshine with

beautiful flakes of clouds floating before a fresh mountain wind.

The broad plains that have been the battleground of so many races and so many ages were green and peaceful under the primitive husbandry of the contadini.

Everywhere under the long lines of the yet unbudded vines the seed was springing, and the trenches of the earth were brimful with brown bubbling water left from the floods of winter, when Reno and Adda had broken loose from their beds.

Here and there was some old fortress grey amongst the silver of the olive orchards; some village with white bleak house-walls and flat roofs pale and bare against the level fields; or some little long-forgotten city once a stronghold of war and a palace for princes, now a little hushed and lonely place, with weed-grown ramparts and gates rusted on their hinges, and tapestry weavers throwing the shuttle in its deserted and dismantled ways.

But chiefly it was always the green, fruitful, weary, endless plain trodden by the bullocks and the goats, and silent, strangely silent, as though fearful still of its tremendous past.

Day came and night again, and all the heavy, chill, bitter, lonely hours jumbled themselves away in some dreary chaos. The journey had become horrible to me. I was stiff and cold and miserable. I lost all heart to look out at the spaces between the leathern curtains on to the country beyond. I had lost all power to watch for the first outline of Tasso's "grand' Apennino."

We had passed through Padovà in the darkness.

and I had not noticed the young Tirolese descend
there. But I found the sheepskin left about my knees,
and was touched by this little gentle wayside flower
of kindness.

I suppose I must have slept some portion of the
time, but the beat of the horses' hoofs never ceased
to thunder through my brain.

There were red flashes of lights on my eyes as we
stopped to change at a posting-house; wonderful
purple and rose sunsets and sunrise; a sense of endless gliding green distances that never grew any one
whit the nearer; a confusion of cruel noises; a continual sense of pain and of unrest; and then at length
the cumbrous vehicle paused under an immense vaulted
gateway; a sentinel challenged; a guard looked in,
holding up a lantern; the gates unclosed and closed
again; and as we rolled over the stones I heard the
tired travellers mutter the name—"Bologna."

I trembled, and felt afraid as the tired horses
toiled wearily over the pavement underneath the ink-
black shadows of those vaulted footways.

It seemed to me as though they would never end;
their silence, their gloom, their architecture, the
enormous height of the walls, the vista of the in-
terminable arches, the hollow echo of the stones that
had been trodden for fifteen hundred centuries by
the feet of men and beasts—all terrified me with
a vague poetic awe which yet was, in a sense, de-
lightful.

Every old Italian city has this awe about it—holds
close the past and moves the living to a curious sense
that they are dead and in their graves are dreaming;
for the old cities themselves have beheld so much

perish around them, and yet have kept so firm a hold upon tradition and upon the supreme beauty of great arts, that those who wander there grow, as it were, bewildered, and know not which is life and which is death amongst them.

To enter Bologna at midnight is to plunge into the depths of the middle ages.

Those desolate sombre streets, those immense dark arches, dark as Tartarus, those endless arcades where scarce a footfall breaks the stillness, that labyrinth of marble, of stone, of antiquity; the past alone broods over them all.

As you go it seems to you that you see the gleam of a snowy plume and the shine of a straight rapier striking home through cuirass and doublet, whilst on the stones the dead body falls, and high above over the lamp-iron, where the torch is flaring, a casement uncloses, and a woman's hand drops a rose to the slayer, and a woman's voice murmurs, with a cruel little laugh, "Cosa fatta non capo ha!"

There is nothing to break the spell of that old world enchantment.

Nothing to recall to you that the ages of Bentivoglio and of Visconti have fled for ever.

The mighty Academy of Luvena Juris is so old, so old, so old!—the folly and frippery of modern life cannot dwell in it a moment; it is as that enchanted throne which turned into stone like itself whosoever dared to seat himself upon its majestic heights.

For fifteen centuries Bologna has grimly watched and seen the mad life of the world go by; it sits amidst the plains as the Sphynx amidst her deserts.

CHAPTER VII.
Under the Garisenda.

I SEEMED to awake roughly from some marvellous dream, when the vehicle stopped at a post-house with a great gilded sign of a golden boar projecting far out in the dull lantern light across the shadow of one of the narrow streets.

The entrance to it was through a deep archway into a paved court; from within there was the feeble light of oil wicks burning in iron sconces; beyond I could see the kitchen, with the glimmer of its copper and pewter and the sturdy padrona in a kirtle of orange and green, who was sending her people right and left in her eagerness to retain for the night all travellers by the stage.

The diligence stopped for good at the Cignale d'Oro, and I thought that I could do no better. The inn folk came round me eyeing me with some amazement and with some suspicion; but an Italian's first impulse is always one of ready kindness; the vociferous padrona softened her voice for me, her household smiled on me, and when I asked them for a little bed where I could sleep in peace, a black-browed damsel showed me up a wooden stair to a little bare chamber with a radiant gleam of her white teeth and laughter of her dusky eyes, such as might fairly have made sunshine in the shadiest place.

That sunny smile of Italy!—it has in it all the youth of the earth's golden ages—all the faith of man's first dreams of God.

My little chamber was very bare, very narrow with

a floor of red brick and a casement that looked only on to a pigeon-house in the roof. But I had been used to simple ways of living, and I was very tired; I wanted nothing but rest; and being young, rest came to me as soon as I stretched my limbs out and closed my eyes upon the hard grass mattress.

I slept all night dreamlessly; and when I awoke with the sun shining full on my face, and the pigeons, white and grey, pluming themselves upon the roof outside, I sprang up refreshed and fearless; eager to begin again this strange new story of life, whose first chapter I had read and turned down for ever when I had looked my last at sunset on Verona.

There is nothing in any after times, however radiant with pleasure or success those latter times may be, so perfectly happy as the buoyant and fearless ignorance of the creature who has just left childhood for youth, just first thrust out its head from the shell of dependence and ventured alone to survey with dazzled and delighted eyes the illimitable domain that lies in the mere Possible.

To any other than myself it would have seemed, as it had done to the Tirolean, that nothing in the whole range of human fate could be more desolate or more appalling than my fate; there was a child of fifteen years let loose upon the world with a dozen gold florins for her solitary possession, without a friend, without a refuge, and with no relative in all humanity, except a father who had abandoned her, and of whom she knew not even so much as whether he were living or were dead.

Nothing could well have been more lonely or less to be envied surely than I; and yet when I had flung the cold water over myself and tossed the hair back over my shoulders, and looked out of the window to say good morrow to the pigeons opposite, I laughed quite happily in the face of the bright day and was not afraid.

It seemed to me that nothing could long go very ill in that fresh spring air, in that warm living light, in that pleasant murmur of birds' wings, and of drowsy bees, that rose upward on the stillness of the city from the little garden court below.

It was early as I unslid the wooden bar of my door and ran downstairs in the mirthful sunlight; but the padrona was up and about, and all her stout damsels at work with her, coming and going in their many-coloured garments to and fro in the brightness and the shadows of the open court and the sombre archways.

Great turkeys were ruffling and strutting about the passages, hens were squatting by the stoves, a big white owl blinked his eyes on a butter tub, and grey rabbits ran between the swiftly flying feet of the inn-maidens as they vied in haste to obey the shrill commands of their mistress.

In the square court they had set out the winter-housed store of lemon trees.

There was a thread of water bubbling from a sculptured Medusa's mouth into a huge earthen amphora; on the door sill an old woman was slicing carrots; above her in the carved lintel was a Lucca della Robbia worth its weight in gold: it was such a scene as might have stayed there unchanged since Guido had first dipped his brush in oils.

I had all the forenoon before me, and not liking

to take up room there in that busy tavern, I wandered out to look a little at the city.

A winding passage-way led from the court-yard straight out in front of the two leaning towers, with their coppersmiths' workshops beneath them and above the clear blue sky of the Romagna.

It was about nine o'clock and a market day, and all the town was astir; throngs of busy, laughing hurrying people were crying their goods aloud, or lustily chaffering for the goods of others; whilst around them were those old sun-burned walls, those dim gigantic frescoes, those austere arcades, those mighty stones that had borne the fires and the furies of a thousand years of sack and siege.

Mules brayed, dogs barked, poultry cackled, the charlatan screamed his sing-song recitative, the hawkers vaunted their dried pumpkin seeds, their little fried alardi, or their barrowful of many-coloured woollen socks and kerchiefs; the bells clanged sonorously, the old scriveri held solemn court within their dens, the peasants rode in on their asses laden with cabbages or with poultry; the ringing hammers of the countless coppersmiths and pewterers resounded from a hundred workshops; and it was all life, mirth, tumult, business; and amidst it all rose the old unfinished mournful pile of the Duomo, the ancient palaces with beggars' rags fluttering from the balconies, the slanting shafts of the twin towers, the arched footways brown and sear with the passing of a thousand generations.

In the gay sunlight it was not so terrible as in the darkness of night; but it was perhaps more melancholy still.

I wandered on and on, looking now at the contention of some buyer and seller under the leathern awning of a market-stall, and now at the grandeur of some decaying fresco dying slowly of neglect and age above on the sculptured houses.

I stood gazing up at the Garisendà, where it leaned above against the delicate blue of the immense Romagna skies, whilst beneath in their dusky workshops the brawny bare-armed coppersmiths beat the ruddy metals, their hammers rising and falling with steady and deafening rhythm.

I stood gazing at the Garisendà and the Assinelli that in their day had seen the slender hands of Properzia de' Rossi at work upon the monumental marbles; and had heard the last Bentivoglio called from his workshop to a crown; and had watched the scholars come from all far countries—from wild Ireland, away in the mists of the northern seas, as from fountain filled Damascus rose-girt on the edge of the desert,—trooping by thousands and tens of thousands to pace the stones and learn the lore of the great Academy.

I loitered long in the old stone labyrinths of the Bentivoglio's city. It awed me, it oppressed me, yet it allured me.

The Past is very gaunt and grim in the old University, but it is noble for all that. It is like the lofty skeleton of a dead knight wrapped in the black cloak of the Misericordia.

The people chattered with me gladly; and told me where to find the Raffael, the Guido, the Domenichino, the Tarini, above all their darlings — the Carracci.

In Verona I had felt but little the genius of the place. Verona had forgotten so much; the foe's heel had stamped out her brain; and besides, her great Paolo, ages ago, was stolen utterly from her by wanton Venice.

But here in Bologna it was beautiful to find how dear and living to them their three Brethren were.

Stendahl was astonished to find his cobbler in Bologna able to tell him all sorts of traits of the Carracci, and really full of sorrowful reminiscences, because Luigi had died of grief at some bad drawing of his own in the angel of the Annunciation. Stendahl adds that a cobbler in Paris would have had a gilt chair in his shop, but would have told you nought of Greuze or of Gros.

It is just this tenderness of the past and knowledge of it, which make the Italian populace unlike any other under the sun:—in these peoples' eyes there are always dreams, and in their memories there is always greatness.

Wandering full of these thoughts, vivid and yet confused in my brain, the hours sped away uncounted by me.

That there was pain or danger or singularity in my position, I had utterly forgotten. I was only glad to be free and to be amidst these places which had lived so long for me only in the light of imagination and of history.

I was standing under the Garisendà picturing that old academic life and thinking how good the days of a student must have been in those times when the meaning of scholarship had just touched the world with its light; I was just standing there, when the voices of men and women beside me caught my ear, speaking of an opera which had been given the previous night with unusual pomp before all the great people of the Romagna.

Its name arrested me; for it was the Alkestis.

"A German opera!" said one with a shrug of his shoulders. "We have to swallow it."

"Nay, it is fine music; music that has held all the stages of Europe forty years," said another. "And it is more Italian than anything; the man studied always in Milan——"

"But what good thing has he written since?"

"Mere *roba*," grumbled the first speaker. "It is that which beats me; and he gets such prices!—he is as rich as all the Ghetto—whilst look at our Rossini."

"Those German hogs get all the truffles of Europe," said the other with a sigh. "But there is this Rothwald, the guest of the Grand Duke, to-day, and to morrow of the Cardinal, and what not, and good Italians starving their naked bones over a pinch of charcoal in their garrets, with more melody in their do, re, me, as they sing to themselves as they saunter about, than this fellow in all his long lifetime."

"Caro, caro, be just," laughed the others. "The Alkestis is perfect, quite perfect; our fathers settled that long ago; but then of course it is due to Milan, since he studied there. Rothwald is a great old man, that we are bound to confess, and his music is as fresh to-day as though some youngster had just penned it. The chorus people sang his great Cora degli Dei, under his window in the Palace this morning early. He was quite touched; he came out into the balcony, and there threw down a handful of gold whilst they tossed him carnival flowers."

I heard, and my cheek burned, and my heart beat high with hatred: I thought of Ambrogiò Rufi as I had left him stooping over his wretched and solitary hearth.

"They honour Rothwald like that!" I cried to the students, heedless who my hearers were, as it was my careless childish fashion to be, everywhere and always.

They looked at me in surprise, and no doubt I had a strange enough aspect, glowing in my purple and yellow against the darkness of the coppersmiths' dens, and above me the quaint Garisendà.

"Why not, signorina?" they cried gaily to me, possibly amused at the rage of disdain that doubtless quivered over all my face. "Because he is a Tedesco? —a good reason, we grant."

"Because he was a traitor!" I said to them, and then could say no more, but turned away with a burning face and a swelling heart, for there seemed to rise before me the broken-hearted, weary, deathstricken form of my dear old master, and the thought of this man who had betrayed him was unbearable to me; this man, who dwelt in princes' palaces, and scattered gold broadcast, and received the songs and the flowers of the nation he had robbed.

In the fury against injustice and the passion of longing to redress it, which are part and parcel of all youth that is at all generous or at all unworldly, I felt strong enough to force my way to the palace itself up high on the hill there amongst the cypresses, and fling the truth in the face of this perjurer whose lie had been for forty years fair and fruitful before the world.

"Oh! why does God let such things be?" I cried in the rebellion of my heart against the cruelty of creation, as I dropped down under a little shrine in a twisting passage-way out of the public square.

Bologna had lost its charm for me; it seemed only a great dark, dusty, noisome, cruel place, with its strange city of the dead walled up beyond its gates.

What was it to me that my old master sat alone by a wretched hearth whilst the man who had betrayed him was feasted by cardinals and honoured by nations? What was it to me?

Nothing indeed.

And yet I sobbed bitterly as I turned from the streets into an old dark church, ashamed that the people should see the tears upon my cheeks.

CHAPTER VIII.
The Maidenhair.

THE church was quite empty: an immense naked marble desolation, with a white Christ looming vast and sad above the altar.

I sat down on an oaken bench and cried my heart out, as the children say: most for the cruelty of Ambrogiò's fate, but also a little for the utter loneliness of my own.

I had little hope of finding my father; and if I found him, how could I tell he would not disown a little travel-stained penniless wanderer, as he had disowned the child with the peacock's plumes in the painting chamber of the Veronese students?

I dreaded his calm cold smile; I dreaded his icy incredulous response; I resolved within myself, if I found him not at Florence, to seek him no more, but to go on and try my fortunes at Rome.

For once, when I had sung in the streets to a little knot of people in Verona, an old man had come up to me and had told me he was the director of the Corea, and had bidden me, if ever I had a mind to appear in public, to betake myself to him there in the Eternal City.

"Might I not help you a little, illustrissima?" said a gentle, timid voice. I started, and saw the young Tirolean, the bright colour in his costume glowing in the gloom of the dusky aisles.

I was not sorry for companionship, yet I was wounded to be seen in my sorrow. I stared at him stupidly through my tears.

"You did not stay at Padova, then?" I asked him at length, seeing that he seemed more ashamed than I.

"No, signorina," he answered shyly, and then was still.

"You have business in Bologna?"

"No."

He spoke with downcast eyes, and swept the dust of the pavement with the long plumes in his hat.

"I was sorry for the little eccellenza," he stammered humbly. "And it seemed so terrible for her to be alone; so young, and with such a face as that; and so I dared to travel on with her. I was on the roof of the diligenza all the way from Padova."

Then he was silent; lifting, timidly, his brown, honest, dog-like eyes, that were wistful like a dog's that dreads a beating.

But I was too used to the comradeship of Il Squarcionino and all his boyish brethren to be in any whit embarrassed by this act of the young mountaineer. I took it as a kindly piece of thoughtfulness, no more.

"It was very good of you," I said, brightening a little, "and—and—it is true, I am all alone. But no one would hurt me—why should they? I am not afraid."

"The little illustrissima is hardly more than a child," murmured Marco Rosas, with a pity in his look I did not comprehend. "It is so damp and cold in this church. Would the signorina come a little in the country? There is a great Madonna here to see, they say, and the day is long."

I hesitated a moment, then consented. What harm could there be? And anything was better than being alone; and the young man was so gentle, so simple, and so frank, that he seemed to me only like a bigger Raffaellino.

So out of the gates I went into the white wide country, with the sun on its dusty roads, along which the bullock waggons were crawling.

Anywhere else I should have been stared at—in my yellow and violet, with the hood lying on my shoulders and my hair uncovered to the sun, and the young Unterinnthaler in his picture-like dress of velvet, and broad red sash, and hat with the drooping myrtle-green plume.

But in Italy—blessed Italy—no one noticed.

There is such immunity from observation in a country where colour is a household fairy brightening every rent and ruin, in lieu of an unknown god at once dreaded and derided.

So I went on in the sunshine along the road that leads to the Madonna of S. Luca high on her green hill.

We made our obeisance at her shrine, and gazed through the wonderful breadth of the plains with their countless cities and towns, and the low lines of the circling mountains lying curve on curve in endless undulation.

Then we came down from the height and wandered whither we knew not exactly amongst fresh-turned fields and vines just set with leaf, and orchards of olive and mulberry, where many a little quiet paese nestled with white-walled houses and red-roofed dovecotes. At one of these poderi there was a woman with a merry handsome face and a scarlet kirtle sitting spinning on the top of a flight of steps under a dark archway hung with convolvulus.

Marco Rosas asked her if she could give us a draught of milk.

She assented joyfully, and brought out not only milk but honey and pomegranates and black sweet bread, and set them out on a stone bench on the top of the step under the convolvulus; and would have us eat there and then, she spinning all the while and telling us her own history and her grandmother's before her, looking across the great sunny plains that stretched away like the sea-green ocean, some white tower rising here and there out of the sun-mist like a seagull on the wing.

She was a cheery, good-hearted creature; she lived on the most wondrous battle-field of all Europe, but she knew nothing of that; she only knew that her eggs sold well in Bologna market, and her bit of land was fruitful, and her husband was a good man though careless, and her olive-trees had been bit by the frost and would bear ill that summer.

We had a pleasant hour with her there on the sunny steps facing the low tumbled crests of the Apennines, hyacinth-hued in the clear spring weather.

We bade her farewell with many good wishes on either side, and went on our way to the city. The sun was not far from its setting.

During those long sauntering walks the Unterinnthaler had told me still more about himself and his birthplace in the high mountains.

As we drew under the city walls he began to speak again, and a little confusedly, of his country, of his home, of his people. His millet-fields and his mountain cattle were dearer to him than all the dead glories of Bologna.

"The châlet is large," he told me, "and Anton, my brother, is a good, gentle lad. There is a great store of linen, for my mother and her mother before her were great spinners; and there is some little silver in the plate chest, for our people have been there for generations. It is not so very cold in the winter-time, for everywhere we have double windows, and we can afford to burn as many oak logs as we like. And then in the spring it is so beautiful—all the waters leaping as though they were mad, and the loose snows rushing, thundering down, and the cattle lowing with delight to get once more up on their pastures, and the hyacinths and gentian springing up everywhere—oh, signorina, you do not know how beautiful it is upon our mountains then!"

"No doubt," I answered him, dreamily, my thoughts not being with him.

"Much more beautiful than all this!" he said, with a sweep outward of his hand to the country. "Here it is just maple and mulberry, mulberry and maple, over and over again, and those endless vineyards everywhere—so flat, so pale and tiresome."

"No doubt," I said again to him, indifferent, watching the white bullocks come through the gates with an open waggon of the past year's hay.

He was silent a little while; then he spoke again; his voice was swift and low.

"Signorina, did ever you hear of a tale that our priest told us once? There were terrible times across the mountains, amongst the Francesi, I think, and the peasantry rose against the aristocrats, and everywhere they slew the nobles; and at one place the nobles were drowned by thousands in a river. Do you know?"

"You mean the Noyades of Nantes?"

"It may be. I cannot tell the name. It was in some time of revolution, and they did not spare even the women. All the wives and daughters and mothers of the nobles were bound and flung into the water. There was only one way that anyone of those young noble maidens could be spared; it was if one of the men of the populace asked and took her in marriage——"

He stopped abruptly. I, gathering some tufts of maidenhair off the city wall, laughed a little.

"The waters were better, I should think. Well?"

"Signorina," he began once more, and as I looked up, astonished at the tremulous sound in his voice, I saw his eyes fastened on me in pathetic entreaty, still as of a dog that prays of you not to beat him. "Signorina, I have been thinking. It is almost as ill with you as with those young noble Francese maidens. You are all alone, and you have no home and no friends—you have told me so; and surely your father cannot be amongst the living, or he had never been silent so long. Now, I am only a mountaineer, I know that, and ignorant, and altogether beneath you, and yet if you would let me give you my home so long as ever—as ever—you want one. The world is bitter and bad for a motherless child."

He paused and grew very red, then hurried on with his explanation.

"I meant—if you would come to us—my mother is so good: the little illustrissima would get to care for her; and the place is humble indeed, but sweet and wholesome—and safe. I would go straight back with the donzella, and not rest till she was safe with my mother on the mountains. And I—I know well the donzella would never look at me, never think of me—I should never dream of it. But if she would only let me be of use to her, only let me put a roof over her head, I should be so thankful! I would serve her like a dog. For—for—in this one little short day I have got to love her so well!"

Then he stopped abruptly, and grew very white, and I could hear his quick hard breathing as we stood together outside the gates of Bologna in the red sunset light.

My first impulse was that of ungrateful waywardness.

What! escape from Verona only to end my gorgeous dreams in a peasant's shieling on northern mountains! I, who had set my face to the golden south, dreaming of my Sordello of the winter's masque, of my Romeo of the fairy roses.

I am ashamed to say that, like a spoilt and cruel child as I was, I flashed on him a contemptuous glance and laughed aloud.

The moment my laughter had struck on the evening silence I was sorry. I shall never forget the look on the frank fair face of Marco Rosas.

"The donzella is right and I was mad—no doubt," he murmured, humbly; then he fell behind, and followed me in silence through the gates into the grim old town.

My heart smote me a little as I went. He had meant so well; perhaps it was cruel in me to wound him.

I heard his slow firm tread behind me until I had passed into the open court of the Cignale d'Oro.

Then he stopped, and his voice—quite changed in tone—muttered in my ear—

"Signorina, I will never see your face again. Say you forgive me once?"

I turned and looked at him, relenting a little. It was so absurd; and yet some sense of his thorough goodness, of his perfect simplicity and sincerity, stole on me and moved me despite myself.

I stretched my hand out to him with the little shaking maidenhair as a peace-offering.

"You were very good," I said to him, half laughing, half crying. "I thank you very much indeed; only, it was so absurd, you know;—go away and forget me; pray, pray do, or I shall be so sorry!"

He took the little tuft of grasses and looked at me with a wistful sadness in his eyes that haunted me for many an hour after.

"I shall never forget, dear signorina. Never—till I die."

Then he bent his head very low, and turned away and left me.

One little short day, and a life was won!

I felt a strange thrill of conscious power, yet a sense of some wrong thing done by me, as I watched him pass wearily through the entrance passage and disappear into the blackness of the shadow.

I let him go in silence, and went upstairs to my little room under the eaves.

CHAPTER IX.
The Snow-flower.

I WAS pained and yet incensed.

It seemed as though all the cares and sorrows of mature years crowded in on me in one moment. I had been so happy in my heedless goodfellowship with any one who smiled on me, and was willing to be idle and mirthful with me for an hour.

I do not know how others have been moved by the first utterance of love to them; but to me it brought a weary sense of burdensome power and of lost liberty. All the golden hazy glory of my future seemed to have faded suddenly. The future was only now to me a blank uncertainty, which might hold anything—or nothing.

All the gay elastic hopefulness of the previous day was gone from me. I leaned on the edge of my little casement, tired, and with an aching heart.

It was another red and gold evening.

The voices were merry in the cortile below. The little boy of the house played dominoes with his granddam on the stone steps. The padrona and her maidens hurried in and out, for the inn was full of travellers passing through towards Padova and Venice and Milan.

The whole was a little bright busy picture in the sombreness of this great old city, which had seen so much bloodshed, so much genius, so much woe, so much splendour, and now lived on, on its past, as childless greybeards do alone amidst their palaces.

I had no heart any more that day for the streets of Bologna. I shut myself in my little chamber and watched the pigeons plume themselves upon the roof, and heard the chattering, laughing voices down below, and vexed my soul as young things will over the perplexities and the cruelties of human life.

The warm sunset was just tinging the solemn greys of the city into all manner of tender hues, when above the clatter of the voices I heard the little shrill voice of the child of the inn crying as he ran out into the court,—

"Oh, mother, mother! give me a scudo—just one to spend to-night."

"Fie, you naughty soul!" grumbled the mother; "you are always spending money. You will come to no good, Berto. The Frate says you do not know your alfabeto, and you with those blessed Scolopi Fathers over two years!"

"Give me a scudo, mother!" pleaded the little lad. "Only one! I will win it back at ruzzola to-morrow."

"Oh, I daresay," sighed the padrona; "all my dear little cheeses bowled away down the streets. You are a wicked one, Berto, and you my only child, and I a widow; seven years old too, as you are!"

"Give me a scudo!" cried Berto, clinging to her skirts, and, in fine, helping himself without more ado from the leathern pouch that hung at her girdle.

"What is it for, Berto?" she asked, catching the child by his long hair.

"Pascarèl, mother mine!" shouted the little scapegrace, who might have seven years at the uttermost. "To-night—just to-night—and then on to Florence. Will you come too? Do, mother!"

"I do not mind if I do," said the padrona, casting her lace veil about her head. "There is only that little donzella in the house, and two traders from Ferrara. I do not mind if I do. Pascarèl is as good as a winning number at lottery. Here, Pasquà, Gilla, Marta,"—

She called her maidens round her, and set them their tasks of cooking, spinning, poultry-feeding and the like, standing in a circle of red light in the black and white paved court under my casement, and then went out with her little son down into the dusky tunnel of the passage-way.

Pascarèl! the name bewildered and yet comforted me. What would it be, I wondered; a game, a show, a dance, or the name of a living creature?

The name of the man who had chosen the bright melting snow as its emblem?—the snow-flower that glittered a day in the light, and then vanished?

Anyway, it had a solace for me when I leaned there in the red evening, while the place grew quite still as the pigeons went to roost, and the old chimes called to vespers, and the inn maidens ran to chatter within-doors to the Ferrarese as soon as their mistress's back was turned.

Whatever it might be, this mystical Pascarèl, it went before me southward to Florence. If it were only a snow-flower that would melt at a touch, it seemed to me better than all the deathless flowers of Paradise.

As I leaned there watching the silvery birds fly against the reddened sky, I thought—why I do not know—of Properzia de' Rossi.

I knew her story. I had often pondered over it, and looked at the delicate sad face of her, with its drooped lids and its Madonna's eyes. She had dwelt here, in this mighty Bologna; and Bologna had made her its saint and sovereign whilst her short life lasted, and in her death had mourned her almost as Rome Raffaelle.

A slender, dainty, girlish thing, she had a name of power even in that age of giants. She dared to wield, and to wield well, the chisel and the burin in the days when Michaelangelo and Marcantonio held them as their sceptres. Her city honoured her, and the envy and injury of Amico gave her the surest warranty of triumph.

And yet,—she had no joy in any of it; she won one by one all the laurels only to find them bitter on her lips; the marbles chilled her as though they were dead children, and the shouts of the Romagnese homage was dull and without music on her ears. For why? for this;—so little and yet all. That one, only in the city's width, saw no beauty in her, and no wonder in her deeds: and this one,—alone of them all,—she loved.

And he, not knowing, and when knowing, caring nothing, but turning away his beautiful cold face into the light of others' smiles, Properzia grew weary of her work, and changed to hate her lavish gifts of nature; and left undone the public sculptures she had sought so eagerly; and would not for all the city's wooing use her power again, but drew herself in from life and light like a sea-flower that is thrown by tempest on the rocks. And so, when Clement came into Bologna to crown great Charles, and asked, as the first of all the wonders of the place, for that Properzia whose fame had spread from sea to sea in Italy, the Bolognese, weeping bitterly, could only lead him to the hospital to look upon the fair dead body of a girl.

I thought of her wistfully as the tawny evening colours spread themselves like an emperor's pall over the desolate city.

I only saw the beauty and the sadness of the story. What there was of evil in it passed by me; the passion and the shame shadowed out in that terrible sculpture, which was the last her genius wrought, had no meaning for me; of the poison of unrequited desire which had burned up and ruined all the delicate grace and innocent loveliness of her nature and her life, I had no sense or suspicion.

I was only sorry for her—dead all those centuries before—here in the city of Guido. And a strange new wonder awoke and thrilled in me;—what could it be, this marvellous thing called Love which had thus killed her?

And then I thought,—I knew not why,—of the dark and tender eyes of the Florentine Masquer.

The owl had awoke from his watch-tower on the tub, and had begun to boom to and fro hunting bats through the shadows of the angles and roofs.

The deep bell of the Misericordia boomed over Bologna in the stillness. The old woman, spinning at her wheel, stopped to cross herself and say a prayer or two for the poor passing soul.

I saw the stars come out, and thought of how they were shining there away across the plains on those lowly graves beneath the shadow of the Alps; and then I threw myself wearily on the little bed, and cried myself to sleep.

At daybreak I rose and went down and paid my slender score. Then I bade them farewell, and went out into the white and glistening light that heralds morning in the Italian plains.

An hour later I was on my way across the wild gorges of the hills to Florence.

CHAPTER X.

La Reine du Moyenage.

ALL day long, and all night long, the heavy diligenza creaked and rolled upon its course over the grey heights, and through the dusky ravines of the Apennines.

I slept and dreamed, and woke and gazed, and slept and dreamed again; it was all blent to me in a confused tumult of light and darkness, rest and pain.

It was again daybreak, when, with a shock and a dull crash, the great vehicle reeled over on its side and fell broken and crushed upon the stony way, the poor beasts struggling under their entangled weight of leather, rope, and links of brass. It had been urged too swiftly down a steep and angular slope.

I rose with a confused sense of pain, but I had received no hurt.

There were stir and strife and lamentation. Then some one told me that it would be hours ere the vehicle could be again upon the road, and that it were better to go on foot to Florence: we were on the hill-side, not a league away, and very soon night would have fallen. They pointed me the way; I followed it; a rough road winding between high stone walls, descending always abruptly, and without beauty, white with dust, and rugged to the feet; above, a wondrous sky; sapphire blue in the zenith, all to westward glowing with a million cloud-flecks of intensest rose; the rose of the deep carnation buds when they blush into life with the spring of the year.

I followed patiently the windings of the path, always between the pale stone walls, a little solitary figure, purple and yellow, as though the violets and crocuses of the woods had dressed me.

Suddenly, with a sharp bend, the road sheered downward into a wide valley, white and grey with the blossoming woods of the olive. In the midst of that silvery sea was stretched the fairest city of all the empires of the world.

The sun was setting.

Over the whole Valdarno there was everywhere a faint ethereal golden mist that rose from the water and the woods.

The town floated on it as upon a lake; her spires, and domes, and towers, and palaces bathed at their base in its amber waves, and rising upward into the rose-hued radiance of the upper air. The mountains that encircled her took all the varying hues of the sunset on their pale heights until they flushed to scarlet, glowered to violet, wavered with flame, and paled to whiteness, as the opal burns and fades. Warmth, fragrance, silence, loveliness encompassed her; and in the great stillness the bell of the basilica tolled slowly in the evening call to prayer.

Thus Florence rose before me.

A strange tremor of exceeding joy thrilled through me as I beheld the reddened shadows of those closely-lying roofs, and those marble heights of towers and of temples. At last my eyes gazed on her!—the daughter of flowers, the mistress of art, the nursing mother of liberty and of aspiration.

I fell on my knees and thanked God. I pity those who, in such a moment, have not done likewise.

My eyes were dim, but my heart was strong, and beat high with hope as I rose and stumbled down the rugged way, onwards, to the entrance of her gates; always with the great dome shining before me in the golden haze; always with the clouds light as a breath, scarlet as a flame, hovering above me in the windless air.

The afterglow was still warm in the heavens when I reached the city walls and entered the shadows of her historic streets.

I wandered all the evening, unconscious of fatigue, until the streets were all ablaze with lights, and all astir with people. I remembered then, for the first time, that it was the last Domenica of the year's Carnival.

The great white Seasons of the Santa Trinità rose like snow against the golden air. Monte Oliveto towered dark against the rosy glory of the west. There was a sweet sea wind blowing which fanned out as it went all the spiced odours of the pharmacies, and all the scents of the budding woods. The shops of the goldsmiths, and mosaic sellers, and alabaster workers gleamed and sparkled in the light. Everywhere there was some beauty, some fragrance, some treasure; and above it all rose the wondrous shaft of the campanile, glancing like gold and ivory in the sun.

Where lies the secret of the spell of Florence?— a spell that strengthens, and does not fade with time?

It is a strange, sweet, subtle charm that makes those who love her at all love her with a passionate, close-clinging faith in her as the fairest thing that men have ever builded where she lies amidst her lily-whitened meadows.

Perhaps it is because her story is so old, and her beauty is so young.

Behind her lie such abysses of mighty memories. Upon her is shed such radiance of sunlight and of life. The stones of her are dark with the blood of so many generations, but her air is bright with the blossoms of so many flowers; even as the eyes of her people have in them more sadness than lies in tears, whilst their lips have the gayest laughter that ever made music in the weariness of the world.

Rome is terrible in her old age. It is the old age of a mighty murderess of men. About her there is ever the scent of death; the abomination of desolation. She was, in her days of power and of sorcery, a living lie. She called herself the mother of freed men, and she conceived but slaves. The shame of her and the sin cling to her still, and the blood that she shed makes heavy and horrible the air that she respires. Her head is crowned with ashes, and her lips, as they mutter of dead days, breathe pestilence.

But Florence, where she sits throned amidst her meadows white with lilies, Florence is never terrible, Florence is never old. In her infancy they fed her on the manna of freedom, and that fairest food gave her eternal youth. In her early years she worshipped ignorantly indeed, but truly always the day-star of liberty; and it has been with her always so that the light shed upon her is still as the light of morning.

Does this sound a fanciful folly? Nay, there is a real truth in it.

The past is so close to you in Florence. You touch it at every step. It is not the dead past that men bury and then forget. It is an unquenchable thing; beautiful, and full of lustre, even in the tomb, like the gold from the sepulchres of the Ætruscan kings that shines on the breast of some fair living woman, undimmed by the dust and the length of the ages.

The music of the old greatness thrills through all the commonest things of life like the grilli's chant through the wooden cages on Ascension Day; and, like the song of the grilli, its poetry stays in the warmth of the common hearth for the ears of the little children, and loses nothing of its melody.

The beauty of the past in Florence is like the beauty of the great Duomo.

About the Duomo there is stir and strife at all times; crowds come and go; men buy and sell; lads laugh and fight; piles of fruit blaze gold and crimson; metal pails clash down on the stones with shrillest clangour; on the steps boys play at dominoes, and women give their children food, and merry maskers grin in carnival fooleries; but there in their midst is the Duomo all unharmed and undegraded, a poem and a prayer in one, its marbles shining in the upper air, a thing so majestic in its strength, and yet so human in its tenderness, that nothing can assail, and nothing equal it.

Other, though not many, cities have histories as noble, treasuries as vast; but no other city has them living and ever present in her midst, familiar as household words, and touched by every baby's hand and peasant's step, as Florence has.

Every line, every rood, every gable, every tower, has some story of the past present in it. Every tocsin that sounds is a chronicle; every bridge that unites the two banks of the river unites also the crowds of the living with the heroism of the dead.

In the winding dusky irregular streets, with the

outlines of their logge and arcades, and the glow of colour that fills their niches and galleries, the men who "have gone before" walk with you; not as elsewhere mere gliding shades clad in the pallor of a misty memory, but present, as in their daily lives, shading their dreamful eyes against the noonday sun or setting their brave brows against the mountain wind, laughing and jesting in their manful mirth and speaking as brother to brother of great gifts to give the world. All this while, though the past is thus close about you the present is beautiful also, and does not shock you by discord and unseemliness as it will ever do elsewhere. The throngs that pass you are the same in likeness as those that brushed against Dante or Calvacanti; the populace that you move amidst is the same bold, vivid, fearless, eager people with eyes full of dreams, and lips braced close for war, which welcomed Vinci and Cimabue and fought from Montaperto to Solferino.

And as you go through the streets you will surely see at every step some colour of a fresco on a wall, some quaint curve of a bas-relief on a lintel, some vista of Romanesque arches in a palace court, some dusky interior of a smith's forge or a wood-seller's shop, some Renaissance seal ring glimmering on a trader's stall, some lovely hues of fruits and herbs tossed down together in a Tre Cento window, some gigantic mass of blossoms being borne aloft on men's shoulders for a church festivity of roses, something at every step that has some beauty or some charm in it, some graciousness of the ancient time, or some poetry of the present hour.

The beauty of the past goes with you at every

step in Florence. Buy eggs in the market, and you buy them where Donatello bought those which fell down in a broken heap before the wonder of the crucifix. Pause in a narrow bye-street in a crowd and it shall be that Borgo Allegri, which the people so baptised for love of the old painter and the new-born art. Stray into a great dark church at evening time, where peasants tell their beads in the vast marble silence, and you are where the whole city flocked, weeping, at midnight to look their last upon the face of their Michael Angelo. Pace up the steps of the palace of the Signoria and you tread the stone that felt the feet of him to whom so bitterly was known "*com' è duro calle, lo scendere è'l salir per l'altrúi scale.*" Buy a knot of March anemoni or April arum lilies, and you may bear them with you through the same city ward in which the child Ghirlandajo once played amidst the gold and silver garlands that his father fashioned for the young heads of the Renaissance. Ask for a shoemaker and you shall find the cobbler sitting with his board in the same old twisting, shadowy street way, where the old man Toscanelli drew his charts that served a fair-haired sailor of Genoa, called Columbus. Toil to fetch a tinker through the squalor of San Niccolò, and there shall fall on you the shadow of the bell-tower where the old sacristan saved to the world the genius of the Night and Day. Glance up to see the hour of the evening time, and there, sombre and tragical, will loom above you the walls of the communal palace on which the traitors were painted by the brush of Sarto, and the tower of Giotto, fair and fresh in its perfect grace as though angels had builded it in the night just past, "*ond' ella toglie ancora e terza e nona,*" as in the noble and simple days before she brake the "*cerchia antica.*"

Everywhere there are flowers, and breaks of songs, and rills of laughter, and wonderful eyes that look as if they too, like their Poets, had gazed into the heights of heaven and the depths of hell.

And then you will pass out at the gates beyond the city walls, and all around you there will be a radiance and serenity of light that seems to throb in its intensity and yet is divinely restful, like the passion and the peace of love when it has all to adore and nothing to desire.

The water will be broad and gold, and darkened here and there into shadows of porphyrine amber. Amidst the grey and green of the olive and acacia foliage there will arise the low pale roofs and flat-topped towers of innumerable villages.

Everywhere there will be a wonderful width of amethystine hills and mystical depths of seven-chorded light. Above, masses of rosy cloud will drift, like rose leaves leaning on a summer wind. And, like a magic girdle which has shut her out from all the curse of age and death and man's oblivion, and given her a youth and loveliness which will endure so long as the earth itself endures, there will be the circle of the mountains, purple and white and golden, lying around Florence.

Who, having known her, can forsake her for lesser loves?

Who, having once abode with her, can turn their faces from the rising sun and set the darkness of the hills betwixt herself and them?

CHAPTER XL
The Midnight Fair.

So beautiful was it all, so strange, so wild, so fantastic, that all hunger, fatigue, and fear were forgotten by me in its curious delight. I wandered on and on, asking nothing, only for ever looking and looking and looking. I thought that I had strayed over the border land that parts us from the past, and was amidst the breathing burning life of the Cinque Cento.

By many and various streets—all made noble with frowning fortress, carven statues, walls massive and lofty as alpine slopes, ornament delicate and wonderful as frost on woven aspen boughs,—I came at length into a great square, which I needed none to tell me was the place where the soul of Savonarola had been sent forth on fire. For there the standard of the people rose on the tower of the Commonwealth, and the lustrous moonlight lay calm and broad about the feet of the bronze Perseus.

The Hercules and the David stood white and serene against the darkness; the battlements of the magisterial palace were set like jaws of iron hard against the night; the moonshine caught the colours on the blazoned shields that edged the walls; the beautiful Judith knit her brows against the world from under the black arch of her loggia. How still it was there, where only the shapes of marble and of bronze kept watch and ward in the gathering-place of the Republic.

Yet—a stone's throw, and all Florence laughed,

and danced, and reeled, and sang, and gamed, and shouted in the open gallery of the Uffizi. A stone's throw,—and in the very shadow of the Vecchio standard, under the very gaze of the Donatello, Florence in her wildest gaiety held her riot and her revelry.

It was the midnight Fair of the Carnival.

All the length of the arcade was filled with the bright and motley throng. In open spaces on the flagstones the people were dancing to shrill clamour of fife and drum. Here a white Filatrice with powdered face was whirled down by a scarlet Mephisto, and here an Arlecchino all ablaze in squares of colour, spun round a black domino ready masked for the Veglione. There a débardeur, sunny-faced and stout-limbed, toyed with a Neapolitan Pulcinello; and there a lithe contadina, with eyes of jet, galloped like a Friuli filly down the pavement, tiring out a panting and piteous Stenterello.

On either side in the niches between the marble figures were ranged the little gay canteens and stalls of the traders; wines and straw work, and flowers and woollen goods, and all the merchandise of the whole contado, were decked out with coloured lamps and painted devices, and streaming ribbons, and all fanciful follies of gay ornamentation.

Aloft on a barrel, the charlatan, in a flourish of scarlet cloth, screamed forth the praises of his pharmacy and of his life-pills; whilst his compeer of the lottery, in tissue of silver and a conical hat an arm's length high, with flaunting peacock's plumes, rattled his dice and shouted forth the winning numbers. Peasant girls with penthouse hats of straw, grave fattori watching the selling of their wares, little children hugging loads of stracciataunta, maskers flying in a blaze of crackers, the people everywhere, in crowds, pushing, shouting, anticking, sporting, but always in glee and always in good humour, while here and there amidst them some patrician idler sauntered with some mistress of the hour, masked, upon his arm, smiling together as they watched the humours of the fair.

Amidst it all stood the white statues; here the quiet face of Arretino,—there the bold brows of the Uberti; here the austere sadness of Dante,—there the old man's smile of Sant' Antonino.

And away at the far end of the great gallery the white arches crossed each other high above against the blackness of the night; and in the gleam of the tossing lamps the drooping banners of the Lost Liberties hung, crimson as the blood of Campaldino and Custozza; and out further in the stillness beyond the stone parapet rolled the broad moon-lightened Arno water; and above all were the clear skies, breathless as in summer, the eloquent luminous purple skies of a Florence night.

This is how I saw the city first; this is how she will lie in my heart and in my memories for ever.

I was but a child; I was entranced by the goodly chaos of mirth and colour, by the beautiful outlines, by the zestful masking, by the gaiety and the grotesqueness that were framed in that stately setting.

I found a quiet nook under the marble shelter of the figure of old Taddeo Gaddi, and rested there and watched the whims and vagaries of the Florentines.

It had grown quite late. I heard all the chimes of the belfries striking and ringing the twelfth hour of the night.

Acrobats were tumbling, musicians were braying, the dancers were flying faster and faster, the swift crackers were running along the stones like stars, the buyers and sellers were raising shriller and shriller their clamour, the winners at the lottery were darting hither and thither triumphant, hugging their prizes of wines and capons and kerchiefs and sugar-loaves; and every now and then, amidst the noise and uproar, there would come a sweet, short ripple from a lute that broke in the air like sea spray; or there would pass through the crowd young, barefooted, with dreaming eyes that saw heaven afar off, and were blind to all the stir around him, some monk, with the head of Fra Angelico.

For in Italy life is all contrast, and there is no laugh and love-song without a sigh beside them; there is no velvet mask of mirth and passion without the marble mask of art and death near to it. For everywhere the wild tulip burns red upon a ruined altar, and everywhere the blue borage rolls its azure waves through the silent temples of forgotten gods.

As I stood against the stone figure of old Taddeo, a man went by me swiftly, laughing, and chased by the people. He was clad in the gay and many-coloured dress of the Neapolitan Pulcinello, bound, no doubt, later on, for the Veglione.

He had a scourge of bladders and little gilded bells in his hand, and he struck his pursuers deftly, casting amongst them wild words of the shrewd Tuscan wit that is sharp and silver like the leaf of the Tuscan olive.

The people flew after him, laughing, tumbling, shouting, frolicking, and as they chased him called out, "Pascarello! Pascarèll!"

It was he who had given me the onyx. It was my Romeo of Verona, my Florindo of the scarlet plume, and unconsciously I sprang forward and tried to touch him as he flew.

Alas! it was in vain.

He passed me like the wind, and caught a girl of the Casentino about the waist, and whirled her into the maze of the waltzing. He did not notice me where I leaned in the grey shadow of old Gaddi; and I soon lost him from sight in the mass of blending hues, and the strange chiaroscuro of that shadowy ballroom, with its torch lights flaming amongst its banners and the blue night sky for its roof.

A sense of deadly chillness and of blank disappointment stole over me.

He was but a stranger, and I had seen his face but twice, and yet I was stung to a passionate grief and humiliation to think that he had passed me by and gone to fling about in the wild dancing that black-browed, red-kirtled contadina.

The beauty and the frolic of the fiera were all over for me.

CHAPTER XII.
With the Wild Crocus.

I LEFT it with my eyes dim and my heart beating fast with a sickening pain; left it in the height of its revelry, the people streaming in faster and faster to join the merriment and take their chance at the lottery.

I had no knowledge whither to go or where best to rest the night. I moved across the piazza without quite well knowing where I went, and casting one look behind me at the Judith where she knit her dark brows in scorn against the folly of it all, I left the square by a little dusky passage way.

Some man accosted me as I turned into the gloom, but I hurried on, my hood well over my face, and he was in haste to reach the Uffizi and let me pass. In the street that is named of the vine I saw a little homely-looking hostelry called the Silver Melon. I was very tired and sad now that the excitement of my entry into the city had passed by. I asked them if I could have a bed there, and when they assented I crept up to the little chamber that they offered me, and, after a little space, cried myself to sleep with the shouts of the populace and the strains of the music in the gallery hard by keeping the air astir all night and mingling with my dreams.

When the daylight came, a certain hope and gladness came to me with it.

There was so much to see in this wondrous city, and I was so young,—and, after all, things would surely go well with me.

The people had always said that I was fair to see; and those who knew had told me that I had a fortune in my voice. After all, I was in Florence, and I had a dozen broad florins in gold, and I was a child, and I was not afraid.

When I had broken my fast, I left my little load of clothes in pledge of my return, and went.

> "Where, white and wide,
> Washed by the morning's water-gold,
> Florence lay out on the mountain side."

It was past ten by the clocks and belfries, and a flood of sunlight streamed on the Valdarno. In its delicious brilliance I moved on and on and on, enthralled, entranced, in rapture of the present, in meditation of the past.

> "River, and bridge, and street, and square,
> Lay mine, as much at my beck and call,
> Through the live translucent bath of air,
> As the sights in the magic crystal ball."

And of my magic crystal I was never tired.

All the town was astir, eager to make the uttermost of the last days of Carnival. The bells were ringing madly, in as much tumult and confusion of metal tongues as ever called the Trades together in the old days for a raid upon Oltrarno. The long, covered gallery of the Medician tyranny hung in the air like a black cloud. I thought of the day when to build it they had pierced through the cobbler's dwelling, and had laid bare to the tyrant's eyes the beauty of Camilla Martelli. One seems to see her sitting there in the little, dusky den, with the smell of the leather and the tic-tac of the shoemaker's hammer, her only companionship all through the weary hours, until the crash of the axes and mallets broke down the wall of the chamber, and, with the flood of the daylight, let in so wondrous a blaze of changed fortune. Beneath it, on the old bridge, the penthouses of the jewellers and of the workers in gold and silver sparkled with colour and glistened with treasure, whilst the men and the mules pushed by, and to right and left through the arches shone the sunny stretch of the river, the trireme-like group of the boats cutting sharply and darkly against the gold. I thought of that awful morning when over that bridge there had ridden the gay young bridegroom of Buondelmonte, with the white garland on his golden locks, whilst at the feet of the statue of Mars the avengers had waited with naked blades and souls set hard on the slaughter. One seemed to hear the shiver of the steel against the marriage jewels, and to watch the Easter lilies fall, trampled on the blood-red stones

Everywhere the people were about, they had danced till daydawn at the Veglione and the Fiera, what of that?—they tossed down a little red wine, and fastened new signal ribbons to their shoulders, and swept out in troops into the sunshine, ready again for the masquing and motley. There were bursts of music; notes of mandolines; ripples of laughter; chattering at all street corners; great clusters of scented roses torn from castello walls beyond the gates; sweet clusters of rosy cyclamen blushing faintly like seashells; baskets of yellow muscat grapes and great black figs, and the red hearts of cut pomegranates. And above all the warmth, and stir, and glare, and mirth, and tumult, there rose the spiritual beauty of towers and spires, such as sculptors see in cities of their dreams, and on the high standards there flashed the scarlet cross of Florence that once had burned triumphant above even the walls of Rome herself.

It was past noon as I came out on to the river's side, and saw to right and left of me, far as the eye could strain, the lovely reaches of the sun-burnished water, the near hills silver with olive, dark with ilex and cypress, and, far, far away, the green plains, the lines of Lombard poplars, the golden sea of light, the purple shadows of the mountains, sown with their countless villages and villas as a lake with the whiteness of its summer lilies.

So near they looked, so ethereal, so worthy to be some mystic border land of Paradise, those soft Apennine and Carrara ranges, lying fold on fold in their loveliness, that my steps were irresistibly drawn towards them until I had passed out through one of the city gates, and was in a wooded place upon the river, with deep ilex shadows above my head, and near me thickets of acacia, with their budding branches quivering in the light; and in the distance always those soft, dreamy hues of the Carrara marble flashing in the noonday sun.

Then, being tired and warm, I sat down upon a stone bench where the trees grew very thickly and bordered a meadow sown at every step with crocuses, until the grass was pale and purple with them.

I did not think what was likely to become of me, nor of how little probable it was that I should find trace of my father and of Florio. I was only dreamily happy, half-stupidly conscious of the charm of the soft southern air and the spell of the stretching mountains.

All was quite still: a rabbit scudded swiftly amongst the crocuses, nibbling here and there: a hawk flew by: beyond the canes that grew thick by the water there were some sweet bells ringing away there where the grey shadows of Monte Murello sloped upwards against the sun.

After a while an old creature, with a basket full of Roman lilies and Parma violets, came across the place where I sat. She cast some lilies into my lap, and called me her dear signorina, and begged of me a coin for the love of God.

"What bells are those?" I asked her, lifting the lilies, with their long green leaves, doubtfully, for I was too poor to buy them.

"Perretola, dear signorina," she said, sadly. "I was born there eighty years ago. It is hard to live eighty years only to sell flowers for a bit of bread. It is a little place. Step out, and you can see it across the vines. Yes, the bells are fine. They rang when I was married. I thought marriage a fine thing. He was a worker in stone. He got into trouble in the old Duke's time when the French were about the place; and was in prison, and what not; as if married men should do aught but find charcoal to boil the souppot—but it was the way of them all at that time. And now he is dead; dead a matter of twenty-five year, and we are no nearer all the fine free things he used to be mad to talk of, at least so they prate; and I sell lilies for a bit of bread. It was better in the old Duke's time—better in the old Duke's time—so I say."

Poor soul! It was "better in the old Duke's time" to her. To her, nothing the liberties of Italy, the rise of the People, the expulsion of the Gaul, the rebound from bondage into aspiration and free-drawn breath. It was "better in the Duke's time"—when she had had youth and health, and love and dreams, away there where the bells were ringing in the white village just across the vines.

I felt sorry for her, she was so old, so old: and to stand in the sun when one was as old as that, and hear the very bells that once rung in one's bridal hour and find no music in them, but only desire to mumble a crust in one's toothless jaws—it seemed horrible to me, very horrible.

"Give me something—some little something, dear signorina," she murmured, holding out her withered hands. "The lilies die so soon in the sun, and I have walked in from Perretola without bit or drop!"

Wisely or unwisely, my heart was won. I slid my hand into the little leathern pouch bound round my waist by a thong, in which all my little worldly store was kept. Oh Dio! the horror of that moment. The purse was empty!

In lieu of touching coin either of gold or of copper, my fingers slid down the bag, meeting nothing in their way. I sprang to my feet with a scream; I tore the pouch off my girdle; I pulled it inside out with the horrible vehemence of a deadly terror; not so much as a brazen scudo fell upon the ground. In the chamois leather there was a straight slit, as though cut through by a knife: the pouch was empty. No doubt I had been robbed the previous night in the press of the Carnival Fair.

I did not cry out; I stood like a frozen thing, in cold, gazing at my empty hands. The sunshiny country reeled before me; the white road seemed to heave to and fro like a sea. Everything was sickly, and blinding, and unreal.

I knew the meaning of poverty too well not to measure in one moment the whole extent of the ruin that befell me. The old contadina stood still and looked at me, appalled, no doubt, by the despair of my face and of my attitude.

"The signorina has nothing?" she stammered, thinking, doubtless, poor wretch, of her own empty hearth and her own aching hunger. The words broke the spell of the terror that kept me motionless and silent.

"Nothing!" I echoed, and I know I laughed aloud —laughed wildly, in riotous hilarity, in my unutterable horror. "Nothing—nothing—nothing in all the whole world. My God!"

Then I threw myself down prostrate at the foot of the marble bench, whilst the old peasant, aghast and bewildered, stood and looked on, silent and appalled. I could not speak nor weep; I felt as though some huge stone had been flung on me and had stretched me half dead beneath its weight.

With my little store of golden florins, I had felt myself strong enough and hopeful enough to meet all accidents of life and vanquish them, but penniless, I was nerveless, hopeless, homeless. The extremity of my dire despair stifled me, as though some suffocating hand were at my throat.

Alone, without a coin in the world to get me bread! I thought how much more mercy the robber of my little all would surely have shown to me if only he had drawn his knife across my throat.

I do not know how long I lay there, crushed and stunned, down on the beautiful crocus-filled grass of the pasture.

The old woman stooped and touched me gently.

"Have you, indeed, nothing, signorina? Is it stolen, or what? Do not lie like that—you frighten me."

I raised my head, and looked at her. A mist swam before my eyes. The whole green expanse of the meadow eddied giddily about me like a whirlpool. But in the midst of my misery a vague remembrance of how bitterly I must have disappointed her arose to me: she was not poorer than I was now; but then she was so old.

"I am sorry," I murmured, brokenly, "sorry for you; but they have robbed me—I have nothing in the world."

The poor old creature sighed; to her also the blow was heavy. She had argued from my face and my youth some liberal gift. But the generous and tender heart of her country beat in her withered breast.

"Never mind, dear signorina," she said, softly, "you wished to give; Our Lady will remember it to you just the same—just the same. And you love the lilies."

She laid another cluster of the flowers on my lap as she turned away. Poor soul! I hope that act has been remembered to her likewise.

How Italian it was! the little simple sunny kindness done in all the darkness of poverty and age and pain.

I could not speak to her again; vacantly I watched her figure, brown and crooked, pass across the blossoming meadow in the full blaze of the shadowless light. No doubt she went to sell her lilies at the gates.

On the road, which ran through trees beyond the field with all the vast panorama of the Apennines unrolled along its length, I saw a bullock-waggon creeping towards me, and farther yet a little cloud of people, bright against the sun as gold-winged demoizelle.

Instinctively, to avoid sight or sound, I rose and

wandered into the wood which bordered the meadow; it was of ilex and pine, dusky even at noon. I plunged into its shadow, holding the lilies to my aching heart.

I moved on and on through the trees, unconscious of what I did, until I struck my breast against the trunk of a tall fir with a shock that brought me to sharp consciousness of where I was. I sat down beneath its shade, wounded by the momentary pain.

I was all alone. I looked around me with a curious sense at once of apathy and desperation. I knew not what I feared; but I feared everything—I in whose daring eyes, a moment earlier, all heaven and earth had seemed to smile in the smile of Florence.

I dropped my head upon my hands, and crouched there at the foot of the pine. I sobbed as though my very heart would break.

As I sat thus there came the little white scudding figure of a scampering dog; he ran before a little troop of people: they all stopped at some distance from me at the end of one of the aisles of pine.

They were talking and laughing gaily. I could hear the indistinct bubble of their mirthful chatter; they had three dogs with them and a monkey; they threw themselves on the grass, and took some food and wine from a basket, and one of them built up a fire with dry sticks; all the while the dogs frisked, the men laughed, the woman sang little fresh passages of song; they were all so glad and so gay, it seemed to make my misery unendurable.

The sun came down on them where they were stretched upon the turf; I sat alone in the shadow. I saw them; they seemed not to see me.

They had no doubt come out to breakfast in the Cascine woods, as Florentines will do on spring and summer days.

They seemed gay as the grilli in the grasses, and their dress was light and full of sunny hues; and from the broad hats of the men long scarlet ribbons floated. They had only bread and herbs, and some purple wine; but their laughter all the while was like a rippling brook, and they seemed not to know nor to want any better or fairer thing under heaven than thus "in sweet Valdarno to forget the day in twilight of the ilex."

They had a lute with them, and now and then one of them, the one who seemed leader amongst them, sang to it. His voice had the clear, sonorous, far-reaching vibration, like the chords of some stringed instrument, that belongs alone to Italian voices.

I sat there in a sort of stupefaction, listening to them, wondering dully how much longer the sun would only fall on other people and the gloom alone be mine. The slow tears dropped down my cheeks; my sobs had ceased; I had passed into the passive exhaustion of a great grief.

After awhile I think they caught sight of me, for they whispered together in lower tones. The woman with them rose and came towards me—a little pretty figure, plump as a little rabbit, blue, light, and gay, with twinkling feet and a small brown face under the lace headgear of Genoa, that seemed to me as bright and rosy as any tulip-bell amongst the wheat in Maytime.

She came towards me with a fresh charming grace, and paused before me.

"The signorina does not seem happy," she said, hesitatingly. "Has anything gone ill?"

I could not speak to her; I was ashamed and full of pride. I tried for her not to see the tears that were wet upon my face.

"I am sure there is something ill," she persisted. "The donzella is weeping, and all alone; if she would tell us, perhaps we might help?"

I turned my face to the trunk of the pine; but I could not keep from her sight the great mute sob that shook me from head to foot as I leaned there.

Perhaps it frightened her, for she was silent some time, though she did not move away; then, turning a little, she called to her companions.

I heard the step of a man brush through the grasses and approach her.

"Speak to her, caro mio," said the girl, in a low voice. "There must be something amiss with her, I am sure—and she so young too!—only a child!"

"If the signorina will not speak we can do nothing," said the voice of the man. It was very rich and flute-like. It was he who had sung the songs to the lute.

It conquered my pride. I turned and answered without looking at him.

"I had only twelve gold florins in all the world," I cried, in the despair of my heart. "And they have taken them, every one—every one!"

"Who have taken them?"

"A thief—how can I tell? In the fiera, last night, it must surely have been. They were safe when I came into Florence, and now—see here!"

I turned and showed them my poor little slit pouch.

I did not look up in the face of the speaker, for my eyes were blinded by their rain of tears.

He took the bag and examined it.

"Cut through with a knife, no doubt," he said, after awhile. "And you are very sad for the loss of this money, signorina? Someone will scold you if you go home without it, is that it?"

"Oh no!" I cried, with a fresh passion of weeping that I could not repress. "If it were only that! It is all I have in the world, I tell you—all—all—all!"

"But your friends?"

"I have none."

"What! You were adrift on the world with twelve florins—*you?*"

"Yes. Why not? I have no one to give me anything. I made that money honestly; it was all mine. It would have lasted me till I should have got to Rome. And now I have not a farthing in the world—not one—not one. I can sing a little, indeed, but then I promised Mariuccia never to sing in the streets, and I dare not break my word, for she is dead, you know. And I am all alone here in Florence. I do not know a soul. And my brothers are all dead; and no one can tell where my father is. But nothing of that frightened me so long as I had the money. But now I *am* frightened, oh Mother of God! for I have nothing in all the world, you see; I must just starve and die; perhaps even they will not believe what I say, but will take me for a thief, when they find that I have nothing! And if I had only died in Bologna!"

The passionate stream of the words had coursed from my tongue unbroken when once my pride had given way and found a refuge in speech; when my voice dropped in very weariness I stood before them heart-broken and striving with my piteous sense of shame; my cheeks burned dry my scorching tears, and my sobs died silent in my throat.

The man standing above under the ilex leaves laughed, but the laughter was tender and gentle.

"All nonsense, nonsense, *cara mia!*" he cried lightly. "No one ever dies in Bologna that can help it. It is not pleasant, you see, to be walled up in a square of bricks, and labelled dismally in the lump, with a thousand other '*vagabondi*,' or '*ladri*,' or '*bricóni*,' just as it may please the good town complimentarily to classify you. Take heart, signorina, and come and breakfast with us. Your gold florins, after all, may perhaps have been left at the house you slept in —who knows? You may mistake, or the thief may repent, or be found out, which is indeed the same thing. Come along and see my dogs, and taste my wine, if there be any left. Do not be afraid of us; we are none of us very respectable perhaps, except the dogs, but we will do you no harm."

Something in his voice and laugh, something of silvery resounding clearness, "*com' il dolce suonar d'una lira*," ringing on a metal plate, thrilled through my heart familiar and full of solace. I dashed the blinding mist from my eyes and my falling hair from my forehead, and gazed up at him breathless and entranced.

"And you never came the next day!" I cried to him in passionate reproach. "And you never saw me last night! Do you not know me now? I have kept one of the roses—look!"

I took out of the folds of my dress one of the

dead white roses of Verona. His face flushed darkly; he laughed; but his beautiful eyes looked dim.

How had I been a moment without knowing him! partly, because absorbed in the terror of my grief I had paid hardly any heed to anything around me; chiefly, because on the two nights when I had seen him he had been disguised in the gay masquerade of the carnival costumes.

And yet his was a face not commonly seen, nor once seen lightly forgotten; the Cinque Cento face, the face of the old Renaissance when the features of men bore the reflex of the artistic and heroical life which was in its full flower in their midst. The face with aquiline outline, dreaming lids, thoughtful brows; profoundly melancholy in repose, and in mirth gay as a young child's; with eyes sad as death, and a smile frank as sunlight; the face which is the most historical and purely idealic of all human countenances.

Be the reason what it may, lie as it will in climate, race, or breeding, it is a fact that the Italian physiognomy retains as no other nation's does, the impression of the past upon it.

The noble comes to you down the bare stone galleries of his old palace, and it is still the noble of Tintoretto and Tiziano that salutes you with that cold and lofty grace, which can change at will to the joyous and caressing softness of a woman. The peasant of the contado flings his brown mantle across his mouth to screen himself from the mountain blast in the market place, and it is still the model of Angelo and of Sarto that laughs aloud from those glancing teeth, and saunters through the braying mules and bleating kids with those supple and sinewy limbs, and that unconscious harmony of gesture.

Were it not too fanciful one would say that those great centuries, while they gave an immortal soul to the pagan graces of art and produced human genius in its most complex and complete form, had so entered into the blood and bone of these people that their influence is deathless. The sun of that wondrous summer noon of art has set indeed; but the after-glow of its rays shines still in the regard of the living sons of Italy.

Such a face was this which had laughed on me in the moonlight in the streets of Verona, and now in gentle compassion was before me in the City of Lilies.

CHAPTER XIII.
The Great Magician.

I SLID the rose back into its hiding-place a little shyly. The black-eyed girl was gazing at me with wide parted, astonished lips, and a little jealous wonder in her eyes.

"And you never knew me, last night!" I murmured to him. "Last night I almost touched you, and you never saw——"

"Last night! no;" said he, frankly. "When I go mad at the Carnival fair, I know nothing and nobody. But to-day, donzella, oh yes, I recognised you the instant you sat down under the cypress. That you have a genius for adventure is self-evident. How come you here all this way over the mountains?"

"But you never kept your promise!" I cried to him, intent on my one especial wrong.

"But you never came to me!" I cried to him, "You only sent the roses!"

"No, for the best of all reasons, signorina," said he, with a smile. "I had talked sedition that day, or so the stranieri construed it. I had lashed thy people with more than bladders, and had salted their soup with more than jokes; and to crown it all, in the Veglione, after I left you that night, I made an harangue which to Austrians' ears savoured of downright treason. So, in the grey of the daybreak, as I went home singing and dreaming no evil, the good Tedeschi seized hold of me, and marched me out of the gates, and gave me not a second to pack my knapsack or send a word to my people, but set off with me for the frontier in the sleet and the teeth of the wind. They were fifty to one, so there had been no sense in resistance. Hard by the gates I spied a flower shop, just opening its shutters; I asked the soldiers to let me stop and light my sigaretto. Then I picked out a knot of roses, the best I could see, and paid for them, and bade them take them to you. I am glad they did so honestly. It was very cold tramping across Lombardy, at a horse's tail, in that Florindo masquing dress, which looked absurd enough in the midst of the grey and white plain; and it snowed hard, and the tramontàna blew like a knife, but the sharpest thing about it to me was the thought that you would believe I had broken my promise."

He smiled a little as he spoke, that wondrous Italian smile which has so much mirth in it, so much tenderness, so much pathos. Surely that smile of

Italy is the loveliest thing left in all the width and weariness of the world!

Something in his accent made me turn and gaze at him. I breathed quickly in a happy excitation.

"Then you had not forgotten me really?" I cried. "I thought you had; I quite thought you had last night."

He laughed.

"Certainly not. I knew you, cara mia, at my first glance at you under the cypress yonder. You sang too well in Verona that day to be forgotten, and that wonderful black and gold dress, and your hands full of the Carnival roses, and that hair of yours with all the yellow lights in it;—yes, I saw you, and a pretty picture you made, that I grant I should have stayed a little to find you out; but your Tedesco friends and I have no love for one another. They say I excite the people. So I was fain to go out of Verona, not knowing your name, signorina."

"They have not stolen the onyx," I cried, breathless, standing still with the red sun in my eyes, whilst I tore the little silk cord from about my throat and drew the ring from its hiding place.

A flush of pleasure swept, like light, over his expressive face.

"Ah-ah! you kept that stupid thing! Too large and clumsy for your pretty little fingers, and no use to you at all. What did you do with the rest of the treasures? You had a fine lapfull that morning."

"I gave them away," I said, dreamily, not very well knowing what he said, gazing at him in the lustre of that crimson flash of the red and fading light in which we both were standing.

The little plump brown rabbit of a maiden peeped with her pretty, shy, raven-like eyes over my shoulder: she saw the ring with the Fates.

"Why, Pascarèl, that is your onyx," she cried to him; "the onyx you lost in Verona that first day of the Carnival when I was not with you, you remember?"

Pascarèl looked a little impatient.

"Did I ever tell you I lost it? At any rate the donzella found it, and it is hers now by every law of possession. Cara mia, those dismal old immutable Parcæ do not look fit dispensers of the Future to *you*."

"Would you not have it again?" I murmured, seeing that he now wore no ring.

He repulsed it with a sort of gentle impatience.

"Would you insult me because I am poor? Keep it, signorina; though it be a grim and gloomy fashion of gift to you."

I hardly heard him, I was so bewildered at his recognition of me. I slipped the onyx fondly back within my dress. I looked at him, glad and astonished.

"How strange it is!" I murmured.

"Forse il destino!" hummed Pascarèl, in a soft mezza voce, as if in answer.

"Do you believe in destiny?" I asked him, wistfully, in a little awe.

"To be sure!" he answered me. "But it is always feminine, cara mia, whatever our grammarians may say to the contrary. And, now, will you tell me your story a little?"

"What could he be, I wondered, ceaselessly; of

what grade, what habits, what pursuit? A scholar in every accent, a gentleman in every gesture, with the pure inflexions of voice, with the slender delicacy of form, with the indescribable ease and indifference of manner which only come of birth and of breeding, he lived solely, as it seemed, amongst the populace; his white linen garments were worn and threadbare; his meal was of the simplest and most frugal; and his companions were nothing more than populace, little more indeed than vagrants.

Perhaps he caught and understood the speculative wonder in my gaze at him. At any rate, what could he be, I wondered. He did not leave me long in doubt.

"We are strolling players, at your service," he said, with his bright laugh, casting himself down beside me. "She who was so terrified about you is called Brunótta; that short lad with the round head is little Toccò; and the other one owns the time-honoured name of Cocomero. The three poodles are Pepito, Pepita, and Toto. The monkey is Pantagruel. Toto in especial is the star of my troop. Now you know us all. As for me, I am Pascarello or Pascarèl. If you are not afraid of such disreputable companionship, will you narrate us something of your own history, signorina?"

He had made me drink a little of his red Chiante wine and break a crust of bread; it was a solace only to be able to speak of my immense calamity; I told him willingly all my story, warming to the recital of my woes and of my wrongs.

He listened, stretched on the grass and leaning on one elbow; the girl Brunótta lent an eager ear, her little round brown face flushing and growing pale in sympathy; the two lads leaned against a tree openmouthed and breathless; flattered by my interested and reverential audience, I grew a little calmer under my loss, and waxed more and more fluent in the narrative of my sad adventures.

My tale ended, Pascarèl sent the youth, whom he had called Cocomero, into the city to acquaint the guardia with the theft, and make enquiries at the locanda; that done, he threw himself again upon the turf. I wondered if he were sorry for me—he had not said so. All the ejaculations of sorrow and compassion had been Brunòtta's.

I was full of passionate sorrow for myself; the sight of these light-hearted people only made my sense of utter desolation weigh the heavier upon me; when the excitement of the relation of my miseries had passed away, a very horror of despondency possessed me; and, without reasoning very much upon it, to find my Romeo of the Veglione nothing more than a hedge-comedian cast a shadow of bitter disappointment over the romance of my vague dreams.

"So you are absolutely all alone, cara mia?" said Pascarèl, bending his luminous eyes down on mine.

"All alone—yes!"

"And if we cannot find this thief, have not a copper paul in all the world?"

"I have told you so!" I cried with a desperation of pain at being driven to repeat my degradation.

"Altro!" he said, breathing gently that wonderful expletive which comprehends in itself every shade and variety of human emotion.

"Do you know what it is to be all alone and penniless in this best of all possible worlds?" he said, slowly, cruelly, as I thought. I almost burst out sobbing afresh under the torture of the question.

"If I do no harm, can I be hurt?" I asked, wistfully looking in his face.

He laughed, in a kindly compassion.

"Ah! if one does no harm, it goes very ill indeed with one in this world. We are suspected—for ever!"

In the stupefaction of my sorrow the irony was too fine to reach me.

"Is it right to do wrong, then, ever?" I asked, bewilderedly; for I knew that Mariuccia had been my only teacher, and that she, poor soul! had known nothing of the world. Besides,—in Ambrogiò's story, was it not Rothwald who had done the wrong, yet who had thriven?"

"There is only one thing wrong in the world—poverty," answered my new friend briefly.

"It is much the same in the country too," the little Brunótta murmured.

"Assuredly," said the player, stretched on his back in the sun. "The country is only human nature washed in buttermilk; the town is human nature soaked in brandy."

"Why will you talk as though you were a cynic, Pascarèl?" said Brunótta in petulant expostulation.

He held up the ragged sleeve of his old white jacket; it had been, I saw, of finest and silkiest thibetti.

"Every one is a cynic who has a hole at his elbow," he answered her.

"But—as if you cared!"

He laughed, and pinched her pretty rosy ear.

"We do not care; but then we are very disreputable. All respectable people care. It is only scamps who smile."

"A smiling scamp is better than a frowning miser," said the girl; and she set the two white dogs, Pepito and Pepita, to waltz round with each other, whilst she waltzed too, singing a dance tune, down the avenue.

Pascarèl sprang up and caught her round the waist, and set himself whirling likewise; the boy with the fiddle struck out a wild waltz measure: the dogs capered, the monkey chattered loud, the man and the girl span round and round laughing, with their hands on each other's shoulders, and their feet flying like leaves blown in circles by the wind.

The fiddle grew louder and wilder and faster; the ape screamed in chorus; the dogs jumped over each other and sank panting on the ground. Pascarèl and Brunótta danced and danced and danced, with the grass beneath them and the leaves above, and every now and then a blaze of sunshine catching the blue tassels at her skirt and the scarlet ribbons on his hat.

Then, at last, exhausted and laughing, and panting like their dogs, they cast one another aside, and dropped down on the turf in the shadow.

"How well it is to be poor!" cried Pascarèl. "If we were dukes and duchesses we could not scamper like that in a wood! we could only go masked, in the gas, to an opera ball."

As he spoke he laughed, and fanned himself and her with a sheaf of chesnut leaves. I, sitting alone in the depth of the shadow from the cypress, watched them, wondering, and envying their glad content.

Brunótta of the bird-like eyes seeing me sitting

there alone in the dark, rose and crossed to me, and touched me again gently.

"Pascarèl says it is always well for those who love to be poor?" she whispered.

I shivered a little. The double trouble was mine, to be poor without any love to help me under it.

"If both are content, perhaps," I murmured aloud. But I was very doubtful.

"He is;—I don't say I see it so myself," said the little player, as she dropped down by me and wove a plait of grasses, and talked in a cheery, quick, babbling voice like the tinkling of a brook; "we are poor—so poor—but then we are so merry. Pascarèl was not always so poor. He is a great comedian; only the people are all he will play to, and he does not care to be great. Coco's father was a Harlequin and never had any money; and they used to travel much as we do now. He danced for his own bread when he was three years old; and then, when he grew older, he played. He is eighteen now. Pascarèl has a talent—such a talent: I have none. I never did anything until three years ago, except milk the goats and take the insects off the vines, and plait straw, and spin, of course. I can only hop about. We have travelled with three or four companies, but Pascarèl never could get on with the directors; one director made love to me; and another one was cruel to poor little Toto; and a third one failed and ran away in debt to all his troop, and so on and so on; so we are as we are, and we have a merry life. The two lads and the animals love us, and we go about where we like; and Pascarèl can always make the people laugh, and we always get enough to live upon; and it is much better than being at any tyrant's beck and call; and now and then we have a holiday in the woods—like this. In the winter it is a little harder, of course; but even then the little towns are bright and warm, and the people are always glad to be made merry; and before one has romped through Carnival—presto!—the winter is gone! A hearty laugh makes one forget that one could eat more maccaroni, and when one's toes are cold in the snow a dance warms them quicker than anything. Sometimes I am sorry Pascarèl cares nothing at all to make himself great, because he has such a talent; and if he were great one would have such good things to eat every day, and fine clothes and real jewels; but he says one should not care for such things—but then to be sure he does not trouble his head whether he eats a ciambello or a cucumber, a swan or a sparrow! But how selfish I am to run on so!—you are unhappy?"

The little actress saw the whiteness that came over the face above her, and paused in the weaving of her braid of grasses, and said softly again:—

"You are so unhappy?"

"Of course; but it does not matter."

"Yes, it does. Everything seems so unhappy—except just Pascarèl and myself, and the dogs; and it is such a pity, in a sunshine like this, when everything ought to live like the crocuses, being glad and taking no thought. You are unhappy because you are alone, no doubt. Will you come with us? I am sure Pascarèl would be glad! It will be so much better; and we will not teaze you to know what you do not wish to tell—if there is anything——"

"But you know nothing of me——"

The girl laughed.

"Ah bah! We are not great people that dare not taste a pear till they know what stem it was grafted on. We are only poor players; we have nothing to lose; and if we take a liking to a face we are not afraid of its fellowship. There is so much liberty in being poor, you see!"

"Is there?"

I could not see it; it appeared to me that poverty was an ass's hobble, with which one was tied miserably to one place that we had long browsed bare.

"It is the difference between an old shirt and a new," said Pascarèl, rising and lounging near. "The new is embroidered perhaps, and very white and handsome, no doubt, but it is tight and the stitches gall; that shirt is respectable, admirable, and fit for a palace; but comfortable—no. The old is ugly maybe, and looks bad, and in it you will not be asked to a noble's table or a bishop's feast; but it is so easy to wear, and it has so many recollections, that dear old shirt: you pawned it here, and you danced in it there, and pretty fingers darned it in one place, and a rosy-cheeked laundress cobbled it in another; it is picturesque, it is memorial, it is venerable; above all, it never scratches. Those two shirts are Wealth and Poverty."

"Will it not be much better?" said Brunótta, eagerly interrupting him,—"much better, if the signorina come with us for a little space?"

Pascarèl swept the turf with his ribboned sombrero, and declared his willingness in flowery phrases.

"Only—only," he said, at the end of his graceful and gracious sentences, "you forget one thing, Brunótta.

The signorina is gentle-born and gentle-bred; our mode of life would be but a sorry one for her."

"But what can she do?" cried the little Brunótta.

"Ah! what, indeed?" I thought; and I threw myself down face downwards on the earth in a very paroxysm of despair.

Pascarèl threw one gentle look on me, then turned and walked up and down under the trees in meditation.

"Brunótta!" I heard him call; she went to him, and I heard their voices, low and earnest, in conversation at some distance from me, too far away for their meaning to be intelligible.

Then they ceased, and all was quite silent in the wood except the joyous and wild bark of the dogs as they chased a bird or a rabbit. I lay still there with my face pressed on the dry, hard earth.

"If they would only kill me," I thought, "and make an end of it all!"

A little picture rose before my memory of Raffaellino sitting at the coppersmith's door at sunset playing on his mandoline, while his mother and Mariuccia gossiped within over the lamp, and the light shone on the huge red coppers, and the stars came out over the dark quiet piazza.

"Oh, why! oh, why!" I thought, "cannot we know when we are happy!"

I would have given away twenty years of my young unspent life only to have been back once more in that old, despised, safe home in the city of Can Grande!

Pascarèl aroused me, touching me on the shoulder.

"Rise up, cara mia," he said, gently. "That is

not the way anyhow to get back your florins, or to win yourself new ones."

I rose as he bade me, and looked him in the face; my own face I felt was white with pain and desperation.

"I have been very foolish," I said to him, "and you have been very good; you are all strangers, and can care nothing for me. I will go now; I thank you very much—you and yours."

I put out my hands to him in farewell; his eyes were so beautiful, and he had been so kind, I could hardly keep the tears from flooding my own eyes as I spoke to him, and yet I knew I must not trouble them any longer—all strangers as they were.

Pascarèl took my hands and kissed them lightly with the easy grace of all his actions.

He looked troubled and almost embarrassed.

"Not so fast, donzella," he said, gently; "wait awhile; Coco is not back yet with any news, and even if he find your florins, it cannot be said that you are in very fair case for wandering over the country all alone. See here, we are not of your grade in life; we are poor strolling Bohemians; we are not, as I tell you, very reputable people, and we are poor as the devil—altro!—and yet, if you would like to stay with us as—as—Brunótta said, it might be safer at any rate for you than to stray about Italy by yourself as helpless as my little Toto would be if I lost him. We are a sorry resort, I know, but perhaps we are better than nothing, and I may be more able to find your father than you. Say, will you wait with us a little?"

Ere I could answer him, the youth Cocomero burst

through the bushes breathless from having run to and from the town.

"There is no news," he panted, gloomily. "They knew nothing at the Silver Melon, and the guards say there have been many foreign cutpurses in the city of late. They have had a score of such robberies this winter."

Pascarèl shrugged his shoulders and lifted his hands with that indescribable gesture in which an Italian expresses consummate disgust and resignation.

"It is destiny!" he murmured, resting his eyes on me with a look I did not understand. "Well, signorina mia, will you stay with us?"

"I should be glad!" I said, with a little sob in my voice. "It is so horrible—so very horrible—to be alone!"

"Of course it is horrible," he echoed, as he took my hands afresh within his own, and cast himself down upon his knees before me where I stood; in that easy unstudied abandonment of himself to each impulse and emotion of the moment which makes grace of posture as natural to an Italian as it is to a deer or an antelope.

"You will stay?" he murmured, still lightly holding my hand in his. "That is well—at least for you it shall be well; that I swear. Riches we have not, and glory we have not, and the ways of our life will be hard—for you. But all that we can do we will."

"You are very good!" I said to him, scarcely knowing what indeed to answer him.

He was a stranger, seen but half an hour before, and yet already he seemed like a familiar friend.

A shade of sadness and impatience swept over his speaking face.

"Che-che! Wait to praise us till you know us. We are good for very little, cara mia. We will make you laugh sometimes, that I can promise, and perhaps that is much in this life."

"But if I stay with you?" I said, a sudden fear and remembrance striking me with its shame, "if I stay—I have nothing; I will not be a burden to you; never, never! Is there nothing I can do to get my bread? My voice is good——"

"Yes! You sing like all the angels."

"About the angels—I do not know. But anything;—always."

"But you are so young——"

"Not too young for that—only I promised dear dead Mariuccia—— But I will not stay with you unless you tell me of some way to get my bread."

"Bread! Nonsense! You eat, I daresay, as much as one flings to the swallows. But, if you are in earnest, you might be one of us."

"A player! I?"

I echoed the words half in affront half in delight. My pride rebelled, my fancy was allured.

"Why not?" said Pascarèl. "Do you know aright what it is to be one?"

"Surely!" I answered him, with a little gay contempt—had I not seen them scores of times in Verona? "It is to be no longer a man or a woman, but only a mere wooden *burattino* that has to dance or die, to swagger or shrink, just as its master chooses to make people laugh for a copper coin. A fine thing, certainly!"

Pascarèl released my hands and sprang to his feet erect. His mobile face flushed darkly; his changeful eyes flashed fire.

"Is that all you know!" he cried, while his voice rang like a trumpet-call. "Listen here, then, little lady, and learn better. What is it to be a player? It is this. A thing despised and rejected on all sides; a thing that was a century since denied what they call Christian burial; a thing that is still deemed for a woman disgraceful, and for a man degrading and emasculate; a thing that is mute as a dunce save when, parrot-like, it repeats by rote with a mirthless grin or a tearless sob; a wooden doll, as you say, applauded as a brave puppet in its prime, hissed at in its first hour of failure or decay; a thing made up of tinsel and paint, and patchwork, of the tailor's shreds and the barber's curls of tow—a ridiculous thing to be sure! That is a player. And yet again,—a thing without which laughter and jest were dead in the sad lives of the populace; a thing that breathes the poet's words of fire so that the humblest heart is set aflame; a thing that has a magic on its lips to waken smiles or weeping at its will; a thing which holds a people silent, breathless, intoxicated with mirth or with awe, as it chooses; a thing whose grace kings envy, and whose wit great men will steal; a thing by whose utterance alone the poor can know the fair follies of a thoughtless hour, and escape for a little space from the dull prisons of their colourless lives into the sunlit paradise where genius dwells;—*that* is a player, too!"

His voice trembled a little over the closing words, and, ashamed of the passionate eloquence into which the sting of my idle slighting phrase had hurried him, he turned away and began to romp and laugh and gambol with Pepito and Pepita.

I listened; ashamed myself; moved, I knew not very well why; and regretful to think that I had wounded him.

I waited a little while; then I went up to him where he stooped over his dogs, and laid my fingers on his arm.

"I spoke idly," I murmured. "I did not think. And—and—I will try and be a player too."

He lifted his head, with a flash of light over all his face, and touched my hand caressingly with his own.

"Altro!" he said. "It is a fate. Come with us. But as for being a player;—wait and see. You must not choose your future in blind haste."

Then he bade me sing to him, which I did, and Toccò touched his violin in quaint accord with me; and Pascarèl himself raised the echoes of the wood with half the popular songs of Italy.

So, laughing and singing, and pausing to watch the dogs at play, we idled time away under the black pines and the budding chestnut trees.

I was only a child; I was almost happy again. Sometimes I started and wondered if indeed I had been so wretched, there, in that very place, an hour before.

Was he a magician, I wondered, this Pascarèl?

I was ungrateful to the supreme magician—Youth.

BOOK III.

THE DAUGHTER OF HERCULES.

CHAPTER I.
Under the Red Lily.

The day rolled onward, growing chill something early, for it was still but the very first commencement of the spring.

I seemed to have known them all my life long—this little gay, good-humoured band; and the poodles frisked and fawned upon me as impartially as on Brunótta.

She—this pretty little brown thing—was not jealous of their sudden transference of caresses; she was about six years older than I—a girl of the people, no doubt, but with something so good-natured, so confiding, and so gay about her that one could not choose but trust in her and like her. She was so fond, too, of her brother, that one could see at a glance, and very proud of him, and a little afraid of him also.

He was very different in mind and manner to her; though a strolling player, as he said, he had the tone and the temper of a scholar: whilst little Brunótta confessed to me, half in glee, as one who had escaped a gruesome penalty and peril, that, like the padrona's son at the Golden Boar, she knew not her alfabeto.

What did that matter to me?

Raffacllino only knew it just enough to carry him

through the offices of the Church: it never seemed to me a science indispensable in people ere I took them for my friends, which, no doubt, was a grave error on my part, and due to my running loose in my babyhood amongst these Bohemians at Verona.

The shadows and the cold came early in that dusky wood; we were almost in darkness, whilst the road and the plain were still in full sunlight. Pascarèl gave the signal for moving towards the city.

We emerged from the ilex groves on to the highway—Brunótta and I, Pascarèl and his dogs, and the two lads following us with the monkey and the fiddle.

"You have seen good players!" he asked me, as we walked on towards Florence, whilst the silver bells of Perretola and the deep toll of the city churches crossed each other ringing the Ave-Maria.

"I have seen the Burattini hundreds of times, and the Personaggi too, in melodrama," I answered him eagerly, proud of my experience, which was due to Cecco and the rest of the students.

Pascarèl gave his charming gesture of ineffable disdain.

"Fantoccini and melodrama! Oh, cara mia! how much you have to learn,—and to *un*learn,—which is much the harder of the two at all times! No wonder you think little of the stage."

I thought that I was willing to be great as Lillo was great, who had had the showers of gold and of lilies in Verona; but I could see no possibility of any greatness in a strolling player, as we passed over the white dry road, out of the rosy reflex of the sunset, on into the shadow of the Florentine walls.

"Even Destiny loses the light out of her hair here," said Pascarèl, with a laugh, as we passed into the deep gloom of the Borgognissanti.

He looked as if he meant to call me Destiny; but how could I be that, I wondered—I who was but a poor little stray leaf blown and buffeted by the hazards of every breeze of fate?

As we crossed the Carraia bridge and entered the heart of the city, into the twisting streets that curve all around the red dome of the Santo Spirito, and the frowning front of the Pitti, we passed by a cobbler's stall planted against the roadway; the old man, who was stitching at his leather by the aid of a dim lantern, called out gladly to him:—

"Che-che! is it you, Pascarèl? You are welcome as figs in summer!"

Some urchins standing idly near caught up the name; the street became quite noisy with the cry of "Pascarèl! Pascarèl! eccô il Pascarello!"

The people were all sitting in their doorways, or half out in the street, after the manner of Italian dwellers and traders, with little lights burning before some pile of faggots, some stall of chestnuts, some tray of amaretti, some stand of pizzicheria fare, or some image of San Giovanni. They incontinently left their trades and their pastimes and clustered round him in vociferous homage—whom would he sup with?—where would he drink?—did he play to-night beyond the Prato Gate? Beppe and Pippo had been fighting in the Sdrucciolò, he had been wanted badly;—had he heard?—who was that pretty purple and yellow thing he had got with him?—a new dancer? So their stream of questions poured out rapid and mellifluous as olive oil from a tilted flask.

But he shook himself free of them, and leaving the laughing, clinging, delighted crowd as best he might, he took me into the little tavern where they tarried in the town. It was a smaller place, and humbler than the Golden Boar; a great fig-tree climbed over it, just coming into leaf, and on an iron stanchion swung its sign of two crossed halberds, a relic, no doubt, of old Bianchi and Neri strife. But it was clean, and its people worshipped Pascarèl; and their laughter and their welcome, and the colour and pleasantness of the little place made it bright and cheerful in the midst of the dusky old age of grim Oltrarno.

There we dined frugally, as became Italians, whilst the brass stands of the lùcernati threw a feeble light over the pretty black head of Brunótta, and the golden folds of my poor Court dress, and the Florentine face of Pascarèl.

It was only a poor little tavern; the chamber we dined in was only parted from the kitchen by an open arch.

We saw the food stewed and fried ere it came to us, and near at hand to us were some smiths and tapestry-workers playing dominoes and drinking innocent bibiti; and yet—I do not know how it might have been in other countries—but in Italy it was not vulgar, was not even common, but was only a homely, picturesque, pretty scene, full of colour, and movement, and mirth; a noble might have shared in it, an artist would have been happy in it.

They have suffered so much, these people, and yet through all they have kept their hold on so much; for they have kept the smile on their eyes and they have kept the grace in their limbs, and they have kept the poetry in their hearts.

When our meal was over, the clocks chimed the half-hour after six. Pascarèl rose, and we went out into the clear and cold evening, where the young moon was rising above the immense dark masses of the city buildings.

"You play to-night, caro mio?" cried the smiths and the weavers, and they flung their dominoes in a heap, and rose and followed us, talking and laughing with him.

I gathered from their talk that it was his habit to stroll through the country, taking the large towns and the little as they came, sometimes even pausing in the smallest villages, and setting up for himself a little theatre of canvas and wood, in the midst of any breezy pasture on the plain or sheltered nook upon the hills that took his errant fancy.

Brunótta and he and the two lads were all the little company which wandered as it would, subject to no dictation except that impulse of the moment, which was always law to Pascarèl.

By the enthusiasm displayed to him, he seemed to have a strange power to charm, or, at any rate, to amuse the people; and as I listened, the seduction of this nomadic, changeful, careless, adventurous life bewitched me, as it has bewitched so many in their youth.

From their discourse and the confidences of Brunótta I gathered that Pascarèl was always a bohemian, often a beggar; he led an idle, roving life, and preferred it to any other.

His stage had often been any plank across a cart or any board in a fair booth that might offer to him; he wrote the pieces he played that they might serve for his little troop, of which the dogs and the parrot were the stars; he rarely knew one night where he would lay his head another; he often ate his supper at a trattoria, trusting to his skill that same evening to pay off the score; when he made money, as sometimes happened—for he was popular everywhere, except with the directors of theatres—he spent it royally in a mingling of revelry and charity that left him as poor as ever on the morrow.

He was a stroller and a vagabond, so far as social status went, an idle rogue, and a dissolute; but at his heart he was a great artist; and in many a little village, and township, and country fair, and wayside tavern the people had found it out, and the cry of "Pascarèl" brought men and maidens, old women and young children, poor students and day-labourers, in a great eager crowd round any place where his changeful face, with its speaking eyes and its flexile lips, laughed out its mirth upon them.

"He studies nothing; he outrages all traditions; he violates every precedent and canon," said the directors whom he quarrelled with.

The people did not care for that; they only knew that Pascarèl, with a dog for his sole supporter, and a rag of carpet or a broken bough for all his scenery, could make them laugh or cry, hate or love, be miserable or be in ecstasy, whichever he chose in the irresistible dominance of genius.

At a stone's throw from the Cascine woods was an open space; the moon was already shining clearly upon it; a large tent, braced with timbers, was set up in the centre of the place; the canvas was fluttering in the cool evening breeze.

"There is my theatre, donzella," said Pascarèl. "Oh, your Burattini have finer abodes; I know that. When one only hangs on wires and has wooden legs, one must have a fine house, or who will come and look at one? But an artist, if he be worth his salt, can make his temple in the minds of his audience, if he have only the roof of a barn over his head and theirs."

These were not the golden showers and Easter lilies of Lillo! and a little contempt for this nomadic drama rose up in me.

It stood on a breadth of meadow land outside the Prato Gate, with the shadow of the mountain sides behind it, and around it the scents of growing grasses from the fields that had been sown for hay.

The people were trooping to it eagerly; townsfolk of all trades and crafts, cobblers, tinkers, smiths, alabaster workers, mosaic workers, conscripts, carabineers, market women, mule drivers, heaven knows what not; and in from the villages of the Val de Grève there were coming in the opposite direction many country women who plaited their straw as they walked, and contadini who had stuck a flower behind their ear as evening dress.

It was a pretty little wooden house, light and cleverly put together; sometimes its walls were open to the sky like the old Basiliche of the Latins, sometimes its canvas roof fluttered over spectators as close packed and as eager as ever the canvas roof of the Coliseum shaded.

It had the flag of Florence with the red lily flying merrily above it, and above its entrance place was painted in gay letters the words "Dell' Arte."

I asked Pascarèl what the name meant.

"Oh, I broke a flask of wine against it, and named it so ages ago," he answered me. "Why? Because the first wooden home of Pulcinello and his brethren was called so when it rolled one fine Carnival day into Venice.

"A presumptuous name? Oh, I don't see that. We are all the arts in one, if we are worth anything at all.

"And besides, when they grew up in Italy, all that joyous band,—Arlecchino in Bergamo, Stenterello in Florence, Pulcinello in Naples, Pantaleone in Venice, Dulcamara in Bologna, Beltramo in Milan, Brighella in Brescia, masked their mirthful visages and ran together and jumped on that travelling stage before the world, and what a force they were for the world, those impudent mimes!

"'Only Pantomimi!' When they joined hands with one another and rolled their wandering house before St. Mark's they were only players indeed; but their laughter blew out the fires of the Inquisition, their fools' caps made the papal tiara look but paper toy, their wooden swords struck to earth the steel of the nobles, their arrows of epigram, feathered from goose and from falcon, slew flying the many-winged dragon of Superstition.

"They were old as the old Latin land, indeed.

"They had mouldered for ages in Etruscan cities, with the dust of uncounted centuries upon them, and been only led out in Carnival times, pale voiceless frail ghosts of dead powers, whose very meaning the people had long forgotten. But the trumpet call of the Renaissance woke them from their Rip Van Winkle sleep.

"They got up, young again, and keen for every frolic—Barbarossas of sock and buskin, whose helmets were caps and bells, breaking the magic spell of their slumber to burst upon men afresh; buoyant incarnations of the new-born scorn for tradition, of the nascent revolts of democracy, with which the air was rife.

"'Only Pantomimi?' Oh altro!

"The world when it reckons its saviours should rate high all it owed to the Pantomimi,—the privileged Pantomimi—who first dared take licence to say in their quips and cranks, in their capers and jests, what had sent all speakers before them to the rack and the faggots.

"Who think of that when they hear the shrill squeak of Pulcinello in the dark bye-streets of northern towns, or see lean Pantaleone slip and tumble through the transformation scene of some gorgeous theatre?

"Not one in a million.

"Yet it is true for all that. Free speech was first due to the Pantomimi. A proud boast that. They hymn Tell and chant Savonarola and glorify the Gracchi, but I doubt if any of the gods in the world's Pantheon or the other world's Valhalla did so much for freedom as those merry mimes that the children scamper after upon every holyday.

"And we players are all their sons and their successors; and so I baptize my house after them 'Dell'

Arte.' Why not? If we be not artist we have no business to profane a stage at all."

And therewith he bade me adieu, and ran in his room to dress.

We entered the booth—for in truth it was hardly more—as the Florentine clocks tolled the quarter before seven. The people were already gathering thickly in the meadow, and he could only break free of their vociferous welcome by reminding them that if they kept him there without, he could not play within; a sober fact which they recognized at last, though with some reluctance.

Pascarèl drew me to a place where I could see both actors and audience, unseen by the latter; the portion of the tent where the stage was made was divided from the public part of it by a curtain; behind this I was stationed.

They all left me and disappeared; Toccò ran round to light the oil wicks which were to illumine the performance. In an incredibly short space, so brief that it seemed to me Pascarèl must first have whisked a sorcerer's wand to change them all, Brunótta in short skirts of tinsel, and white and rose, and Cocomero in the vari-coloured dress of Arlecchino, and the dogs in quaint little brilliant coats—Toto pre-eminent by cap and plume—all bounded pell mell on to the boards together.

The curtain swung aside, the violin of Toccò thrummed a gay melody, whilst a drum, ingeniously beaten by his foot, rolled now and then its deeper melody.

They commenced one of those pretty and unintelligible dumb dramas of gesture, which are so popular in Italy, and hold the stage longer than opera, or tragedy, or comedy of voice, whether in their grander form of ballet at the Pergola or the Fenice, or in their humblest species such as that in which Brunótta and Cocomero now danced.

Brunótta danced with all the agility and vivacity of a girl who had spun round in the fairs and feste from the earliest days of her existence; Cocomero was a comic and untiring harlequin, and the quaint tricks and astounding intelligence of Maestro Toto were beyond all praise and would baffle all description.

The spectacle was received with glee and good humour by an audience which was by far too large for the limits of the theatre, and stretched far out into the open air in a sea of out-stretched throats and eager faces, in a curious chiaroscuro from the dark without and the oil lamps within, whilst they hummed the melody of the dance tunes all the way through themselves—a detestable mode of testifying musical delight, from which the most patrician musical audiences of Italy unhappily are not free.

The curtain fell, Toto as primo-uomo was thrice summoned and received a shower of sweet cakes and sugar, plaudits which were to his comprehension.

Then loud and imperious rose the cry:

"Pascarèl! Pascarèl! Il Pascarello!"

Pascarèl soon obeyed the summons, amidst the tumult of delight that greeted him from the throngs of coppersmiths, and carpet-weavers, and craftsmen of all kinds, and students, and beggars, and idlers of every sort who made up his motley clientela.

The little piece he played in was called "Le

miraculose fortune e gli amori pietosissimi del Calzolajo e del Conte."

It had been written by himself, to suit the resources of his scanty company; a thing of the slightest and the simplest, in which he played himself the two chief parts, those of the cobbler and the count.

It was only a trifle; but it abounded in wit; it sparkled with irony, it contained epigrams worthy of the palmy days of Pasquin, and every now and then, amidst the rippling exuberance of its play of nonsense, it deepened and had an exquisite pathos hidden in it; it was like a blue forget-me-not that the rains have just dashed where it lifts its blue eyes in the sunshine.

With the utmost ingenuity, the play was constructed so that the old man and the young, the cobbler and the noble, whilst rivals throughout for the love of a contadina, never met one another in all the accidents of their fortunes.

His transitions from age to youth, from youth to age, were so sudden, so marvellous, so perfect, each in its kind, that none who had not known him could have told which years were the real with him or which the assumed.

Other actors in their youth have counterfeited as wonderfully the age of Richelieu or of Louis XI.; but they have been elaborately prepared by costume and by paint, and have sustained the one part unbroken; but here Pascarèl changed from youth to age with scarce breathing time between the phases, and made his personification a vivid living fact by no aid but that of his own consummate powers.

It would have been impossible to say with which

impersonation the sympathies of the public were the stronger; each won them in its turn.

The youth of the young noble was so charming, so full of happy insolence, of generous impulse, of audacious ease, of irresistible assurance, of gay, good-tempered grace.

The age of the old cobbler was so full of sad genuine irony, of wistful loneliness, of pathetic fear of mockery, of trembling tenderness that scarcely dared be uttered; no slippered pantaloon, no palsied dotard, shrunken target for the gibes of fools, but Age—faithful, venerable, true to its own self-respect; but Age—unutterably sad because—alone.

It was a trifle, unaided by any scenic deception, or any delusion for the senses; but it was perfect as only the exquisite delicacy, the unerring truthfulness, and the supreme histrionic instincts of a great genius could make it; and as such it swept away to itself, with the rush of the storm wind, all the pity and all the passion that throbbed in the countless hearts of its audience.

When it was over, and the "Fuori! fuori! fuori!" of the enraptured people had brought him for the last time before their hurricane of applause, he came to me where I stood.

"Well!" he said, with the smile in his eyes.

I trembled before him, burning, breathless, entranced, amazed; so wondrous did his power seem to me, I could have cast myself at his feet and worshipped him for the divine force of the Art that was in him.

"Well!" he said again; but his voice shook a little,

though it had a laugh in it. "Well!—say—is it better than the Burattini?"

I could not answer him; but I burst into tears.

When we left the wooden Arte that night where it stood, with its flag dropping in the quiet air, and its gay scroll facing the line of the Apennines, we were escorted in royal honour homeward by a half hundred or so of sturdy popolani, singing, laughing, shouting, dancing in universal acclaim and fellowship, as only Italians can sing, and laugh, and shout, and dance, when the moon is high, and a mandoline is making tinkling melody before their steps.

It was late, and a beautiful, lustrous, cold night, full of the smell of the young spring, as the breeze blew in from over the budding contado.

We passed through the Porta al Prato, and glanced up at white Fiesole, and went on under the limes of the piazzone and along the edge of the glancing water.

The music of the mandoline drew the steps of the loiterers, of whom there were many about in those luminous, tranquil night-hours.

A youth with a guitar slung across him joined us, and a man with a violin ran out from under an archway, and caught the strains, and skipped before us in many grotesque capers; some people above, on a lighted balcony, threw some violets and daffodils at us as we went by; the moonlight lay broad and white upon the river; all the towers and spires rose clear against the stars; the music passed on, glad as the singing of Pan.

So we went homeward through Florence.

CHAPTER IL
The Rose and the Florins.

WHEN we reached the little tavern, our escort utterly refused to let him enter it.

They claimed Pascarèl as theirs by every human right, and insisted on bearing him off amidst them to supper to a noted wine-house, where the alabaster workers that night were about to hold high revelry. Pascarèl laughed and consented to go with them, but before he turned away, he swept the earth with his sombrero in a good-night to me, and murmured some parting counsel in the ear of his sister.

Then off he went; the rapture of his comrades no longer restrained by the presence of the "donzella," at whom they had glanced as a new and not altogether welcome addition to his little party.

They lifted him fairly off the ground and bore him along aloft on the shoulders and backs of half a dozen sturdy craftsmen of Florence, the mandoline twanging cheerily before them, and all their far-reaching voices blending together.

It was not the white lilies of Lillo; but it was a homage full as genuine in its way.

I stood in the doorway and watched them pass down the sombre, darkling ancient street; the moon shone whitely here and there upon their path, the grim arcades and the mighty walls were upon either side; above, between the roofs, was the dark blue sky of night. Their riotous glee died softly in the distance as they turned out of sight by the base of the old Guadagni Palace, and the last echo I heard was the shout of their homage, "Viva il Pascarello! Pascarèl! Pascarèl!"

How long I stood there, lost in a dream of this strange and wonderful life which had opened upon me, I cannot tell; Brunótta touched me in kindly impatience:—

"Do not dream in the moonlight like that, signorina. It makes people mad, they say. I have some hot soup here; come and drink it, and let us get to bed."

"When will he be back?" I asked, as I followed her withindoors.

"Pascarèl? Oh! not till daybreak, I daresay. He is often out all night long. Come, do not let the soup get cold. And so you thought him wonderful, did you? Ah! did I not tell you only the truth?"

She sat opposite me, with the little brass soup-kettle between us, toasting her feet on an earthen scaldino; she had not changed her pretty short white and rose skirts; she had still her little starry crown on her forehead. She was a little gay, rosy, cheery soul, and yet I thought she seemed hardly worthy to be of the same race as this marvellous Pascarèl.

"I never could have dreamed of anything like him!" I said, under my breath, for I had been too deeply moved to be able to talk of it easily: "but the whole world ought to know it; he ought to play before kings!"

"He likes this best," said Brunótta, keeping her airy skirts off the hot charcoal of her footstool. "He is so free, you see. He does just as he likes: in the world fame would be bondage. So he says, and no doubt he is right. Besides, I do not think he cares so much as this brown pot would care for either riches or fame. He loves his freedom, and he loves the people, Pascarèl."

"But he wrote that piece himself?"

"Oh, yes. He writes everything that he plays."

"But that is genius!"

"I do not know what you mean. He is very clever, no doubt, wonderfully clever; there is no one like him. But then he is a great scholar, you know; he took his degree at Pisa."

"At Pisa? And you do not know how to read?" I cried, forgetful in my astonishment of all laws of courtesy.

"No. I cannot read," said Brunótta, with a little confused laugh.

"But a degree at Pisa, and not to know the alfabeto—that is a great difference."

Brunótta coloured; perhaps she was vexed.

"Yes. No doubt it is a good deal of difference. But then I was always a very lazy little thing, and never cared to do anything but to dance in the streets, whilst Pascarèl,—oh, you cannot imagine what wonderful things he has it in him to do. He might be very great—very great—there is no doubt, if he liked."

"It is odd he should not like?"

"He has no ambition, I suppose—that is it: he likes to be free."

"But who can be free if they be poor?"

"Anybody, signorina," laughed Brunótta, with the philosophy which she had acquired from Pascarèl; "that is, if they do not try to be rich, you know. Of course, if you be always struggling to be something you are not, you never can be at ease—rich or poor."

There was a profound wisdom in this, no doubt; but it was too profound for me.

"Pascarèl might have made an enormous deal of money, no doubt," pursued the little dancing girl, "but he would never bind himself; that is where his fault is; and people will not pay you, ever, unless you will put yourself into harness for good and all. He is happier as he is; playing just as the fancy moves him.

"And you cannot think the good that he does, for all he looks so careless. That poor little Toccò there; he was the son of one of the brigands at Pæstum. The law took the father and the whole gang. They shot some, and sent some to the galleys, poor wretches! and little Toccò they turned adrift on the streets, for he was only twelve, and nothing proved against him. Of course, in time, he would have been a thief like his father, but Pascarèl got hold of him and kept him; and now there is not an honester or better little soul in the whole length of Italy than Toccò; and I am sure he would be cut in a million pieces for Pascarèl.

"At the great flood, too, two winters ago, in Tuscany, when the whole land was under water and the bullocks and sheep drowned by thousands, and the people were only saved here and there by getting up on the tops of the towers, and the great stacks of hay and corn, and the trees, and often the roofs and very bodies of the houses were tossing down the great yellow sea of the flood like so many little cockle-shells in a gutter, you should have seen Pascarèl that day: we happened to be up high on the hills where the flood did not reach, but he heard of it at sunrise, and down he went and he got a boat, and he rowed about hither and thither on the white horrid face of the torrents, shaming the cowards that dared not stir, of whom there were hundreds and hundreds; and ever so many times he was within an ace of being swept to his grave, and not a whit did he care—not he.

"He worked on and on till the night fell and the force of the waters abated, and the men and women and children, and the flocks and the herds that he saved, you would never believe if I told you.

"There was much talk after that of some public reward for his goodness and courage, and some of the towns wanted to make great feasts in his honour and have jubilees in their churches, and give him money.

"But when Pascarèl heard that, he fled out of the country as though the black death itself were after him, and went along the Corniche into France, and would not return into Italy till time had gone by long enough for the people to forget what they owed to him. It does not take very long for people to forget a benefit, you know, signorina.

"But it is nearly midnight, donzella mia," said Brunótta, rising after a pause in her chatter, and shaking the embers in her earthen pot, "and Pascarèl said you were to sleep early and wake late, because you were tired and not used to our life. Let me show you your room; it is a very poor and small place, but it is clean; and I hope you will not mind it."

Then she led the way with a lantern, and we

climbed a rickety ladder-like stair, and I found my little chamber—a mere nook in a wall as it were, and bare of comfort, but still clean, as she had said, and on the little hard bed was cast a cloak of skins.

"That is Pascarèl's; he thought you might be cold; the nights are chilly, and so he told me to put it there," said Brunótta, busying herself in a hundred kindly girlish fashions after my comfort as well as she could.

After she had bidden me thrice good-night, she stood, with her light in her hand, looking at me wonderingly as I unloosed my bodice and shook down all my hair, and took my shoes and stockings off my tired feet.

"The donzellina is beautiful to look at," she said, meditatively, with a sort of astonished inquiring pleasure in her voice: "and what white little feet, though she is so tall, and what a white skin!—it is wonderful! I wish Pascarèl could see you now. He says he never saw anything like you. He says you would do for the Angelica in that poem he is so fond of, you know! He is always running his head on that kind of rubbish, as if it would do one any good."

"You are very flattering, Brunótta," I said, laughing, as with some vanity, I fear me, I displayed to her all the thickness of my hair, which always delighted Italians, because of the yellow lights it had in it, which never darkened with the sun as their own did.

"I only say what is just true. Is that generous?" said the good little honest soul, as she turned at last fairly away with her lantern, and drew my door close behind her.

For myself, I was so confused, so excited, so full of a mingled pleasure and pain, that, though I threw myself at once on my bed, it was long before I could sleep.

When I did at length fall asleep, the grey streak fo the dawn had already begun to stray through the narrow casement across the bricks of my floor; and I dreamed feverishly of rushing floods, of drowning cattle, of dancing harlequins, of the onyx with the Fates, of old forsaken Verona, and of Pascarèl.

It was broad day when I awoke; the iron rod on a wall opposite, which served for a sun-dial, showed that it was ten o'clock. I heard a voice that I knew —a voice with a clear, careless laugh in it.

"Oh, good little soul," it said, as in a mirthful expostulation, "what possessed you to go aside in that wood yesterday? We were so well as we were; and women will never let well alone. They will always paint their lilies, and, of course, the poor lilies die of it. We were content as we were, and now—. What possessed you to bind up with our hedge-row flowers a stray hothouse rose like this?"

"You saw it before ever I saw it," the voice of Brunótta replied to him. "And you must have liked the look of the rose, Pascarèl, or you never had given away for it your onyx."

I heard him laugh, self-convicted.

"That was for the pure love of music, carina. Don't you believe that? Oh, little sceptic! Nay I will make no bones of it; I will say the truth. The donzella is too noble for us; it is that which troubles me. When I saw her standing first in the square of Verona, I said to myself: What can she be, that young princess, with her golden skirts, singing in a crowd for a few baiocche? I could not understand it; and it troubles me now. She is too good for our life, and we have no other."

"Let her go her own way, then, and go we ours," said Brunótta, with tranquillity.

"No, by heaven, never!" retorted Pascarèl, with a fiery force in his voice. "What! Leave a beautiful, fearless, innocent thing like that adrift by itself in the world? Fie for shame, little Brunótta!"

Brunótta laughed; but there was a little sadness in the ripple of the mirth.

"Do you remember, Pascarèl, in the great flood that winter, when everyone was safe, as far as one could know, and it had grown quite dark; you could just see the outline of a young bull drowning far off; and nothing would do but you would launch the boat afresh, and ride the flood again, and go for it? And you got to it as it was sinking, and dragged it into the boat, and came to land with it with such a struggle that everyone thought all was over with you, and you were indeed half dead. Do you remember?"

"Yes. What of that?"

"Well, do you not remember, too, that as soon as the bull had strength enough to stagger up on to his legs alone he rushed at you, and struck you in the breast with his horns, and scampered off to the hills as fast as he could go? And you were very ill for many days; and they said if the blow had been an inch nearer to the heart, you might have died of it?"

"Well?" said Pascarèl.

"Well," answered Brunótta, "I was only thinking —if the signorina should be like the bull!"

Then their voices ceased, and I heard a casement shut; they seemed to have been speaking in the chamber next to mine.

I sprang off my bed, a little indignant and a little touched, too.

Like the bull! I thought—no, never, never.

Brunótta seemed a traitress to me only to have breathed the possibility of such a parallel.

I dressed quickly, threw my hair back loose over my shoulders, and ran down the stairs into the common room. Pascarèl was there alone, standing by the window, looking thoughtfully out into the open air, with Toto at his feet.

It was the Berlingancio — the Mardi gras — the maddest madness of Carnival; all the fury and frolic already were ringing all over the city with deafening clash and clangour.

He turned swiftly, and saluted me with that cordial and easy grace which characterised all his movements.

"Ah, good day, my donzella. I have good news to shine on you with the sun. We have got your golden florins."

"My florins!" I echoed, doubting my own joy. "My florins! How?—when?—where? Can it be possible?"

"Very possible," he said, gaily, and he proceeded to count out on the stone seat of the window a dozen round, bright, golden Austrian florins. "How? Oh, never mind how. It is always an ugly story—a thief's. You know I told you the rogue would repent as soon as he should be found out; they always do. You see the guardia of the town went to work in earnest for you. But you must be more careful of your wealth in future."

I was too enraptured to heed much what he said. He might have told me the most improbable romances, and I should have credited them at that moment, so supreme was my ecstasy over my recovered treasure.

He watched me with a certain melancholy in his handsome eyes.

"So now—you are free again, you see," he said, after a pause. "You can go away from us when you like, cara mia—if you like; what do you say? Twelve florins, even when they are of gold, are not a large patrimony with which to scour the earth. But still, you thought them enough for you rashly to run away from Verona on the strength of them alone."

His words clouded the heaven of my restored happiness. I had been kissing my florins, laughing and almost crying over them. As he spoke I stopped, and looked him full in the face.

"Signor mio,—I ought to tell you,—I heard what you said this morning in the room next mine to Brunótta."

His face flushed hotly.

"By heavens you did! How much did you hear? What about? Tell me quickly."

"I heard you from the time that you called me a hothouse rose to the time when your sister said that I should be like the bull you saved out of the flood."

Pascarèl laughed; his face was a little flushed still, but he looked relieved.

"Is that all, carina—honour bright?"

"Quite all. But—you seemed sorry she spoke to me in the wood yesterday; you seemed to think that I should be some trouble or burden to you. If that be so indeed, tell me the truth; I will go."

Pascarèl stood before me, with the lights and the shadows swiftly succeeding each other on his changeful countenance.

"You do not wish to go, then, signorina?" he asked at length. "I thought you might, now you have back your florins."

"No, I do not wish to go; I wish to be one of you, and to learn your art."

I could not trust my voice to say more, for my heart was full at the idea that I should be again adrift by myself with those poor florins, which no longer seemed to me the brilliant safeguard and the omnipotent possession which they had done ere I had lost them.

Pascarèl rolled towards me a little table spread with a white cloth, on which coffee and wheaten rolls were set ready.

"Breakfast first, cara mia; then we will talk. Do you mind my smoke? No? that is right."

Therewith he stretched himself out on the stone sill of the window embrasure, and rested at his ease, sending the smoke into the air in almost absolute silence, glancing now out into the street, already filling with processions of the Berlingancio fooleries, now glancing back at me where I broke my fast with pleasure, knowing that I could pay for what I took.

The radiance of the sunshine came through the open casement and bathed the large square red bricks of the floor; from without there came the smell of tossed flowers, and the noise of many bells, and the sound of countless feet pacing over the stones of the streets: above everything, there was the sweet, youthful scent of the Spring that dreamily breathed itself from the vineyards and fields, even through the dark and blood-stained old age of the Medicean streets.

When his spagnoletto was smoked out, and my coffee ended, he came across the room, and sat astride on an old walnut-wood chair, with his arms crossed on its back, and so gazed at me long and gravely.

"What do you wish for most in this world, cara mia?" he asked, at last.

"Money, of course," I answered him, with widely opened eyes and a little impatient laugh of wonder. Was it not what I had missed and wanted all my life long—always?

"You have no genius in you, then!" he said, with a dash of scorn.

My answer had offended all the artist's instincts in him. No doubt it seemed half puerile and half vile to him—so true an artist in every pulse and fibre of his being, that so long as his audience laughed or wept with him, he could not bring himself to consider whether gold pieces or copper bits filled the box at the door of his play-house.

"Perhaps not," I said, in my own turn a little offended. "But——"

I glanced at the queer little bit of mirror which hung on the rough stone wall between a waxen Jesù and a portrait of the last brigand known in the Valdarno.

He followed the gesture and laughed.

"Oh, you have the best genius for a woman, no doubt. I would not deny that. But I thought you might, perhaps, have a touch of the other too."

"It is a large word," I said, more humbly. "And no one ever seems to know very well what they mean by it."

"No. Some people say it is all your days to carry about with you a torch which illumines everyone's path except your own."

"Perhaps. My old music teacher used to say that to have genius was to be a fool."

"That I deny. It is to be alone amidst fools— a thing much more bitter. And *such* fools! Dio mio! But, after all, what does it matter? If the world were only human, it would matter hideously; but, thank heaven, the world is so much else besides. When one is choked up to the throat with fools, one can always get away to the woods, to the mountains, to the birds, to the beasts, to the hills in the rain mist, to the sea when the sun breaks. If it were not for that, one would go mad straightway, no doubt. And even with that one feels small sometimes— choked, fenced in,—Do you not know? One wants to push back the clouds, to thrust away the skies, to see beyond the horizon, to look close at the sun. If one only had wings!—but let us talk of yourself. You want money, you say; well, that certainly will not come to you on the stage for a long time. To many —to most it never comes at all; and myself, I always think that whether it does or not matters very little, after all."

"But money is everything!" I cried to him—I, who

knew so well by the want of it all that its possession must imply.

"Is it? Well, no doubt, to those who think so it *is* everything: I am not amongst them. But you are a woman-child; I am a man. We shall never think alike on that theme.

"A man, be he bramble or vine, likes to grow in the open air in his own fashion; but a woman, be she flower or weed, always thinks she would be better under glass. When she gets the glass she breaks it —generally; but till she gets it she pines.

"As for my art, the art of the stage needs much study, though, I dare say, to you, as to all lookers on, nothing seems easier than to rattle through a part.

"The actor must be born, like the poet, the painter, the sculptor, no doubt; but also, like them, he must be made perfect by study. Gesture, glance, feeling, passion—all these come by nature: but accent, knowledge, oratory, effect—all these are the mechanical parts of the whole, which only long application will acquire.

"To the art of the stage, as to every other art, there are two sides: the truth of it, which comes by inspiration—that is, by instincts subtler, deeper, and stronger than those of most minds—and the artifice of it, in which it must clothe itself to get understood by the people.

"It is this latter which must be learnt; it is the leathern harness in which the horses of the sun must run when they come down to race upon earth.

"Do I talk nonsense? Never mind, if you know what I mean."

I think my face showed him I knew, for he went on without pausing for my reply.

"We Italians have always needed less of this harness than men of other nations. The French and the Italians are the only great actors that the world ever sees. The northern races cannot act, just as they cannot paint.

"After all, both acting and painting are a matter of colour, and the northern peoples have no feeling for colour, no sense of it. Perhaps because it is not about them in their daily lives, nor visible in their landscapes. They are great in very much, but they are not great in art.

"The French are great, but they are three-parts artifice; it is a very perfect study, but it is a study always. With us we do hold closely that *ars est celare artem;* and we are infinitely more natural than the French are upon the stage. This is national in us, no doubt; we are always ourselves at home and abroad, and we concern ourselves very little as to what other people may think of us. We carry this happy immunity on to the stage with us, and the result is, that on the stage Italians are without rivals.

"But, with all this, it is not the happy-go-lucky hit-or-miss sort of thing that you may fancy it. No art can be good unless into it be brought something of all other arts.

"A man may be a passable actor if Nature has given him the trick of it; but he will not be a great one unless he study the literature of his own and other nations, unless he know something of the intricacies of colour and of melody—above all, unless he can probe and analyse human nature, alike in its health and in its disease.

"To be a great artist one must be a student, and a sincere and humble one, at the foot of every greatness—ay, and every weakness—which has preceded us.

"The instrument on which we histrions play is that strange thing, the human heart. It looks a little matter to strike its chords of laughter or of sorrow; but, indeed, to do that aright and rouse a melody which shall leave all who hear it the better and the braver for the hearing, that may well take a man's lifetime, and, perhaps, may well repay it."

He paused, while a dreamy thoughtfulness cast its shadow over his features; he had been speaking rather to himself than to me, I saw. I thought of what Brunótta had said of him, that he had been a great student of many sciences once, away there in old Pisa.

And yet he had no ambition: it seemed to me very strange.

"You are a great artist, surely," I said, slowly. "And yet—yet you play only for the people."

He looked up with the quick, contemptuous flash of his eloquent eyes.

"Only for the people! Altro! did not Sperone and all the critics at his heels pronounce Ariosto only fit for the vulgar multitude? and was not Dante himself called the laureate of the cobblers and the bakers?

"And does not Sacchetti record that the great man took the trouble to quarrel with an ass driver and a blacksmith because they recited his verses badly?

"If he had not written 'only for the people,' we

might never have got beyond the purisms of Virgilio, and the Ciceronian imitations of Bembo.

"Dante now-a-days may have become the poet of the scholars and the sages, but in his own times he seemed to the sciolists a most terribly low fellow for using his mother tongue; and he was most essentially the poet of the vulgar—of the *vulgare eloquio*, of the *vulgare illustre;* and pray what does the 'Commedia' mean if not a *canto villereccio*, a song for the rustics? Will you tell me that?

"Only for the people! Ah, that is the error. Only! how like a woman that is! Any trash will do for the people; that is the modern notion; vile roulades in music, tawdry crudities in painting, cheap balderdash in print—all that will do for the people. So they say now-a-days.

"Was the bell tower yonder set in a ducal garden or in a public place? Was Cimabue's masterpiece veiled in a palace or borne aloft through the throngs of the streets?

"I am a Florentine, donzella; and I have enough of the blood of my fathers in me to know that the higher and truer the art, the more surely should it belong to the people.

"It is the people that make your nation great or vile in the sight of the universe. Shall you nourish them, then, on the garbage of ribald feebleness, or on the pure strong meats of the mind? As you feed them, so will be their substance and sinew; as you graft them, so will be the fruit that they bear.

"How would it have been with Florence if she had not perpetually borne that vital truth even as the very marrow of her bones?

"Her great men gave their greatest—not to the empire, not to the pope, not to princes only, whether temporal or spiritual, but into the very midst of the populace, into the very hands and hearts of the people, so that through the blackest ages of oppression and superstition, through the deadliest losses of liberty and of peace, she was still as a shining light in the face of the nations, and still held fast, to bequeath them to others, the unquenchable fires of freedom and art."

The rapid words coursed like fire off his lips in passionate enthusiasm; then, as his habit was, he laughed at his own emotions.

"Forgive my vehemence, cara mia," he said, as he lit another spagnoletto. "As I told you, I come of Florentine race."

"What were your people?" I asked him, expecting from him any one of the great names of the great Republic.

"My father was a tinker," he said brusquely, but with the shadow of a laugh about his mouth.

"A tinker! Impossible!"

He laughed outright at the accent of my voice.

"Not impossible at all. An Italian tinker, mind you; that is something very different to a tinker anywhere else. You know us; we are never vulgar."

"But a tinker!" I murmured, in unconquerable disappointment.

Pascarèl laughed on, radiantly and inextinguishably, and busied himself with his little paper roll of tobacco.

"That is why Brunótta cannot read, I suppose?" I said, after a pause, trying to shake off the curious coldness of disenchantment which this announcement of his cast upon me.

He got up, and walked to and fro about the room.

"Of course! A poor devil of a tinker has to mend several millions of stew-pans and braziers before he can solder the alphabet to the empty heads of his children.

"I went to Pisa? Yes: who told you that?

"Poor blind old Pisa! She was very glad to be rid of me, I fear. I won all her honours, but I played her very sad pranks.

"Poor old widowed Pisa! she always seems to be lamenting, Dido-like, her lost lover the Sea. She is unutterably sad; and yet I am never abroad on a moonlit night without wanting to watch it shine on her wonderful palaces, on her empty desolate squares, on her perfection of desolation.

"Do you remember how the Florentines went forth in arms to guard the gates of her, when her walls were weak because her sons were all away on the high seas subduing Minorca? She was their old hereditary foe, but they defended her honour for her in her day of weakness. I doubt if there be anything in all history manlier than that is.

"But to talk of yourself, mia bella.

"Is it indeed true that, lacking all better friends, you would like to wander awhile with us? Nay, no fair words. Let us speak honestly. I know that it is not the least likely that if you had any other sort of protection you would seek that of a set of strolling players. But you have no other, and so—"

He came back, and cast aside his cigar, and stood

by the table looking down on me; his eyes grew almost melancholy, and his voice was very grave when he spoke.

"See here, donzella; you are but a child, as one may say, and know nothing of life but its dreams. It is but fair to warn you; to be a player for the populace with us may hurt you in time to come. I told you yesterday we are not over reputable people.

"We are honest, and we hurt no one, it is true; we may, perhaps, even do some little good in our way; but in the very nature of things we cannot be respectable. We could not be if we wished, and I am afraid we don't wish. Well, all this may hurt you in some time to come. I dare not say it will not. At any rate, it is only fair that you should know so much.

"You are much above the life that we lead; you heard me say so; above it in temper, and tastes, and, no doubt, by your birth. On the other hand, friendless and lonely as you are, worse may easily befall you than to stay with us.

"You shall hear no evil, and shall see none that I can keep you from; that I swear.

"We owe no man anything, and we do the best we can that no creature shall go out from our little house of canvas baser than he entered by even so much as a licentious thought. We are poor, indeed, but, as you have seen, we are none the less glad and gay for that; and we find, perhaps, a fairer side to daily life and human nature than do those whose honey of gold draws the thieves and panders and liars to lick them over with tongues false and foul. As you are now, your fate is a very terrible one for your sex and your age."

His voice had a sweet, persuasive force in it, and lulled me into a dreamy silence; I did not answer to him; I listened as to some delicious music.

"I have been thinking, donzella," he pursued, after a while, "that it may be ill for you to associate yourself with us. Association, you know, is like a burr off the hedges; it clings ere we know it, and we can scarcely free ourselves of it without losing something, be it only a shred.

"The life of the stage—it is only fair you should know—at its best has a certain slur in it. You spoke thoughtlessly, but you spoke as the world speaks, when you uttered your scorn for us living Burattini. At its greatest the life of the player has only false glitter in it, and never true honour. We are toys for the rest of mankind; and the world, having done with us, laughs and then breaks us.

"Why not? We are only its playthings.

"Yesterday, when you said this, I rebuked you, for you wounded me more than you knew. But, to be frank with you, as it is only just I should be, I confess that your gay disdain had its grim root in fact, whilst my reproaches were baseless and worthless, because they were only the fanciful utterance of a fanatical enthusiasm. Sincere, indeed, in its way, but, for all that, self-deceiving.

"Perhaps we never so fatally deceive others as when we are ourselves the first dupes of our falsehoods.

"Altro! I love the life that I lead, but I will not wrong you by saying that it is a fit one for you.

Nevertheless, perhaps a broken crust is better than no bread whatever at all. You must choose for yourself. I have said all there is now to say."

I stood and thought bewilderedly, withheld from him by my pride, drawn towards him by the nameless seduction which existed in all his words and ways.

The brightness of the sun shone across us; the brazen tumults of the bells filled all the air; the people streamed past the casement, laughing, chattering, dressed in their best, and eager to enjoy.

The fulness and gladness of human life was all about me; I had not courage enough to turn away from them and go out into the darkness and the loneliness by myself. I was but a child, and I was afraid of gloom, of solitude, of misfortune. This man, with his passionate tones, with his radiant courage, with his eloquent eyes, had an influence over me that I hardly attempted to resist, and attempted not at all to dissect.

What matter if he were only a bohemian, an adventurer, a strolling player, a tinker's son; he was an artist, a poet even; it was surely better to laugh with him than to perish miserably all alone in the very onset of my warfare with the world.

So the thoughts drifted vaguely and restlessly through my brain; self-centered as the thoughts of all young creatures are. He spoke of my future, but it was not of that I then thought; the present was enough for me.

"If I remain with you, can I earn enough to pay my way?" I asked him, suddenly.

He gave a gesture of impatience.

"Certainly. Your florins will last for all eternity in so simple a life as ours; and even if they do not, we can find a place for you, no doubt."

"Then I will stay," I said, on an eager impulse that I did not dream of defining; and I remember that I held my hands out to him with a little triumphant laugh.

That wonderful luminance, which gave so subtle a charm to his face at such times as it lightened there, flashed over his features.

He caught my hands and touched them lightly with his lips, as one may brush with a kiss the leaves of a rose or the curls of a child.

"Altro! So be it!" he cried, with a laugh which covered, I thought, a deeper emotion. "Ah, dear donzellina, did I not give you the Fates? For me it was ill, very ill, I fear; but for you it shall be well, if the will of a man count for aught in this world."

"Does it not count for much?" I asked him.

And he answered sadly:

"I have lived to think not; for in this world there is—Woman."

CHAPTER III.
The Golden Celandine.

My future being thus determined, Pascarèl said no more about it; it was a thing resolved on and done with; his sunny temper threw off its momentary shadow, and he gave himself up, as his habit was, to the easy, light-hearted, debonair enjoyment of the present.

All that day we enjoyed Berlingancio, and the next

he sauntered about Florence with me, whilst Brunótta stayed in to mend her torn kirtle. He was bent upon making me happy, and he succeeded. That day lives now, golden, and long, and clear, in my remembrance —a very king of days.

The weather was so radiant with the coming of the spring that even in those deepest shadows of the walls it was bright with the sweet youth of the year.

There were great masses of violets and of the snow-white wood anemoli selling at all the corners of the streets. The people sat out before their doorways, working and talking, laughing and chaffering, glad of heart because the winter was gone for nine good months, in which they would be free to live at pleasure in their heaven of the open air.

Between the grey grim piles of the war-worn stone, looking up, one saw the smile of the blue blue skies; beyond the gates there was the silver gleam of the loosened waters, of the budding fields, of the fruitful olives, of the far-off hills.

All the day long we sauntered there, he talking often of the city's past, with phrase so teeming with the colour of language and the poetry of history, that one listened in enchanted breathlessness as to some sorcerer's tale.

Lelio Pascarèllo, whom one and all called Pascarèl, was artist in every fibre of his temperament. Passionate, sensitive to external influences as any woman, full of poetic thoughts and impulses, he joined to this the vivid Florentine energy and the gay Florentine ardour.

There was much in him of the bright vivacious humour which was in Buffulmaco and Bramante; of that love of sport and of ready jest which laughs like so much sunlight over the great memories of Giorgione and Da Vinci.

Linked to an incapable companion he would have rid himself of the burden with the same witty skill as Brunelleschi, and locked in his study by an exacting patron, he would have escaped by the window to enjoy his pleasures in the streets, in the same ardent and amorous determination as Fra Lippi's.

He seemed to have just left those wise, fearless, gay, tumultuous times when the great sculptors went laughing to buy their eggs and cheese in the market; when the great painters challenged each other to gay duello with pencil and with chisel; when the great artists held their rapiers no less ready than their brushes; when men worked and loved, and fought and jested, and swept all the Arts within the one magic circle of their universal genius in that easy strength which looks the miracle of saints to this weakling world.

He loved light, and air, and indolence, and mirth; the mere sense of living sufficed for him with a voluptuous content which those of northern lands can never know; to lie and dream on a grassy slope, and watch the lithe brown arms of a girl as she washed linen in the brook below; to go singing through the luminous moonlight with a dozen comrades, waking the echoes of old, dim, marble streets; to laugh and jest round the charcoal fires in the winter *veglie*, or lying in the deep corn on the moonlit threshing-floors at harvest time; to toss a draught of wine behind the thick screen of a pergola foliage, whilst bright eyes laughed at him and bright sunbeams darted on him through the leaves, and made his year as one long holiday, from the Beffano to the feast of Ognissanti—these were enough for Pascarèl.

Sometimes, as we went that day, he stopped before some cobbler's stall or some stove where the last chestnuts of the year were toasting, and exchanged with the Florentines presiding over them fantastic passages of drollery and wit. Sometimes he encountered some barrow rolling on its way with woollen stuffs and silken handkerchiefs, or some truckful of oranges and lemons, and took the sale of these out of the hands and the mouths of their vendors, and made the crowd around them split their sides with his quaint and subtle Tuscan humour. Sometimes he would enter some old dusky church where some world-famous picture made a glory in the darkness, and, standing before it, would let his thoughts and his words roam dreamily over the deepest meanings of art and the remotest mysteries of history in all that abstract meditation which is the most precious indulgence of the scholar.

Half a hundred times a day his mood and his manner altered with that ardent vitality in every phase of their countless changes which was the life and soul of the man himself. Not for one whole half hour together was he the same throughout; and yet, grave or gay, riotously laughing with the crowd, or dreamily questioning the lost secrets of the old masters, selling a yellow bandana to a housewife at a fair with buoyant raillery, or straying through the dim arcades of the old academies tenderly recalling the heroism and the learning of their earliest ages, he was always, in all his contrasts, Pascarèl.

He was like the child's toy of the kaleidoscope, with every moment his moods changed their shapes with unpremeditated caprice; but the hues which made them did not alter.

"Were you truly a tinker's son?" I asked him, late in that day, when we were stretched again upon the grass of the Cascine woods.

"Che diamine!" he cried, in the expressive Tuscan affirmative. "Utterly and simply a tinker's son. But, to console you, though tinkers we had become, we were of a race that yielded in ancientness of blood to none. I think old Malispini even accounts for us as amongst those who, on coming out of the Ark after the Deluge, bestirred themselves in the building of Fiesole. In the old, old days, my people were of that territorial nobility beside which the Medici are mere rubbish of yesterday. We were Ghibellines, and in their ruin fell, of course. Our utter destruction came when one of us would have a palace fashioned by Orcagna, to pay for which his descendants in the third generation had to sell nearly all their worldly goods and lands, like that hapless fool Luca dei Pitti. Jews of the Oltrarno got the little there was left in time. Old races die hard with the load of long debt round their necks; but—they die. For two centuries we had been poor, poor, poor. Poor as the devil. At last we worked for our daily bread. Old races have done worse. My grandfather toiled to and fro as a facchino in the country where his forefathers had scowled defiance on Carlo di Valois, and mowed down the burghers round the red Carroccio on that terrible day, 'che fece l'Arbia colorata in rosso.' From a facchino to a tinker is hardly a fall; perhaps it is even a rise, for a tinker must own some little stock in trade of tools, whereas the facchino only toils underneath the goods of other people. At any rate, a tinker my father was, God save his soul! and a man of most infinite humour. I know he scratched a prince's coronet on his smelting pot. Coronets have been in worse places. He was weak enough, I am ashamed to say, to be ever proud of his lineage, and fed me when I was a little fellow on all sorts of dead glories out of Dino Compagni and Villani. But I ran about with bare legs over Tuscany, and cared nothing that I ran over the graves of my ancestors. At any rate it was more harmless than to run about with a bare sword as those Pascarèl princes did. It was queer, perhaps, to blunder into some old church in some little hill-town or city of the plain, and see a great white statue, and read the record of some mighty Pascarèllo; and all the while one was a Pascarèllo too, though only a little mischievous dog, ragged and hungry, scouring the country for saucepans to mend. It set one thinking, no doubt. But, after all, what did it matter?"

"It would have broken my heart!" I cried, where I sat beside him amongst the crocuses.

Pascarèl laughed.

"It was likelier to break my head. For, being a little fool, and strong for my years, I would get fighting for that coronet on the smelting-pot times out of number with half the boys of half the villages we entered. They thought a coronet on an old iron pot ridiculous, and they surely were right; but I was resolute to have both pot and coronet respected, being my father's; and perhaps I was right also. At any rate, I had the courage of my opinions, and got half killed for them over and over again, as all people rash enough to keep such ticklish possessions as opinions invariably do. A princely couronne and a travelling tinker! Supremely ridiculous, that is certain; but would they have been less so if I had whimpered and had not fought? It is stupid to have a bad cause, no doubt; but after all, as far as we ourselves go, perhaps it is not the cause that matters so much as it is one's way of upholding it. The Carroccio was a sorry childish emblem in itself enough; but does that take from the grandeur of the deaths of the Tornaquinci round it? My Carroccio was my father's old tin pot; but I am glad even now to think how many sucking Tuscans I in my babyhood thrashed for sheer love and honour of that sacred household god. Not love of the coronet, mind you, but love for what he had put there; if he had scratched a cat's head on the pot, and they had laughed at it, it would have been the same to me, and I, Pascarèl, should have been bound to fight for it."

"Did you ever work with him?" I asked, glancing at those long, slender, brown hands of his which were weaving some rushes together.

"Altro! of course I did. Tinkered many an old woman's copper kettle all along the country, east and west, from Livorno to Venice. But I never took to the work. I had a natural genius for making holes, not for mending them. The people used to call me the Marchesino, in derision of the leaves and balls on the tin pot. But they dropped that after they found by frequent experience that I could make holes in their sons' skulls past all power of apothecary's soldering. Not that I was a bully, believe me; but when they shouted their 'Marchesino' in derision I thought of the marble Pascarèlli in the churches, and hit out—a little too straight home sometimes. I was a little lad at that time, trotting on bare legs after my father's barrow from house to house all over the land. It is all forgotten now. I buried his tin pot in his coffin with him, as his forefathers were buried with their golden crowns, and I have buried all the old follies with it. I was fifteen years old when he died."

"And you are the last Pascarèllo?"

"The very last. Much good may it do me. The people, God bless them! have forgiven me all the broken heads of my boyish time, and have learnt to love me—well. I am afraid the Ghibelline Pascarèlli who live in marble in the churches could never say as much."

"And you are content with that love?"

"Eh, Dio! I should blush for myself if I were not."

A great darkness stole over his face as he spoke —that melancholy of an Italian face which is as intense as is the sunlight of its happiness.

"Oh, cara mia, when one has run about in one's time with a tinker's tools, and seen the lives of the poor, and the woe of them, and the wretchedness of it all, and the utter uselessness of everything, and the horrible, intolerable, unending pain of all the things that breathe, one comes to think that in this meaningless mystery which men call life a little laughter and a little love are the only things which save us all from madness—the madness that would curse God and die."

A little laughter and a little love! Across the brilliant fancies of my supreme ignorance the words fell with a pathetic meaning. Was this all, indeed, that the wide world could offer? And was it worth while to wander so far to reach so little?

"Yes, cara mia," he said, with his quick divination of another's thoughts. "Yes. They are all that are really worth the having in this world; and they lie so close to us sometimes, and we flee away from them, not knowing, and perhaps we never meet them face to face or have them in our reach again. For neither of them will come for the mere asking."

"How, then, shall we gain either?" I asked.

He smiled.

"There was once a youth who was a shepherd. He was all alone in the world, and sorrowful. No man tarried with him, and no woman found him comely.

"A fairy took pity on him, and gathered a yellow blossom of celandine, and put it in his hand. 'Breathe on the flower, and wish thrice,' she said. 'Three times you shall have your desire.'

"He breathed once on the golden flower, scarcely believing in his own good fortune. 'Let me laugh as other men do,' he wished. Immediately he laughed on and on, not pausing, over a flagon of wine that was never emptied; but there was no joy in his mirth, and he grew sick of it.

"He breathed a second time on the flower. 'Let me love as other men do,' he wished. Instantly a young maiden kissed him on the mouth, and he toyed with her, and yet was not content; it seemed to him that her lips were cold and her eyes without any light.

"Then he breathed the third time on the flower

and cast it down weeping, and crying, 'Let others
laugh and others love. Joy is not for me, I see.'

"Then, strange to say, all at once his heart grew
light, and he was glad, and sang aloud with rapture,
and the maiden rejoiced beside him, and the kisses
of her lips were warm and sweet as the suns of
summer.

"The fairy took from him the golden flower.
'Now laughter is yours and love,' she said. 'For the
wish that you wished was for others, and pure of the
greeds of self.'

"Do you know what the story means? No; you
have only just got your yellow celandine, and have
scarcely breathed upon it."

But I knew what it meant enough to know that
he himself used his golden flower for the gladness of
others—always.

CHAPTER IV.
Beside dead Fires.

UNDER the financial government of Pascarèl my
florins seemed endlessly to expand. As yet I did not
appear upon the stage with any of them, though he
trained me for it sedulously with all the skill and
subtlety that were given to him by the unerring instincts and the long practice of his art.

We were completely happy; Brunótta was a little
humble merry soul, quick as a mouse, bright as a
bird, honest, I thought, as the day. Cocomero and
Toccò worshipped the ground that their chief even
trod on, and would have laid their lives down willingly
to do his bidding in the merest trifle. Whilst Pas-

carèl himself, the life and soul, the alpha and omega, of the small community, governed it with that gentle sway which lends to obedience as sweet a charm as lies in liberty.

He inquired everywhere, as best he could, for tidings of my father and of Florio. But either the people knew nothing, or those who knew anything had been bidden not to reveal it; we learned no intelligence of any sort, and at the post in the Uffizi he heard that letters from Verona had been addressed to the name of Tempesta, and were still lying there unclaimed. Doubtless, these neglected things were those which old Maso Sasso had penned for Mariuccia in the den of his loggia.

Pascarèl sought, honestly and unweariedly, on my behalf; but he did not affect to be sorry for the result.

"No one who has once caught hold of destiny likes to lose that slippery sovereign," he would say, with a laugh; and so I remained with him and his, through the cool weeks of the Quaresima.

At times, indeed, he spoke to me—like one who does an unwelcome duty—of seeking shelter for me in some convent's safety and stillness; but my passionate terror of the captivity disarmed his wiser resolves; and, indeed, to have won the money necessary to secure such a refuge was as impossible to me as to draw down the moon; and to take it from him, as he sometimes hinted,—for he said he had a few hundreds of lire laid by in the hands of a goldsmith of Florence, lest any evil should befall him and leave his troop adrift,—would have been a debt from which, child though I was, all the instincts in me revolted.

Before we left Florence on the springtide wanderings, he betook himself to Verona, to see, for his own satisfaction, what could be learned of my father. I heard long afterwards that he went at great peril to himself, and in disguise, from the hatred of the Austriaci against him; but of this he said nothing to me at that time. Of danger to himself he never spoke. This was only a week or so after I had first fallen in with the merry little party in the ilex woods, and I was vaguely startled to feel how deadly a blank his absence caused to me. The skies lost all their light, and the city all her golden and transfigured beauty.

He placed me, whilst he went, at a house on the other side of the river, where a good friend of his, Orfeo Orlanduccio, a master worker in mosaic, dwelt.

Orlanduccio was a widower, with one little, pretty, merry child called Bicè. They were very good to me in the dusky ancient house, through whose grated casements one looked out, like prisoners, on the world, and whose massive chambers were all rich with carving, and scented with that curious old world incense-like aromatic odour of which the Florence streets are full.

It was in the Via de la Pergola, not far off the house that the Duke gave to Cellini; and as I leaned against the barred windows I used to think of the bronze-workers in that little garden, and of the fierce molten metal seething out under the flame from the oak timbers; and of the stream, hot and red, like blood from a murdered man's throat, crushing in to fill the beautiful mask of the Perseus, and of the artist—breathless, agonised, torn betwixt hope and fear, rent by the noble rashness of genius and the feebler human dread of accident—coming out under the dark hanging fig-leaves with armsful of his household gods of silver and pewter and copper and gold, and casting them all into the furnace, as children were cast to Moloch, so that his Thought might arise from the fires and live for all time in men's light.

Orfeo Orlanduccio was a grave, melancholy, stern, good man; he had been lamed in the wars of Carl-Alberto, and was subject to suspicion for his advanced political creeds; he had a noble grey head like Luca della Robbia's, and it was a picture to see him in his dark workshop piecing the tiny fragments so deftly into all manner of delicate arabesques and dainty flowers with his lithe slender fingers that had used to grasp a sabre to hard purpose, they said, in earlier days.

I stayed with him and the little, saucy, smiling rosebud of a Bicè whilst Pascarèl went northward. Brunótta did not come with me there; indeed the mosaic maker seemed to me to know little or nothing of her existence.

On the fourth day of my stay with them, the good Orfeo, coming from the market-place, was arrested and borne to the Bargello under some accusation of conspiracy. I know not what, but all liberal thinkers were under suspicion in those days.

His apprentices brought word of his misfortunes, and little Bicè, a merry babyish thing, of nine or ten, cried her pretty eyes red with weeping for her father, and in the evening time her foster-mother, a peasant of the Casentino, came in and bore her off to dwell in the country till her parent should be set free, which might not be for many months, they said.

I remember the sense of desolation, of belonging to no earthly soul or thing, that shivered over me that night as the little heedless child went, laughing through her tears to hear the mule bells ring, and the apprentices took down their caps and stared at me stupidly, and the woman who did the housework there in the daytime, having cleaned her pots and pans and swept up the kitchen, came and looked at me with her arm in her side, and asked me, meditatively:—

"The signorina will betake herself to her friends? the lads sleep out, and then I will bar the place up safe. Orfeo has been in this sort of trouble before. Men are such fools;—they will craze their heads for things that have no concern for them. Will the signorina go; I want to bar the doors; it is dark now."

I begged her to let me stay a little. I had promised Pascarèl not to leave this house until he came for me, and no force in Florence, I think, would have availed to make me disobey him.

A rebel to all other authority since my babyhood, I took a passionate delight in obeying this stranger's mere glance and gesture.

The donna di fatica, moved by my loneliness and my supplications, lit me a lamp and left me, promising to return in an hour, when go I must, she said, for she had served Maestro Orfeo twenty years and more, and was not going to leave his bottega open to thieves for all the yellow-haired signorini in Christendom.

Her heavy steps trod slowly out of the stone passages, and the massive nail-studded door closed behind her. My heart sank as I was left alone in the empty house with its unfinished mosaics strewn over the floor, and its dreamy aroma from the millions of pine cones and oak logs that had burned on those old hearths in the fires of five hundred centuries.

It was one of the oldest dwellings in Florence. Its massive stones and iron stanchions had stood against sack and siege, flame and mob. It was only antique and strange with the 'prentices' merry feet on the stairs and Bicè's rosy round face at the grated casements, but when one was alone in it, at night, there seemed dim clouds of ghosts in every dusky chamber.

My heart leaped with the sweetest gladness it had ever known as I heard a light swift footstep on the stairs, and the clear sweet ring of a Tuscan voice.

"My donzella!" it called, in the gloom, "are you all alone here?"

I sprang to him in joyous welcome, and did not notice till he had sat down beside me on the oaken settle by the fireless hearth that his face looked worn and weary.

"Yes, Orfeo is imprisoned," he said, impatiently. "There is nothing to be done. He is known to be in the confidence of Mazzini, and papers have been found—do not let us talk of it. His child is safe, and he will come back to his old place in a year or less. He is a good man and true. We must have patience."

He was silent. The lamp burned dully. The old house was silent around us.

"I am vexed for him—and for you," he said, after a long pause. "I thought, dear signorina, that it would be better for you to stay with little Bicè than to roam with us. Orfeo is the only man whom I can trust. My friends lie amongst poor people—very poor—or men honest, indeed, but reckless and given over to wild work, who can be of no sort of good to you. Orfeo, indeed, I could have trusted. He would have given you a safe home, though a poor one. But it seems willed otherwise."

"But I am to go with *you!*" I cried, aghast at this disposal of me.

He smiled gently, but a darkness and impatience passed like a mist over his face. He was silent, trimming the wick of the oil-lamp.

"Well, so it seems, dear donzella," he said, after awhile, with a certain hesitation not natural to his frank, free, rapid modes of speech. "Well, I will do my best by you—God help me, and forgive us sinners! Nevertheless, if Orfeo had not fallen on this evil chance, it had been better."

"If I be any trouble to you," I began——

He stopped me with a tender gesture.

"Never say that—it is not that I mean. It is—a safe and quiet home were better for you. But since fate wills it otherwise, oh, cara mia! credit me, you shall be as sacred to me as though my dead mother lived to care for you."

I looked up at him in wonder at the emotion in his voice; his thoughts were in nowise clear to me.

There was a long silence in the dark old house.

He leaned against the wall, lost in meditations that my imagination failed to follow.

He looked down suddenly, and spoke:

"I have learned nothing at Verona," he said, with a certain tone of sadness that wounded me, for it seemed as though he were regretful not to be rid of me. "No one has seen your father, nor could anyone give me any news of him. Nor do they appear to know any more of who or what he really is than you do. But there is one sad story that I heard for you, and that is of your old master."

"Ambrogiò?" I cried, and all my heart went back to the poor old lonely man whom I had forsaken in a child's eager desires for fresh fields and pastures new.

"Yes, dear donzella," answered Pascarèl.

I sprang to my feet eagerly; he answered me with a slight, hopeless gesture of the hands that chilled me into a great awe.

"He died the night you left Verona. They found him dead over his empty brazier in his garret—all alone. The children saw him first; going to take their lesson in the morning. He is buried by now."

The simple words seemed to pierce my heart as I heard them.

My poor dead master!

I saw the place — the still lone garret, the uncurtained lattice, the robin singing on the sill, the dreary roofs, and the snow mountains far beyond; the miserable home, with the grey ashes of cold fires in the earthen brazier; the children at the half-opened door, peeping with pale scared faces, and whispering together, and pointing at the figure on the hearth—all the sad, dreary, colourless picture, drawn in the black and white of Age and Death, arose before me as I listened.

I sank down on a bench, and cried bitterly, as for a woe all my own.

Was this the end—the only bitter end—of all those years of wrong and want? One other nameless grave in the snow under the bleak blasts in old Verona!

Pascarèl let me sob on, and did not seek to console me; but I poured out all the history to him in my sorrow, and he listened gravely, there, in the old, dim, lonely room, heavy with the scent of the long-died-out fires that had warmed so many faces and forms that were now dust in the crypts and sepulchres of the city.

"You must never tell the tale but to me, my child," he said, at length. "The secret belongs to the dead. He chose to keep it in his life; you must keep it for him in his death. Rothwald is rich and famous? Yes; why not? Justice is not of this world."

"But why does God permit such things?" I cried, in the despair of my poor lost master's wrongs.

Pascarèl gave an impatient sigh.

"Oh child! Has the human race solved that problem in all these many thousand years since the first men dwelt in the first lake-cities? We shall never know that till our souls leave our bodies——"

"But for no punishment to fall!" I cried, and sobbed afresh, weighed down with the burden of all those long, lone fruitless years, whose end was a beggar's grave in sad Verona.

"Ay! if the bolts would smite, and the heavens

would open, life would be so much easier, and hope so much easier too," said Pascarèl; "but, perhaps, even in this world, there may be more punishment than we can know.

"Listen, donzella," he pursued. "Did never you hear the story of Andrea dal Castagno, who lived here in the street hard by? No? Well, then—

"He and the bright Venetian Domenico dwelt together in great and close friendship; so much so, that they shared the same chambers, painted in the same studio, were inseparable in pursuits and pleasures, and aims and endeavours, and were cited all through the city as the very symbol of faithful comradeship.

"Well, one night, the Venetian went forth as usual, with his lute under his cloak, to serenade his mistress in the moonlight; and there, in the dark archway of the street, a dark figure lay unseen in wait for him, and he was stabbed through and through, and his love-song was stifled in his throat, and he was slain.

"Who had killed him?

"The city could not tell.

"Andrea was found painting quietly by lamplight when they bore the dying man home; and he tore his hair and rent his garments in agonised lamentation over the bleeding body of his dear dead friend.

"Yet Andrea was the murderer.

"For greed of the secret of the oils and varnishes, some say; some say for envy of the woman's love. Which no one ever rightly knew.

"Andrea lived in honour all his days. He was a

great artist, and all men spoke well of him. Suspicion never fell on him. Had not Domenico breathed his death-sigh in his arms, blessing him to the last? Nay, the State even employed him to paint the traitors hung on the city walls by their heels—and his brush did not falter.

"He had long life, I say, and everything to make it good and even glorious. Yet, though he had riches, and fame, and, as men call it, happiness, he never once in all that time could ever quite forget. He never once forgot; he never ceased to see the kindly faithful face dead there in the lustre of the summer night; he never ceased to hear the familiar voice in the last love-song ere he had stifled it in its death-struggle; he never ceased to be pursued night and day by the remembrance of his guilt; never, that we are sure; for, though he kept his secret close all his life long, he could not keep it to the very end. On his death bed he confessed his crime, and Florence, though at the tenth hour, despoiled him, and dishonoured him, and gave him a felon's grave."

I shuddered as I heard.

The tale told in that old dark Florentine room, within a stone's throw of the place of murder, had a terrible ghastly awe in it. I shrank closer to Pascarèl, and he stretched his hand out and took mine.

"Did I tell you too frightful a story?" he said, caressingly.

"No, no," I murmured, "it is not that. But my poor old master! And see here: if Andrea were chastised, what did that compensate Domenico? It could not give him back his life and love——"

"Of compensation to Domenico there was none," said Pascarèl, sadly. "But of chastisement to Andrea I think there was enough. I told you the tale to show you that, where we think glory and gain are most abundant, there sometimes burns the fire that quenches not, which men call remorse. Your master left his vengeance with his God. We must so leave it likewise. And now, donzella mia, you shiver in this cold dark room. Come out, and let us get to the light and warmth again, and forget all these weary meditations. You must wander with us; those Fates on the onyx so will it. Well, I swear to you, carina, that you shall never repent your trust in me."

He touched my hands lightly with his lips, and we went down the stone staircase, and out of the dark and lonely house of the mosaic-worker.

I clung close to him as we went through the now gloomy streets, and I was glad when we reached the little bright archway of the locandà in Oltrano, where Brunótta met us with many exclamations, and with the ruddy flame of a wood fire she had lighted glowing on her little plump figure and her gorgeous silver ear-rings.

The Arte was shut that night, for it was the Domenica di Passione.

She had a little supper ready for us of shining brown alardi, crisply fried, and stewed rice with pears. She, like Pulci's Margutte, was given to swearing "neither by black nor blue, but only by a good capon, whether roast or boiled," and had no notion of starving even on the gravest fast of the Church.

It was all quiet in the quarter of the Silver Dove.

Bells were sounding for the vespers, that was all; and as we sat at our little meal people streamed by the open door, going in flocks to pray in the great white vaulted stillness of the Santo Spirito.

Pascarèl and I were silent that night.

He thought of his friend Orfeo; and I of my old dead master.

Nevertheless, we were both glad, I think, that the morrow was not going to part us; and whilst Brunótta and the boys played together at taròc, I sat and looked every now and then at the delicate profile of Pascarèl against the shadows from the oil-lamp, and felt no trouble or fear for the future.

CHAPTER V.

Giudentu dell' Anno.

WE stayed in Florence through the long, cool, sunny weeks of the Quaresima, broken here and there with the mad frolic of the Mi-Carême, and the fun of the Fairs of the Innamorati and the Curiosi and the Gelosie at the Gates of the City.

The great lilies, white, and azure, and purple, were just beginning to bloom everywhere round the city, and the streets and the woods seemed to shine as snow with the clusters of the stainless anemoli.

There is nothing upon earth, I think, like the smile of Italy as she awakes when the winter has dozed itself away in the odours of its oakwood fires.

The whole land seems to laugh.

The springtide of the north is green and beautiful, but it has nothing of the radiance, the dream-fulness, the ecstasy of spring in the southern countries. The springtide of the north is pale with the gentle colourless sweetness of its world of primroses; the springtide of Italy is rainbow-hued, like the profusion of anemones that laugh with it in every hue of glory under every ancient wall and beside every hill-fed stream.

Spring in the north is a child that wakes from dreams of death; spring in the south is a child that wakes from dreams of love. One is rescued and welcomed from the grave; but the other comes smiling on a sunbeam from heaven.

All the Quaresima we abode in Florence; and he made glad and perfect to me each lenten hour as it glided by; and when the sun set, it left me always tired, happy, thoughtful, full of peace.

CHAPTER VI.
The old Star Tower.

ONE day, I remember, we strolled slowly out by the Romano gate towards the hills as the day drew to its close.

The old frescoes on the house wall were bright in the afternoon light; there was a group of soldiers drinking; there were some asses laden with straw for the plaiters' market on the morrow; a bare-foot, brown-frocked monk went by amongst the soldiery; the cypress and ilex road stretched up into the distance; coming down the Stradone was an old white horse with a pile of fruit upon his back, and a lad in a yellow shirt at his bridle; about the base of the old broken statues of Petrarca some children played.

"How very little that is!" said Pascarèl. "And yet it is all a picture. It is a pity ever to do anything in Italy; the country is made just to lie still in and dream in, with the body half asleep and the mind wide awake, but lost in fancies. Italy soothes us as a mother's arms lull a wayward child, if only we will let her do it: but if we struggle from her natural influences, and try to spend our lives in strife, then her sun stings, and her dust blinds us, and all her charm is gone."

So, talking whilst we passed the people, and followed closely by the three dogs, he took me up to the Star Tower of Galileo amongst the winding paths of the hills, with the grey walls overtopped by white fruit blossom, and ever and again, at some break in their ramparts of stone, the gleam of the yellow Arno water, or the glisten of the marbles of the City shining on us far beneath, through the silvery veil of the olive leaves.

It was just in that loveliest moment when winter melts into spring.

Everywhere under the vines the young corn was springing in that tender vivid greenness that is never seen twice in a year. The sods between the furrows were scarlet with the bright flame of wild tulips, with here and there a fleck of gold where a knot of daffodils nodded. The roots of the olives were blue with nestling pimpernels and hyacinths, and along the old grey walls the long, soft, thick leaf of the arums grew, shading their yet unborn lilies.

The air was full of a dreamy fragrance; the bullocks went on their slow ways with flowers in their leathern frontlets; the contadini had flowers stuck behind their ears or in their waistbands; women sat by the wayside, singing as they plaited their yellow curling lengths of straw; children frisked and tumbled like young rabbits under the budding maples; the plum-trees strewed the green landscape with flashes of white like newly fallen snow on alpine grass slopes; again and again amongst the tender pallor of the olive woods there rose the beautiful flush of a rosy almond-tree; at every step the passer-by trod ancle deep in violets.

The air was cool, but so exquisitely still, and soft, and radiant, that as the old people came out of their dark, arched, stone chambers, and sat a little in the sun, and made up into bunches for selling the blossoms which their children gathered by the million, without seeming to make the earth the poorer, one felt as if the sun shining on them as it did must make them young again—as if no one could very long be very old or very sad in Italy.

It was the thought of a child, and of a happy child. When one is old it must surely be better to creep away under the mists, into the darkness of some chimney-corner, in the chill, short twilight of the loveless and bitter North, than to behold this divine light, cloudless and endless, which seems to beat with all the pulses of passion, and to laugh with all the sweet, soft, foolish ecstasies of love.

Who was it that called Italy the country of the dead? Not they surely who have beheld her in the days of spring.

About the feet of the Tower of Galileo, ivy and vervain, and the Madonna's herb, and the white sexagons of the stars of Bethlehem grew amongst the grasses, pigeons paced to and fro with pretty pride of plumage; a dog slept on the flags; the cool, moist, deep-veined creepers climbed about the stones; there were peach trees in all the beauty of their blossoms, and everywhere about them were close-set olive trees, with the ground between them scarlet with the tulips and the wild rose bushes.

From a window a girl leaned out and hung a cage amongst the ivy leaves, that her bird might sing his vespers to the sun.

Who will may see the scene to-day.

So little changed—so little, if at all, from the time when the feet of the great student wore the timber of the tower stairs, and the fair-haired scholar, who had travelled from the isles in the northern sea, came up between the olive stems to gaze thence on Vallombrosa.

The world has spoiled most of its places of pilgrimage, but the old Star Tower is not harmed as yet, where it stands amongst its quiet garden ways, and grass-grown slopes, up high amongst the hills, with sounds of dripping water on its court, and wild woodflowers thrusting their bright heads through its stones.

Generations have come and gone: tyrannies have risen and fallen: full many a time the plain below has been red with the invader's fire, and the curling flame has burned the fruitful land to blackened barrenness; full many a time the silence of the olive thickets has been broken by the tumult of war and revolution, and the dead bodies of men have drifted thick as leaves in the blood-stained current of the river.

But nothing has been changed here, where the old square pile stands out amongst the flowering vines.

It is as peaceful, as simple, as homely, as closely girt with blossoming boughs and with tulip-crimsoned grasses, now as then, when from its roof, in the still midnights of a far-off time, its master read the secrets of the stars.

You can see it to-day—any day that you will—this quiet shadowy hill-side place amongst the fields.

But come up softly between the old gnarled olive stems; tread noiselessly the winding pathway where the wild hyacinth shakes its blue bells on the wind; be reverent a little—if reverence in this age be possible—as you climb the narrow wooden stair, and through the unglazed arches of the walls look westward where the sea lies, and southward towards Rome.

Be reverent a little, for a little space at least: for here Galileo learned the story of the sun; and here Milton, looking on Valdarno, dreamed of Paradise.

CHAPTER VII.
Due Amori.

WE scattered the pigeons that day as they picked their way amongst the rose trees, and we went across the sombre quiet court, and up the wooden stairs, on to the square roof where the great Tuscan had sat so many and many a night with his listening pupils round him, and, beneath, the dark stillness of the sleeping plains.

"How fair she looks down there!" said Pascarèl, resting his eyes fondly on the City. "I have seen pretty well all the world, but I have never seen anything that can make one forget her. I am of the same way of thinking as was Visino;—better a flask of Tribbiano and a berlingozzo of Florence than all the kings and queens and courts and camps in Christendom. Look at her now; she lies like a golden galley of old upon a silver moon-lightened sea."

Very fair indeed she was, the Lily Queen, that evening.

There had been shadows all day, and in the west there were masses of cloud, purple and blue-black, spreading away into a million of soft scarlet cirri that drifted before a low wind from the southward, tender and yet rich in tone as any scattered shower of carnation leaves.

Through that vast pomp of dusky splendour and that radiance of rose, the sun itself still shone; shone full upon the City.

Leaning on the broken edge of the watch-tower and gazing down below, all Florence seemed like the seer's dream of the New Jerusalem; every stone of her seemed transmuted; she was as though paven and built with gold; straightway across the whole valley stretched the alchemy of that wondrous fireglow, and all the broad level lands of the Valdigreve were transfigured likewise into one vast sheet of gold, on which the silver olives and the dim white villages and villas floated like frail white sails upon a sunlit sea.

Farther—still farther yet, beyond that burnished ocean—the mountains and the clouds met and mingled, golden likewise, broken here and there into some tenderest rose-leaf flush, miraculously lovely, as a poet's dreams of nameless things of God.

We stayed long, and watched it high above on the

wooden roof of the tower; watched it until the sun had set, and the glow had died, and the stillness of evening had fallen over the hills and plain, and past our faces flew a little grey downy owl.

"Your fathers saw Galileo?" said Pascarèl to the bird as it went, "and thought what a fool he was, no doubt, to sit mooning there with his face turned to the stars instead of hunting moths in the night air and slaughtering mice under the olive stems as they did. To be sure:—the owls and the world, no doubt, were quite of one mind concerning him. When there is a nice, plump, black mouse to be killed down on the clay, what greater folly can there be than to stay on high staring at stars? Who would not be an owl ten times sooner than a Galileo?"

"Are you serious?" I asked him, when we leaned against the wooden rail. I had not then learned to disentangle his thoughts from his language.

"Altro!" he cried, sending a pebble down into the olive foliage beneath. "Who would not be an owl? To escape all the toil and moil of the day, asleep in a cosy ivy hole; to doze all the hours away, and only awake to kill and eat; to be able to swear there is no such thing as a sun, because we are too blind to see it—what can be finer than that? It is such a popular type, too; ten thousand times more popular than a Galileo!"

I looked at him where he leaned with his arms on the parapet of the roof, and his profile, clear and dark, against the delicate silvery greys that had followed the rose glow in the heavens.

He had more interest for me than Galileo or the owls; in no way could I reconcile the grace of him, the wit of him, and the look of his face with the mode of his life, which was scarcely above the grade of vagrants and of mountebanks.

It seemed to me so strange that any man of such various learning and such ironical perception should thus willingly pass away his years in the homely and grotesque career of a strolling player.

*   *   *   *

"What could ever first make you take this life you lead?" I asked him, incredulously, when we stood together on the top of the star tower.

"I fell in love," said Pascarèl, promptly, leaning over the roof-wall to watch the shadows steal over the long cypress stradone, and come slowly upward and upward to the heights whereon we stood, "not for the first nor the fifth time, of course, but truly enough for that matter. A set of French comedians came to stir the stately silence of old Pisa. They were merry, poor, happy-go-lucky people who played their way all along the Riviera. Clever people, too—French players always are.

"Amongst them there was a girl whom we called the Zinzara, because of her pungent tongue. I am not sure that she was handsome, but she had a *diable au corps*, you know—no, you don't know—no matter!

"To see the Zinzara play Phædre in the first, and dance the cancan in the afterpiece, was a revelation. I had always maintained that women could not possess genius, but I gave in before her. Her renderings of Racine were miracles, and so were her soups and salads.

"She would scare your very soul out of you with her whirlwinds of passion, and her whisper was like the hiss of a snake, and her eyes seemed a blaze of fire and passion, and then half-an-hour after you would see her in her one poor little room, with her cuffs turned back from her long white hands, and she would mix you oil, and lettuces, and beet-root, or toss you a herb omelette over her stove with a skill that half the cooks of Paris could not have equalled. She was a true Frenchwoman, the Zinzara. I have never seen her like since.

"It was she who made me an actor. I had always had a taste for it, but when I saw this Paris mosquito the die was cast. I had finished all my course in Pisa. For that matter I had swept all before me, and won all there was to win. Indeed, they actually offered me a professorship of mathematics. Never say that I have not rejected greatness.

"I was two-and-twenty; I was an Italian; I was Pascarèl; and they imagined that I should settle down to lead all my life in old Pisa like an owl in a belfry, till I grew as old, and as grey, and as silent, and as forgotten of God and man as Pisa is herself! But they meant well; only they knew nothing of the fitness of things. Academies never do.

"If I had meant to stay, the Zinzara would have swept my intentions to the winds. I had a room I was very fond of, high up in a tower, with the river washing against the walls far away down below. There were scores of cobwebs, and legends, and ghosts attached to it, but I slept too soundly in those days to take heed of any one of them. I had hundreds of books there, and my tubes, and prisms, and telescopes, and I had passed seven years there after the fashion of Faust, only that I had all my life before me, and being young broke up my learning and science with nights of nonsense and days of pleasure that needed no devil's cordial.

"I loved my room, and was loth to quit it, and almost it tempted me to stay in Pisa; but one fine morning, as I read my Plato for the thousandth time, I heard a merry noise and laughter in the street at the foot of the tower; and looking out I saw a little set of people all ready for long travel, and going gaily on their way. It was the Zinzara and her brethren going back towards their France.

"They had the sun all about them; they had great clusters of cherries in their hands; they were eating, and laughing, and singing; they were dusty already, but what of that? they were going to the green country, to the blue sea, to the charm of change, to the tumult and merriment and variety of life.

"The spell of the Wanderjahre was cast on me, to say nothing that I was really in love with that poor Zinzara.

"An hour after I had made over my room and my books and my instruments to my best friend, Ezio Luccone, and I had caught up the mosquito and her friends on the high road for Livorno, just as the sun reached to noon. From that day I was a player.

"I stayed about two years with that troop, all that time on the Riviera or among the little mountain towns of Savoy.

"The Zinzara taught me all she knew. For the matter of that I had found my vocation, which assuredly did not lie in a professorial tribune.

"I used to write comedies and 'revues' for them.

No! I have not a scrap of what I wrote left. What does that matter? If one have any *oro sodo* about one at all, either mental or moral, one never counts what shreds of the good metal one drops along the roads. If others pick it up, let them. To be of ever so little use is all one can hope for in this world.

"At the end of two years the troop broke up; it is a miracle amongst actors when any set of them holds together half as long, and I went by myself to Paris, where, too, I played.

"But I never cared much for Paris. One cannot open one's mouth when one talks that language; and amongst those shining zinc roofs, and that blaze of white paint and of gilding, I grew thirsty for my own great dark palaces, and still historic garden-ways, and moonlit plains song-haunted, and measureless distances only swept by clouds and wind. Do you not know? Oh, yes; anyone who has once breathed in Italy knows. And to anyone who had not, there would be no use in talking."

"What of the Zinzara?"

"Oh, the usual thing of the Zinzara. She loved me very dearly for a time, and then she picked up a Marquis out of Monaco—only a Marchese di Truffaldino I am afraid, poor thing—and flung the salad-bowl at my head.

"Women always fling something at you when they are angry with themselves for having been in love with you; a great genius flings a stinging 'Elle et Lui;' a poor actress can only fling a kitchen missile that comes handy. Perhaps the latter is the better. It is not so disagreeable to be forcibly reminded of the radishes and endive of the past, as it is to see all one's old follies and passions served up with pepper and mustard.

"The poor Zinzara! I have not a notion what became of her. She had genius of a sort indisputably, both for tragedy and cookery. But she never fastened her mark on the world, though she had the making both of a Rachel and a Vatel in her.

"Peace be with her wherever she be; she enlivened two bright summers for me; she taught me the tricks of the stage; and she only broke her wooden supper-bowl, and not either my head or my heart."

I was silent as he ceased speaking; I had only the most vaguely innocent notions of what this his passion for the Zinzara might mean; but I had a vague and restless impatience at hearing him speak of any love for any creature at all.

His gaze went westward as he spoke.

Close at hand, on its own quiet hill-side, stood the little convent-church of Sta. Margheritá, the highest point of all, bowered close amongst olive and fruit-tree foliage, with the village slanting away from it in a dusky line of roofs downward to where the Pazzi tyrannicide was planned amongst the villa gardens.

Pascarèl looked across to it. It is not changed since its beautiful novice left its saintly peace and stole down through the amorous olive shadows to the lawless love of Fra Lippi.

"Do you not see Fra Filippo," said he, "gathering his monk's frock about him, and speeding up there to steal a glance at Lucrezia through the convent grating, if chance favoured? What grace was there in that scamp of the Carmelites, that Rabelais of painting, that Falstaff of the fine arts, that a woman, young

and rich and beautiful, should leave all for him, and
cleave to him so faithfully? Some heart and soul
there must have been. The city saw in him a wild,
frolicsome, mad monk, fitter to worship Silenus than
Christ. But there must have been some soul in him
—some soul tender, pitiful, spiritual, profound,—or he
had never painted his S. Stefano of Prato till it made
the fierce men of his own day weep, and he would
never have loved those green, wide, laughing countries
which made him greater than Masaccio, and the first
of the Florence painters of landscape. Perhaps that
soul in him the young nun saw. Are we ever truly
read, save by the one that loves us best? Love is
blind, the phrase runs; nay, I would rather say Love
sees as God sees, and with infinite wisdom has infinite
pardon."

His voice grew very sweet and still, and the
dreamy look came into his eyes as he leaned there
gazing across at the little red roof of Sta. Margheritâ,
whose solitary bell was tolling the Ave Maria over its
silent woods.

His thoughts were far beyond me; I was but a
heedless child, and of where his mind had wandered
I knew nothing; and of the greatness of such a love
as he was wishful for, doubtless, in his heart even
then, I had no more conception or measurement than
I had of that baser passion such as he had been lured
with by the Zinzara.

* * * * *

He spoke no more; the night had fallen quickly
and completely, as it does in Valdarno when once
the sun's disc has dropped behind Carrara.

We went slowly together down the stairs and

across the court and through the olive downward to
the City, and we passed within the gates again as the
stars began to burn, and the sheets of moonlight to
lie white and wide on river and piazza. The world,
so tired though it be with fruitless pain, so dull in
drowsy apathy, so weary of for ever giving birth to
what for ever perishes when touching on its prime,
the world is once more young again when the moon
shines on Italy.

"To my fancy," said he, softly, as we paused a
moment on the bridge of the Graces to see the silver
width of the stream shine away on either side into the
sweet tremulous darkness of the hills, "to my fancy,
when the gods of the golden age were driven from
earth and walked no more amongst men, they looked
back once, and said, 'that we may be remembered a
little in this land—we, the old banished gods of the
old, fair, dead faiths,—let Paradise return to earth
when the moon wakes above Italy.' Her nights are
gifts of the gods that she has, this Italy of ours; it is
so trite to say so—ay, because it is so true."

Florence was very still that night as we went
through her streets from the old Star Tower.

It was the Holy week.

Here and there, from some low open door, a
Miserere was pealing. Here and there the shadow of
a monk fell across the broad white stones. Here and
there a lamp burned before some street shrine hung
with those scentless flowers that are the joyless Christian symbol of immortality.

But Florence never can be very sad. Her tears
and smiles lie close together. If she draw the saintly
cowl about her, her fair eyes laugh from beneath the

folds, so that you half shall swear the robe of penance is a masker's domino.

She tells her beads with one hand, but she touches her lute with the other.

Even this night as we went, though it was the season of the saintly Quaresima, there was a mandoline trilling from some high casement in a palace tower; in an old dusky doorway there was the glisten of a girl's white dress and a cuirassier's flashing breastplate; from a fretted balcony of stone fashioned with lilies and fawns' heads a beautiful dark woman, gathering about her a mantle of black and gold, dropped a single rosebud to a lover who waited below for the pretty symbol; far, far away, across the great white luminous piazza, there came the sound of voices, in chorus, laughing to light scorn the lenten lamentations; some men and maidens had been in the meadows and were bringing home sheaves of the lilies, they danced as they came in the moonlight, and a young boy played a viol before them.

Pascarèl looked and listened, then went onward with a smile.

"Is not my Florence perfect!" he murmured. "Some say I talk of her as though she were a city of fairie. Well, a fairy city she is to every poet and every lover. Was she not builded in a night by Hercules as a pleasure toy for Venus and Flora, made with the stones from the golden Arno water, and set up in a meadow of lilies? Hercules gave her his strength as a birthright, and Flora being content, touched the soil and said, 'All the year long flowers shall blossom here, and their smile shall not cease in any season;' and Venus, being well pleased likewise, called her son to her, and said, 'When you dart your arrows hither wreathe them with roses, and wing them from the eagle and the dove.'"

CHAPTER VIII
The Lily-queen.

He did indeed love Florence with a tender passion.

Paris is the Aspasia of cities, but Florence is the Heloïse; upon the brilliancy of her genius and her beauty there lie always the shadow of the cloister, and always the divinity of a great sacrifice.

Men, with any soul in them, love Florence reverently; for tuneful and thoughtless though her laughter be now, and although now the strangers of northern isles and western worlds coarsely intrigue in her pleasure-places, and basely cheapen her treasures in her streets, Florence cannot be changed or lowered, for in her day she suffered much and failed often, and aspired greatly, and set her seal with a pure hand on much of the noblest work of the world.

To Pascarèl she was as a living thing.

Not a stone of her but had a tongue for him. Not a dark nook in her quietest ways but for him was filled with some figure of the past standing out in the gold and colours of idealised tradition, like some form that a monk had drawn upon his missal vellum.

Gay and idle, and buoyant and amorous indeed had been the tenour of all his days in Florence; laughed away to the tinkle of mandolines, the chink of wine-glasses, the riot of carnival mirth, the twittering love chirp of women quickly won and lightly lost.

But beneath this life of his there ran another vein, deeper and truer, and filled with the strong heroical blood of the past; and he would go through the Florence ways many and many a time, lost to all the daily stir around him, and seeing nothing but the wistful spiritual eyes of Angelico, or the white bare feet of Ginevra, or the flicker of the torch in the hand of the Black Giàn, or the dread of destiny on the face of Luisa Strozzi.

He would laugh at himself for his joy in it, for he would say that he was a citizen of the world, and entered no narrower classification; but at heart the love of Florence was always warm with him, continual wanderer from her olive valleys though he was.

He knew the story of her every stone and spandril; he would trace the steps of all her heroes and prophets inch by inch along the narrow ways; for him her paven courts were eloquent with a thousand tongues; and all the curling leaves and shining traceries of her sculptures had a million whispers of the great workshops where great men had wrought at them amidst the eager reverent eyes of pupils who, in their turn, took up the glorious tale, and told it to the nations.

And now and then, coming out of the Bargello into the broad silvery sunlight, or leaning on the old Rubaconte parapet, looking far, far away, to the snows of Vallombrosa, now and then he would bestir himself and speak of Florence, with that swift rush of that mellow Tuscan which has the war clang of the clarion and the love-note of the lute together in it.

"Her riches?" said he, in one of those moments, answering some thoughtless word of mine. "No. It was not the riches of Florence that made her power —it was her way of spending her riches; a totally different thing, cara mia.

"Amidst all her commerce, her wars, her hard work, her money-making, Florence was always dominated and spiritualised, at her noisiest and worst, by a poetic and picturesque imagination.

"Florentine life had always an ideal side to it; and an idealism, pure and lofty, runs through her darkest histories and busiest times like a thread of gold through a coat of armour and a vest of frieze.

"The Florentine was a citizen, a banker, a workman, a carder of wool, a weaver of silk, indeed; but he was also always a lover, and always a soldier; that is, always half a poet. He had his Caroccio and his Ginevra as well as his tools and his sacks of florins. He had his sword as well as his shuttle. His scarlet giglio was the flower of love no less than the blazonry of battle on his standard, and the mint stamp of the commonwealth on his coinage.

"Herein lay the secret of the influence of Florence: the secret which rendered the little city, stretched by her river's side, amongst her quiet meadows white with arums, a sacred name to all generations of men for all she dared and all she did.

"'She amassed wealth,' they say: no doubt she did—and why?

"To pour it with both hands to melt in the foundries of Ghiberti—to bring it in floods to cement the mortar that joined the marbles of Brunelleschi! She always spent to great ends, and to mighty uses.

"When she called a shepherd from his flocks in the green valley to build for her a bell-tower so that she might hear, night and morning, the call to the altar, the shepherd built for her in such fashion that the belfry has been the Pharos of Art for five centuries.

"Here is the secret of Florence—supreme aspiration.

"The aspiration which gave her citizens force to live in poverty, and clothe themselves in simplicity, so as to be able to give up their millions of florins to bequeath miracles in stone and metal and colour to the Future. The aspiration which so purified her soil, red with carnage, black with smoke of war, trodden continuously by hurrying feet of labourers, rioters, mercenaries, and murderers, that from that soil there could spring, in all its purity and perfection, the paradise-blossom of the Vita Nuova.

"Venice perished for her pride and carnal lust; Rome perished for her tyrannies and her blood-thirst; but Florence,—though many a time nearly strangled under the heel of the Empire and the hand of the Church—Florence was never slain utterly either in body or soul; Florence still crowned herself with flowers even in her throes of agony, because she kept always within her that love—impersonal, consecrate, void of greed—which is the purification of the individual life and the regeneration of the body politic. 'We labour for the ideal,' said the Florentines of old, lifting to heaven their red flower de luce—and to this day Europe bows before what they did, and cannot equal it."

"But she had so many great men, so many mighty masters!" I would urge, whereon Pascarèl would glance on me with his lightest and yet uttermost scorn.

"Oh wise female thing, who always traces the root to the branch and deduces the cause from the effect! Did her great men spring up full-armed like Athene, or was it the pure, elastic atmosphere of her that made her mere mortals strong as immortals? The supreme success of modern government is to flatten down all men into one uniform likeness, so that it is only by most frightful, and often destructive, effort that any originality can contrive to get loose in its own shape for a moment's breathing space; but in the Colnmonwealth of Florence a man, being born with any genius in him, drew in strength to do and dare greatly with the very air he breathed.

"Moreover, it was not only the great men that made her what she was.

"It was, above all, the men who knew they were not great, but yet had the patience and unselfishness to do their appointed work for her zealously, and with every possible perfection in the doing of it.

"It was not only Orcagna planning the Loggia, but every workman who chiselled out a piece of its stone, that put all his head and heart into the doing thereof. It was not only Michaelangelo in his studio, but every poor painter who taught the mere a, b, c, d of the craft to a crowd of pupils out of the streets, who did whatsoever came before them to do mightily and with reverence.

"In those days all the servants as well as the sovereigns of Art were penetrated with the sense of her holiness.

"It was the mass of patient, intelligent, poetic, and sincere servitors of art, who, instead of wildly consuming their souls in envy and desire, cultured their one talent to the uttermost, so that the mediocrity of that age would have been the excellence of any other.

"Not alone from the great workshops of the great masters did the light shine on the people. From every scaffold where a palace ceiling was being decorated with its fresco, from every bottega where the children of the poor learned to grind and to mingle the colours, from every cell where some solitary monk studied to produce an offering to the glory of his God, from every nook and corner where the youths gathered in the streets to see some Nunziata or Ecce Homo lifted to its niche in the city wall, from every smallest and most hidden home of art—from the nest under the eaves as well as from the cloud-reaching temples,—there went out amidst the multitudes an ever-flowing, ever-pellucid stream of light, from that Aspiration which is in itself Inspiration.

"So that even to this day the people of Italy have not forgotten the supreme excellence of all beauty, but are, by the sheer instinct of inherited faith, incapable of infidelity to those traditions; so that the commonest craftsman of them all will sweep his curves and shade his hues upon a plaster cornice with a perfection that is the despair of the maestri of other nations."

So he would talk on at divers times, as we paced the twisting lines of the streets, or paused on some white olive slope to look backward on the tumult of the roofs, with the battlements of the Vecchio tower rising out like some old sea-galley from the waves of the rippling sunshine. And I grew quickly to share this tender, fantastic, filial affection of his for the City of the Lilies.

Nay, who could do otherwise who has once dwelt within the magic circles of her storied walls?

Say some day at noontide you feel a little weary of it all.

Say it is midsummer, and the strong Leone sun is white on every stone; and the very cicale have hushed their chatter, and have gone to sleep.

Arno is nearly dry; grass grows between its pebbles, and straw is laid to bleach on its deserted bed. The buildings are scorched and colourless; the olives are pallid in the heat; the cypresses strain thirstily upward against the sky, as though seeking a rain-cloud and finding none in all the shadowless wide blue.

Say for once you are almost a renegade to her. The zinzari have been troublesome, and the sun beats against the blinds, and will not be denied. Your eyes ache with the radiance as they do when you throw off your mask after the opera ball.

You, for once in a way, are tired of the city, and think you will arise and go to that old, cool marble court in the villa amongst the hills, where the vine shadows play all the day long, and the waters drip in the deep acanthus shadows. Or else you dream a little in remembrance of clear green alpine rivers, shining in greenest meadows; of Tirol pine-slopes, rising to the snow with deep blue shadows asleep on bluer lakes; of Swabian woods or of Thuringian forests, wet, still, and full of song of birds, into whose leafy darkness no daylight ever comes.

Perhaps in the blazing Tuscan noon you think of these or such as these that you have known, and that are all lying there across the dreamy flush of the rosy Apennines.

Say in the daytime you are thus, for once perhaps,

faithless,—yet with the nightfall she will take up afresh her supremacy.

The long bright day draws to a close. The west is in a blaze of gold, against which the ilex and the acacia are black as funeral plumes. The innumerable scents of fruits and flowers and spices, and tropical seeds, and sweet essences, that fill the streets at every step from shops and stalls, and monks' pharmacies, she fanned out in a thousand delicious odours on the cooling air. The wind has risen, blowing softly from mountain and from sea across the plains through the pines of Pisa, across to the oak-forests of green Casentino.

Whilst the sun still glows in the intense amber of his own dying glory, away in the tender violet hues of the east the young moon rises.

Rosy clouds drift against the azure of the zenith, and are reflected as in a mirror in the shallow river waters.

A little white cloud of doves flies homeward against the sky.

All the bells chime for the Ave Maria.

The evening falls.

Wonderful hues, creamy, and golden, and purple, and soft as the colours of a dove's throat, spread themselves slowly over the sky; the bell tower rises like a shaft of porcelain clear against the intense azure; amongst the tall canes by the river the fire-flies sparkle; the shores are mirrored in the stream with every line and curve, and roof and cupola, drawn in sharp deep shadow; every lamp glows again thrice its size in the glass of the current, and the arches of the bridges meet their own image there; the boats glide down the water that is now white under the moon, now amber under the lights, now black under the walls, forever changing; night draws on, then closes quite.

But it is night as radiant as day, and ethereal as day can never be; on the hills the cypresses still stand out against the faint gold that lingers in the west; there is the odour of carnations and of acacias everywhere.

Noiseless footsteps come and go.

People pass softly in shadow, like a dream.

You lean down and bask in this sweet air that is like a breath of paradise.

Against your hand there are great clusters of the red oleander, that burn against the gleaming snowy globes of the half-opened magnolia flowers. The voice that is dearest to you on earth is low upon your ear.

From some other casement open like yours there comes the distant cadence of a mandoline. A sheaf of lilies is flung from a balcony with a laugh. A woman goes by with a knot of pomegranate in her dark hair. A break of song floats down the silence.

"Addio, gioja mia, addio!" drops tenderly down the wind like leaves shaken from a rose.

On the parapet of the river two lovers lean and watch the stream as it glides to its grave in the grey sea-sand, as their own passion glides to its grave of dead desire.

You smile, and know there is no grave for yours; he says so at the least, and you believe.

It is night in Italy.

It is night in Florence.

In all the width of the world is there aught so perfect elsewhere? With a glad heart you will answer, nothing so perfect anywhere.

In such a night why cannot the lips we love kiss us forever—forever—forever—into the dreams of death?

BOOK IV.

THE WANDERING ARTE.

CHAPTER I.
Il bianco Aspetto.

Do you know the delicate delights of a summer morning in Italy?—morning I mean between four and five of the clock, and not the full hot mid-day that means morning to the languid associations of this weary century.

The nights, perfect as they are, have scarcely more loveliness than the birth of light, the first rippling laughter of the early day.

The air is cool, almost cold, and clear as glass. There is an endless murmur from birds' throats and wings, and from far away there will ring from village or city the chimes of the first mass. The deep broad shadows lie so fresh, so grave, so calm, that by them the very dust is stilled and spiritualized.

Softly the sun comes, striking first the loftier trees and then the blossoming magnolias, and lastly the green lowliness of the gentle vines; until all above is in a glow of new-born radiance, whilst all beneath the leaves still is dreamily dusk and cool.

The sky is of a soft sea-blue; great vapours will float here and there, iris coloured and snow-white. The stone parapets of bridge and tower shine against the purple of the mountains, which are low in tone, and look like hovering storm-clouds. Across the fields dun oxen pass to their labour; through the shadows peasants go their way to mass; down the river a raft drifts slowly with the pearly water swaying against the canes; all is clear, tranquil, fresh as roses washed with rain.

In such a daybreak in the soft spring weather we left Florence by the gate that was once in the old days broken down for the mule of the Vicar of Christ to pass through into the city.

Pascarèl was too inveterate a wanderer by instinct and habit to remain long in one place, even when that place was circled by the hills so dear to him; and he was looked for eagerly with the spring and summer in all the towns and villages through Tuscany and Umbria, and the flowering Romagna and the drear sea-washed Maremma.

The Arte, which was light and cleverly constructed, was at such times sent onwards on the back of mules, on the flat cart of a contadino, on the top of a hay-waggon, on the shoulders of sturdy hill peasants, or any manner of conveyance which best served the moment, and the sight of the red and white flag fluttering from the pile of canvas and wood was a signal for a headlong rush and a shout of joy from the whole population over the face of all the country.

As for ourselves we walked always where there was any beauty, whether along the river-shores, or through the fields and vineyards, or along the brown sides of the hills, or beside the play of the tideless sea, on the hot yellow sands, or across the plain, from one little old walled town to another.

Pascarèl and his little troop had never been extravagant enough to take any other mode of travel than that which their own limbs afforded, except when they needed to get quickly from one province to another.

They always sauntered on from town to town, from village to village, staying on the road as fancy moved them. They had gone on in this way all across Italy, and half across Europe; and as for me I liked nothing better than to do as they had done.

As soon as the sun showed his red disc where he rose above the southern seas and the eastern deserts far away, we used to rise ourselves and set out upon our pilgrimage for the day, so that each portion of it was accomplished before the heats of noon. Or at other times, if they had not played anywhere that night, we set forth when the moon showed herself, and went on our way through the wonderful lustre of her, which seemed to throb everywhere like so much conscious life.

In these wanderings I learned for the first time how beautiful is the beauty of Italy.

In the old town of Verona, I had been nothing but a passionate little rebel, hating my poor, pale prison-house for its poverty and monotony, whilst the people with whom I had dwelt had seen no wonder in that which had been about them from their birth, and had found their vital interests lie in the scantiness of the oil for their lucernate, and the uncertainty of the measure of the soup for their morrow.

With Pascarèl, and wandering thus through the length and breadth of the Romagna and of Tuscany, a surer and higher perception awakened in me, and my heart and my mind alike stirred into sympathy with that ethereal loveliness of air, of distance, and of light, which is, as it were, the very soul of all Italian scenery.

Green plains have a certain likeness, whether in Belgium, or Bavaria, or Britain. A row of poplars quivering in the light looks much alike in Flanders or in Normandy. A rich wood all aglow with red and gold in autumn sunsets is the same thing after all in Rhineland as in Devon.

But Italy has a physiognomy that is all her own; that is like nothing else, which to some minds is sad, and strange, and desolate, and painful, and which to others is beautiful, and full of consolation and delicious as a dream; but which, be it what else it may, is always wholly and solely Italian, can never be met with elsewhere, and has a smile on it, and a sigh in it, that make other lands beside it seem as though they were soulless and were dumb.

It is not the intensity but the ethereality of its colour which is its charm; for it reflects every colour this wonderful "bianco aspetto" of Dante.

Colourless itself it takes by turn every hue, and returns every gift of the sun's rays so exquisitely, that there is no single tone which is not by it purified and spiritualised.

At sunrise and at sunset most especially, but more or less throughout the entire day, this wondrous whiteness beams and blushes into the million hues of the flame opal.

Watch it from one year to another and you shall never find it twice the same.

When the blue mists of daybreak drift across it; when the clouds duskily cast their violet shadows on it; when the tremulous wood smoke curls up in the rosy air; when the whole mountain side is flushed like apple-blossoms, darkening here and there where the pines grow into softest amethyst; here and there lightened where the sun strikes into such glow, that like love it becomes "tanta rossa che appena fora dentro al fuoco nata," in all these changes and in a thousand others that sweep each other away again and again in endless succession throughout each hour of the twenty-four, this "bianco aspetto" is the loveliest thing that the world holds.

It is the loveliness of a dream world; it is the loveliness which all other poets as well as Dante have beheld in their imparadised vision of a life eternal; and compared with it the denser colours and the stronger contrasts of more northern lands are almost coarse, and seem to have no soul in them, and speak no message from the gods to man.

Indeed all lands are soulless where the olive does not lift its consecrated boughs to heaven.

Noble and fruitful though the face of them may be, a certain pathos and poetic meaning will be lacking in them, if on their hills and in their valleys the olive do not hover like a soft rain-cloud shimmering to silver with the light.

For the olive is always mournful; it is amidst trees as the opal amidst jewels; its foliage, and its flowers, and its fruits, are all colourless; it shivers softly as though it were cold even on those sun-bathed hills; it seems for ever to say "peace, peace," when there is no peace; and to be weary because that whereof it is the emblem has been banished from earth because men's souls delight in war.

The landscape that has the olive is spiritual as no landscape can ever be from which the olive is absent; for where is there spirituality without some hue of sadness?

But this spiritual loveliness is one for which the human creature that is set amidst it needs a certain education as for the power of Euripides, for the dreams of Phædrus, for the strength of Michelangelo, for the symphonies of Mozart or Beethoven.

The mind must itself be in a measure spiritualised ere aright it can receive it.

It is too pure, too impalpable, too nearly divine, to be grasped by those for whom all beauty centres in strong heats of colour and great breadths of effect; it floats over the senses like a string of perfect cadences in music; it has a breath of heaven in it; though on the earth it is not of the earth; when the world was young, ere men had sinned on it, and gods forsaken it, it must have had the smile of this light that lingers here.

This beauty, the beauty of perfect outline, of faint transparent hues, of immeasurable horizons, of wondrous silvery effulgence in which the eyes seem to range and reach until the mere sense of sight grows into a voluptuous rapture, all this became known to me as I wandered through those old old lands by the side of Pascarèl.

Some instinct towards it had been with me always; but through him I learned to know what it was that I felt; and lesser things than this became through him also eloquent to me and beautiful.

The fruitful soil where flowers rose at every step, as though the sods still felt the touch of the divine thyrsus. The sad cypress rising straight against the sky's pale gold with stars of cyclamen white about its feet.

The vast, dim, cavernous churches, dark as night, save where the lamps of the high altars burned. The lonely aisles where tired feet of peasants wore their way across the marble pavement where great men were laid forgotten in their tombs.

The radiant glad dawns when through the air came ringing the clear sounds of countless bells across the fields to wake the sleeping world. The old bruised shrine set at the dusky corner of some populous streets, so that men looking upwards saw, and remembered, and went the better for a fleeting thought of God on to the daily labours of their humble lives.

The moonlight, magical, mystical, unutterable with the dense ebon shadows making but the more lustrous the wondrous silver world on which they slept. All these he gave me eyes to see, and, whilst I saw, taught me why they filled me with such soft delight.

CHAPTER II.
Étoile qui file.

WE wandered all over the hills and the plains, along the course of the rivers and through the wide and rich champaign of the Valdarno; pausing here, pausing there, as the whim of the moment served, now setting up the wooden theatre on the hillside, amongst the olive woods, now letting it find its momentary resting-place amidst the fortresses and monasteries of some old God-forgotten city.

Sometimes up amongst the mountains we had need to make our home with the peasants, for there was no inn to go to, and no fare but onions and black bread. Sometimes in the cities the harsh laws which still prevailed at that time in some districts swooped down like vultures on the free discourse of Pascarèl, and drove him forth from the gates, leaving his gains behind him.

Sometimes it happened to us to lose our way, or to have night down on us ere we knew where we were, and we had to camp there where we found ourselves, on some hillside, under the chestnut trees, and raise a bonfire with the dead leaves, and sleep around it as best we could until the sun rose.

But all this was little hardship in that gracious weather of the springtime, and above us there was always the brilliance of the deep blue sky, and around us there was always the gay good humour of the hardy and gentle people.

The life was quite beautiful to me, and would have been so, I think, to any one with anything of the child or anything of the poet in them. The people were so fond of us, or, at least, of him, that all the way we roamed was strewed with endless little acts of tenderness and of goodwill that blossomed like the cyclamen along our path.

Quaint old women in huge straw hats and with smiling, brown, shrivelled faces, would bring us little cheeses or golden honeycombs wrapped up in vine leaves. Girls, with lovely dreaming eyes like the San Sisto Madonna's, would come out from the sun-baked, flat-roofed houses with gifts of eggs packed cosily in rose leaves, or strewn over, for luck's sake, with Our Lady's herb.

Sometimes from the white villages with their watch towers in their midst, there would ring out, for us alone, in the golden silence the sweetest melody of chiming bells that seemed to ripple like so much laughter over the low-lying roofs amongst the vines.

We were always amongst the people. Pascarèl played for no one else.

The opera-houses, where the sweet notes of men's throats were hired with gold and diamonds, were for the rich and well-to-do, for the dainty masked dames in the carnival time, and for the noble lovers who wove their intrigues under the shelter of roulade and fioritura.

Pascarèl's little theatre was for the populace alone; for the bronzed vine-dressers, who laughed herculean laughter in their broad bare chests; for the tanners and coopers and smiths, who came with the heat and the smirch of their labours upon them; for the peasant women who had worked weeding in the fields all day, and sat in the tent with their big brown children sleeping at their breasts; for any and all whose lives were hard, and whose bodies were bruised by toil, and who were glad to forget with him a little while the tax that emptied their bread-pot, and the hunger that gnawed at their vitals.

Give an Italian a copper coin, and though it be the sole thing that he owns in the world, he will spend four-fifths of it on the playhouse.

Pascarèl knew his countrymen's foible; and he loved best of all to play for those who had not even the copper piece, and who must have stood all night outside the longed-for paradise had it not been for the joyous summons which rang out to them from his voice crying,

"Come in—come in; you can pay me with a laugh if I prove worth it. Not a soldo in any one of your pockets?—oh, my friend, you must be either the utterest fool or the honestest man in all the universe. Well, never mind. Come in—come in; laugh or hiss as you like, but come."

And they did come by thousands; it was the audience that he preferred—he who surely by his gifts and graces might have done with the world almost whatever he might have chosen.

"You have no ambition!" I said to him one day.

He answered me, with his bright laugh, "None—absolutely none!"

We were resting on the slope of a hill in the Casentino in the sweet maytime.

It was late in the day. The land beneath us was white with the delicate, sad pallor of the endless olive woods. Above, the west was all one soft flame-radiance of that miraculous rose which is to all the other hues of heaven as the ethereal grace of Petrarca is beside all other odes of love.

"But that is very strange?" I reasoned to him. "Where would the world be if all men thought as you do?"

"Much where it is, no doubt," he answered me, "and unstained, moreover, by the bloodshed of war. Do you think that the world owes anything that is worth keeping in its Arts to so personal a passion as ambition? You are very wrong.

"No true artist ever worked yet for ambition. He does the thing which is in him to do by a force far stronger than himself.

"The first fruits of a man's genius are always pure of greed.

"In time, indeed, the world gets at him and tempts him, and if he be not strong, will bribe and weaken him. That is one reason why the creations of an artist's maturity seldom realise the promise of his youth.

"But no mere ambition ever raised the piles of Brunelleschi, shaped the gates of Ghiberti, created the Inferno and the Hamlet, or gave us the Concerto in C minor of Felix Mendelssohn.

"In these days men are governed by personal ambitions, and, as a consequence, they have ceased to produce greatly. In these days no man will be content to chisel humbly, but to his very best, a corbel or a spandril for another man's St. Peter's; not a whit; every one will have his own building all to himself, be it only a gaze-a-bo or a magnified cucumber-frame.

"After all, it was not only that Michelangelo and Lionardo were greater men than we, it was also because their pupils were content to grind the colours and prepare the earths with uttermost perfectness in their simple share of the great work. Now-a-days, did you ask a young artist to grind your colours, he would tell you with scorn that he was not a shopboy.

"When we can get back that single-hearted absorption into Art which characterised the mediæval schools of Italy, then we shall get back with it greatness of execution in Art.

"You remember Il Parmeggiano, who never heard the tumult of the sack of Rome go on in the streets around him because he was so engrossed with painting at the time? The soldiers broke into his studio and found him, brush in hand, and ignorant that the city had been stormed.

"Well, nothing less than that makes a great artist, and it is just that vital absolute absorption of all personality of which there is nothing—absolutely nothing—in the modern mind. It is always outside its own creations; vainly or coldly always outside them.

"The modern priest of art does not believe in his own God—and in art, above all other religions, who that has not faith can work miracles? Art is the divining rod that will blossom like the almond-tree; but it will be bare and barren if the magician himself half scoff and wholly doubt."

"But, surely," I reasoned with him, wistfully, "surely those men dreamed that they were doing what would keep their memories fresh in the thoughts of men for many ages?"

"I doubt it," said Pascarèl. "I doubt very much that they ever thought at all about it in that light. The true artist does his work because he loves it—because he cannot choose but do it. Do you suppose the architect of Cologne Cathedral would have torn his plans up if he had foreseen his name would have been forgotten?"

"But surely an immortality of remembrance——"

"Fine immortality!" quoted Pascarèl. "Napoleon

was right in his scoff at our Tiziano. Immortality! Bah! the brief noonday that carrion flies take to suck at a dead eagle. Immortality—be so good as to tell me, donzella mia, if you can, who were Eugœan of Samos, Bion and Diocchus, Eudemus of Paras, Lampsacus, Damastes, Xanthus of Sardis, or Phericydes of Leros?"

"I never heard of any one of them."

"No? And plenty of people, more learned than you, are in the same plight. And yet they were all authors of Asiatic Greece who, in their day, looked for as much 'immortality' as Herodotus. To come into our own country—tell me who Trissino was, and what he did?"

I confessed that the name of Trissino said no more to me than the name of any one of the little flowers that sprang up by millions underneath the vines.

"Do you know who Trissino was?" he repeated.

"No."

"There again!—why, he believed that he had restored the epic to Italian verse in all its most heroic proportions, and sneered at his contemporary, Ariosto, as only good for the vulgar. Did never you hear, then, of Tito and Ercole Strozzi?"

"No."

"Heavens! And yet they were, or were thought, famous poets; but the world is like you, and only remembers Luisa Strozzi because men were mad for her face, and she made a picturesque figure coming down the hill by San Miniato that night of the fair at the Feast of the Pardon. But to descend a century or so;—what, pray, were Chauvelin, Daunou, Riouffe, Ganilh, Ginguéne, Larromiguière?"

I confessed my ignorance, looking across at the sapphire lights on the Carrara mountains.

"No, again? And yet those men, with the rest of the hundred Frenchmen of the Tribunal of Ninety-Nine, dreamed, surely, of imperishable renown. 'A line in an universal history!' as my wise Napoleon said again after Cairo. True, he arrived later on at getting a whole page for himself; but to print such a page, you must distil seas of human blood to make the only ink that will not rub out with the wear of the ages. and even then, as soon as a greater conqueror comes, you will have your page blotted and turned into a palimpsest. You remember how, in your old Verona, there is a rude, dusky, nameless grave in the mausoleum of the Scala, and above it a superb equestrian in marble, with three stages of sculptured saints and prophets all to himself in might and glory; the first, the tomb of the assassinated; the second, the tomb of the assassin? Believe me, Fame in the world allots things very much like the Scala's sculptor."

I was silent; I thought of poor old wronged Ambrogiò dying by his fireless and childless hearth, whilst as we had passed through Florence the names of Rothwald and Alkestis had loomed large upon the walls.

"Besides—ambition for a player!" laughed Pascarèl, not waiting for my answer, "you might as well say let the dog-grass blowing there try to root itself and grow like that stone-pine. 'Ci-gît le bruit du vent' is our only fit epitaph.

"Thistle-down, smoke, soap-bubbles, 'les étoiles qui

filent, qui filent, qui filent et disparaissent,' those are all our emblems.

"They reproach us that we only live to laugh and to love, and take no thought for the morrow. Why not? There is no morrow for us.

"The player can leave nothing behind him; not even a memory. 'You should have heard him,' say the old people to the young of the dead actor. 'You should have heard him; he was great, indeed, if you like.' But what do the young believe of that? There is no proof.

"Such greatness as the dead man had went out with his breath like a lamp that was spent.

"We live in the present; we live for the present. Why not, I say?

"We are straws on the wind of the hour, too frail and too brittle to float into the future. Our little day of greatness is a mere child's puff-ball, inflated by men's laughter, floated by women's tears; what breeze so changeful as the one, what waters so shallow as the other?—the bladder dances a little while; then sinks: and who remembers?

"Ambition for such a thing as that?

"Grow oaks from the thistle-down; weave ships' cables from the smoke; change the soap-bubble into a prism for astronomers; arrest the falling star as a fixed planet in the spheres; and then, if you will, talk of ambition for a player!"

He had risen as he spoke, and walked to and fro, brushing the tall foliage of the undergrowth of acacia and cane; he spoke with passionate scorn, and though he laughed, there was for once some undertone of bitterness in his easy mirth.

He jeered at the thing he himself was; no man's heart is wholly free of care and doubt when he trenches on the semi-suicide of any self-contempt.

"But players have been great," I said to him, not knowing well what to say. "Great in their lives at least? And rich?"

"Rich, oh yes!" he echoed, breaking down with one hand a head of iris. "A million francs a week you mean, and diamond snuff-boxes from a prince's hand—oh yes—if that be greatness. Good heavens! before you have fairly entered on a woman's years, how thoroughly a woman's heart beats in you!"

"What do you count greatness, then?" I asked, gathering, as I rested on my arms, face downward on the grass, the clusters of the white anemoni, and all the bright spring flowers of the hills.

Pascarèl, standing beside me, looked away to the rose-radiance of the west with that strange introspective musing look in his eyes which comes so suddenly into Italian eyes, and has so intense a melancholy in it, and also so much of that spiritual beauty which their country has.

"There is an old legend," he made answer to me, "an old monkish tale, which tells how, in the days of King Clovis, a woman, old and miserable, forsaken of all, and at the point of death, strayed into the Merovingian woods, and lingering there, and harkening to the birds, and loving them, and so learning from them of God, regained, by no effort of her own, her youth; and lived, always young and always beautiful, a hundred years; through all which time she never failed to seek the forests when the sun rose and hear the first song of the creatures to whom she owed her joy.

Whoever to the human soul can be, in ever so faint a sense, that which the birds were to the woman in the Merovingian woods, he, I think, has a true greatness. But I am but an outcast, you know; and my wisdom is not of the world."

Yet it seemed the true wisdom, there, at least, with the rose light shining across half the heavens, and the bells ringing far away in the plains below over the white waves of the sea of olives.

CHAPTER III.
The Riband and the Mandoline.

NOT many weeks after, whilst the year was still young, the old city of Pisa came in our way in our wanderings; and Pascarèl would fain turn aside from the bright sea-road, and stay within its walls a little.

I saw the ruined rival of Florence, the city "senza fede," once the mart of the world and now a desert. I saw, too, the scholar Luceone, a gentle, meek-eyed man, with the brow of Ghiberti and the mouth of Fra Giovanni. I saw the old Faustus-like room in the tower, with the owls in its broken masonry, and with the Arno washing its base at one side, and on the other the narrow darkling street that the comedians had gone through with jest and song on that Easter morning which had decided the fortunes of Pascarèl.

The old city was sad and sombre with Orcagna's Death reigning over its solitudes as the only sovereign left to it out of all the arrogance and plenitude of its years of power.

So still it was, so unbroken the shadows slept upon its grass-grown stones, so dully the yellow water dragged its way through the yellow sand, one might have thought that it was only that very day that the deathblow had fallen on it away there where the wanton sea abandoned it to kiss and serve Genoa.

"Do you not see Margharità of France?" said Pascarèl to me in Pisa one evening, as we strayed along, "leaning there out of the old palace window in just such a stormy red and gold night as this, perhaps, sick to despair of the gilded captivity, and planning with the gipsies to escape? I wonder no one has ever painted that scene; the delicate wanton royal head stretching out in the crimson dusk to hold council with the black-browed vagabonds. Can you not fancy the fret of her, and the fever and the revolt, that made a barefoot liberty seem sweeter than all the Medicean pomp?"

But I shook my head, and told him no, which saddened him a little as we went. A barefoot liberty was well in its way, no doubt, but to be a princess, was not that better?

It seemed to me that Marguerite must have been but jesting with the gipsies when she schemed thus with them here in dead old Pisa.

So thankless are we to Fate when it is fair for us.

I had all for which the heart of Margaret had hungered, beating itself like a caged bird under its jewelled bodice; I had it all as I went along the sad, windless, unpeopled streets, which his voice filled with sweetest music for me, and the red sun burnished into ancient pomp and panoply; I had it all and but half valued it—alas! alas!

At Pisa, as I say, I saw that old college friend of Pascarèl, the scholar Luceone. He was a gentle, meek-eyed man, with pensive eyes, and a tender sad face, like the face of Masaccio.

He lived up in the Faustus chambers, with the owls outside his casement, and the river water washing below, and on the other the narrow pent-up street that led away to the gate for Leghorn, and was very content in them, and grateful to his fate, asking nothing better of the gods and men than to dwell there in the heart of the academic city, in the midst of the dreary sand plains, with the zanzari hooting and hissing all night amongst the ancient walls.

He touched the self-drawn portrait of Pascarèl with many beautiful and tender lights, so that I saw that the painter had done himself but sorry justice.

"I am so happy here—so happy," said the gentle philosopher to me one day, as I leaned out of the high arched grated window from which Pascarèl had watched the Zinzara and her troop go by on their seaward way, "and I owe it all to him. He was a greater scholar than I. I was his second in mathematics, but only second, never his equal. Ah! you would not think it, you, who only see him smoking over his little comedies, or gathering beans with a pretty peasant in an inn garden.

"But it is true. There was never a greater scholar born than Pascarèl. So great that though he had been very wild in many of its pranks, and in that manner a constant terror to the academy, they wanted sorely to keep him always for the glory of Pisa, and they offered him the vacant Chair of Mathematics when our poor old Dottore died of apoplexy.

"Now, let Pascarèl tell you what he will, it is a fact that the professorship would have been very welcome to him for awhile at least. He would have tired of it and gone on his own ways in time, no doubt, but he would have liked to have had it, for he loved these rooms of his, and at that time, for all he was so gay and even riotous, he had a passion for science, and for all manners of abstruse study, which he could pursue at his ease and leisure here.

"But he knew that I was very poor, he knew that I had an old mother and a sister to keep, he knew that I pinched myself of bread and oil, and that I was glad to pick up the leavings off the dishes of the younger students, so what does he do?

"He goes straightway to the authorities, and he says to them in his careless fashion, 'Illustrissimi, I thank you for your offer, and the honour you would do me, but do not take my meaning ill if I tell you that you have made a great error. I am only a reckless good-for-nothing, a scamp at heart, a riotous free liver, who, as your excellencies know, have had the gates shut against me scores of times, and black marks against my name always. Do not give your empty Chair to me; but give it to one who is as good a mathematician as I am, as sound a scholar as I am, and who, unlike me, will furthermore do you credit by the simple and blameless life that he leads. Give it to Ezio Luceone, and I, Pascarèl, will hold myself as beholden to your Signoria, as though I filled the Chair myself.'

"That is what Pascarèl said to them, and they were so struck that they gave it to me, and I have held it ever since that time.

"He told you he surrendered it to follow that Frenchwoman and her comedians. Oh! no doubt.

That is just like him. But he relinquished the professorship in the month of March, and the Zinzara and her people only came into the town at Easter time, which fell, as I well remember, towards the middle of April in that year.

"It has been a wonderful thing for me, most wonderful. The stipend is quite enough to keep my mother in perfect comfort; and my heart and soul are in my work; and the college lads love me and I love them; and I ask no better life of God or man.

"But it is Pascarèl I owe it to most surely; only I pray of you do not tell him that I have told you, or he will never forgive me, never. I came to know it through one of the Signoria, which vexed him sorely; he had always tried to make me believe that it was only just the reward of my own merit. But it was all his own doing—all.

"I was the gainer, you see; but nevertheless my heart ached when I saw him go for ever out of the sea-gate with his pack on his back and his mandoline slung from his shoulder; the mandoline he has now? yes. The Frenchwoman put a scarlet riband to it, I remember, sitting just there down in the street in the sun as they ate pomegranates one warm Easter day.

"He does not know what has become of her, so he says; but he was wild about her then; a handsome woman, I remember, with great burning black eyes and beautiful feet.

"She did with Pascarèl what she liked; if it had not been for her I think the world would have heard of him. For he had some ambition in those days; and he is the last of the Pascarelli, you know. And they were really princes once? oh, yes! you may read it in Malespini and Villani."

So the gentle scholar would murmur on, and I would listen, leaning my body over the grated sill, and watching the narrow street far down below, where in other days the Frenchwoman had sat, and wound the scarlet riband about the stem of the mandoline, with the lights of the sun and of Pascarèl's eyes shining on her.

I hated to think of it; I hated to think of that far-away love-lightened past of his, in which I had no memory and no share.

Every woman, at all young and innocent of life, has felt the feeling that I mean when she has loved.

Pascarèl came behind me that day, having heard the latest words of his old friend.

"Ah, yes, cara mia," he murmured, softly, while sadly. "So many hands have tied so many ribbons to the mandoline—yes, I shame to say so—and the ribbons have all fluttered away God knows where, some to the dust-hole, some to the carnival-ball, some to deck other men's guitars, some to lie amongst the cinders in the ragpicker's basket. But after all what does that matter? the ribands never touched the chords of the mandoline; the ribands were only for fairs and feast-days and follies; it takes something stronger and better than a riband to get music from the strings."

I understood him a little though not wholly, and was comforted, leaning there out of the grated window as Marguerite had leaned when she had communed with the gipsies, and thought their liberties and love lore better than the gilded palle of the Medici.

CHAPTER IV.
The Poets' Country.

We did not wait very long in Pisa.

The laughter of the Arno wakened its hollow echoes, and the Florentine pennon fluttered amongst its haunted ways for a brief space only. And whilst it was still springtime—late spring—we left its gates and went over the ghostly plain that had been soaked through and through with the blood of so many centuries of warfare, and so back into the Val di Greve and between the mountains along Arno's side.

Only to one place was he always constant amidst his inconstancy; wander away from it perpetually as he would, no less surely would he ever again come back to where the Vecchio battlements were set sharp as lion's teeth against the sky.

He would always come back thither; and Saint John's Day, and the Beffana, and the Pasquâ, and the Berlingancio, and the Ceppò, and the Capo d'Anno, and the Anna feast, when the flags of the Trades were set round the church, and all the other *giorni festivi* that are as many as the golden eyes in a child's string of daisies, would have been robbed of much mirth and life to the populace of Florence, if they had failed to bring through the gates Pascarèl.

All that lovely May time we were afoot through Tuscany.

Is there anything in all the world so beautiful as the springtide greenery of Italy?

The gold of her sunsets, the wonder of her orange groves, the rose of her evening skies, the grandeur of her sterile mountains, on these and on their like words of adoration have been lavished by the million; but who has stayed to bethink themselves of her homelier and humbler charms?

And yet, of these also, she has so many—so many.

Come out here in the young months of summer and leave, as we left, the highways that grim walls fence in, and stray, as we strayed, through the field-paths and the bridle-roads in the steps of the contadini, and you will find this green world about your feet touched with the May-day suns to tenderest and most lavish wealth of nature.

The green corn uncurling underneath the blossoming vines. The vine foliage that tosses and climbs and coils in league on league of verdure. The breast-high grasses full of gold and red and purple from the countless flowers growing with it.

The millet filled with crimson gladioli and great scarlet poppies. The hill-sides that look a sheet of rose-colour where the lupinelli are in bloom. The tall plumes of the canes, new born, by the side of every stream and rivulet.

The sheaves of arum leaves that thrust themselves out from every joint of masonry or spout of broken fountain. The flame of roses that burns on every handsbreadth of untilled ground and springs like a rainbow above the cloud of every darkling roof or wall. The ocean spray of arbutus and acacia shedding its snow against the cypress darkness. The sea-green of the young ilex leaves scattered like light over the bronze and purple of the older growth. The dreamy blue of the iris lilies rising underneath the olives and along the edges of the fields.

The soft, pretty, quiet pictures where mowers sweep down with their scythes the reedy grasses on the river banks; where the gates of the villas stand wide open with the sun aslant upon the grassy paths beneath the vines; where in the gloom of the house archways the women sit plaiting their straw, the broad shining fields before them all alive with the song of the grilli; where the grey savage walls of a fortress tower on the spur of the mountains, above the delicate green of young oaks and the wind-stirred fans of the fig-trees; where the frate, in broad-leaved hat of straw, brushes with bare sandalled feet through the bright acanthus, beaming a Rabelaisian smile on the contadina who goes by him with her brown water-jar upon her head: where deep in that fresh, glad tumult of leaf and blossom and bough the children and the goats lie together, while the wild thyme and the trefoil are in flower, and the little dog-rose is white amongst the maize; where the sharp beak of the galley-like boats cuts dark against the yellow current, and the great filmy square nets are cast outward where the poplar shadows tremble in the stream; all these, and a thousand like them, are yours in the sweet May season amongst the Tuscan hills and vines.

The earth can be no greener even away yonder in the pine valleys of the Alps; and for the air,— what air can be like this that wanders from Adriatic to Mediterranean across a land of flowers bearing lightly on its every breath and breeze the burden of love songs, the sighs of nightingales, the odours of budding fruits, the warmth of amorous suns?

Poets of every nation have celebrated the great and the gorgeous scenery of this land that is the native land of every artist; its magnificence of outline, its riot of hue on sky and earth, its voluptuous delights and violet seas, its classic ruins, and its dryad-haunted groves; these have been over-painted and over-hymned till half the world is weary; but of its sweet, lowly, simple loveliness that lies broadcast on every hillside and under every olive orchard, amongst the iris lilies in the meadows, and along the loose lush grasses where the sleepy oxen slowly tread their fragrant path—of these, I say, not one in a thousand wanderers thinks, perhaps not one in ten thousand even knows.

All that time we wandered about according to our whim and will, from the blue waters of Spezzia to the green fields of the Casentino, and from the spires of Milan to the shadows of St. Mark.

We never tarried long in any place; the true nomadic temper was in Pascarèl.

The flag of our wooden Arte seldom fluttered longer than two or three evenings under the same knot of chestnut trees, or on the same hillside. A certain restlessness always impelled its owner to frequent change and movement, and though he would lie and dream for hours together in the sun, he preferred that the sun when it rose should seldom find him in the same spot where it had shone on him at its last setting.

We went through all the historic country that the Apennines girdle with their broad belt of vine leaves and marble; the country of the poets that has heard their "sweet singing" through so many centuries, from the love-notes of Catullus to the death-sigh of Tasso.

Beneath Peschiera, that still "sits a fortress" as

in Dante's time, to denote the old Teutonic Tyrol ways.

On the stones of the sad City of the Lake, builded above the bones of that "cruel virgin" who wandered from far Thebes to lay her down to rest amidst the "thousand fountains."

Through the Reggio district at the mountains' foot where Boiardo had sung, and laughed, and loved, and fought his graceful life away.

By sad Ferrara, repenting in widowed loneliness the crimes of her lord of Este against the poet who dared to plead in the teeth of pride "per amor mio."

Far northward as Cremona, where the seeding grass and the wild barley grew above that dreadful ditch, once filled up with the bleeding and stifled peasants thrust into a living death that the knights might spur their horses in safety over the chasm whilst Carlo Malatesta's golden mantle fluttered in all the pride of war.

Southward within the sound of Santa Lucia's bell, in saintly Assisi, when the morning dews were wet on the ivy-grown bridge of the Clausura, and the linnets sang in the same old boughs that had sheltered the birds that once had chaunted their Easter litanies to S. Francis.

To strange San Leo, mighty watch-tower of nature, towering over the wide wild waste of up-tossed rocks and barren mountains.

Along the treacherous moonlit waters of the Pô, where the bridal barge had floated to the moat tower, whilst Lucrezia in her albernia of woven gold bent before her lord, and the torches glowed on the plumes of the Moorish dancers, and the Bacchides was played to the sound of Mantuan music.

On the high hills, once the eyrie of the Eagle of the Montefeltro, where Dante dwelt with the great Ghibelline chieftain, and the hazel eyes of the baby Sanzio opened to the light.

In the green gay country where merry-hearted Pulci strung together his "heaps of sonnets big as the clubs they make of cherry blossoms for May-day."

Amidst the Lombard fields and garden where Ariosto, "'twixt the April and the May" of his life, had loves as many and as roseate as pomegranate blossoms in a July noon.

By old Urbino, in whose gaunt silence the silvery echoes seemed to come of Raffael's laugh, and Tiziano's wooing, and Bembo's wit, and the voices of Vittoria and Veronica, and the applause of that gay and gracious court as it listened to the cantos of the "Furioso" and the pages of Il Cortegiano, in the mosaic-chamber, whilst the sea-winds blew over Monte Carpegna, and the stars rose above the iron-stone of Nero's mountain.

"If I had been any famous personage at all, I think I should have chosen to be Boiardo," said he one day as we sat under the shadow of a fig-tree in a little village of the plains, whilst the white oxen trod slowly under the blossoming vines, and the shallow threads of water were all blue with hyacinth and iris.

"Boiardo's life," said he, "must have been worth the living from first to last in that pleasant and thrice-famous Reggio country, green with the vines as this is. A beautiful life—bold, free, gracious, loving, and well loved; a life full of the deeds of a soldier and the dreams of a poet, a life made sweet and fresh by the open air, heightened by passion and battle, but chiefly absorbed in the ideal, for did he not set the bells of Scandiano all a-ringing until the people all thought a new saint had been canonised, when it was only his joy at having found a fit name for his hero? Boiardo was to be envied, I admit: much maybe for having begun the 'Orlando,' but much more for having his name pass into a proverb for a fair fortune. 'Heaven send Boiardo to your house!' So the country folk of all the Reggio district say still when they wish you well. How a man must have been adored by his countryside to be transmitted *so* down the stream of tradition!"

He spoke thus of Boiardo, nothing arrogating to himself; yet it was hardly less love that was won by him through all his birth country.

The fame of him was not indeed spread like that of the courtly rhymester of the "Orlando Innamorato" amidst nobles' palaces and in kings' circles, but there was not a lowly capanna betwixt the two seas that was not the lighter and the gladder for the fall of his footstep on its threshold, and not a peasant from Alp to Abruzzi that would not bring forth to honour his coming the last shred of the goat's flesh and the last drop of the rough red wine.

Money he had not to give them, but he gave them all the riches he had—mirth and music and goodwill, and a strong hand to part them in their quarrels, and a tender patience to aid them in their wants, and a sunny wit to beguile them in their sorrows.

There was, indeed, always that about him which

made one think of Ariosto and of Gabriello's lines on that great Lombard:—

"Credere uti posses natum felicibus horis
Felici fulgente astro Jovis atque Dionis."

At his coming the people trooped out from all their villages and towns in wildest welcome. The shout of "Pascarèl, il Pascarello!" from some shepherd in the fields or some lads playing pallone on the outskirts, brought the whole population of any place which he approached rushing helter-skelter towards him, running and singing before his footsteps, and almost fighting for the coveted honour of giving him shelter for the night.

He might have drunk a hundred stoups of wine, he might have kissed a hundred women, he might have supped at a hundred tables within any gates he entered.

The poorest hamlet got together some little show of riches in his honour, and the best of everything, if poor that best might be, was dragged forth and spread out in delighted homage before him under the fig-trees or the cork-trees in the mellow evening light.

I grew to understand how and why he was so happy with his life, and how and why he would have been loth to leave it for any other. There were in it such perfect liberty, such continual change; and what touched him most, I think, so great a love for him everywhere.

It was perhaps only a sunshiny form of selfishness, the laughing and indolent life that this man of fine powers and of fine culture led from village to village over the face of his native land.

Yet it had a great influence over me that purified and ennobled my faults and my follies, and I think it had often the same over the populace amongst whom he dwelt.

For once in a hamlet on the plains, when cholera raged, I saw Pascarèl welcomed as though he had been an angel who had brought them healing on his wings; and once in a turbulent street riot in Vicenza, he controlled a furious and death-dealing mob with the mere charm of perfect courage and trick of timely and skilful wit.

I think the earnestness that lies in the Italian character is altogether overlooked.

Its indolence, its gaiety, its love of pleasure, lie on the surface, and are steadily measured; but the depths of it are graver—very grave indeed—grave even to a profound melancholy.

The Italian character is made up of contrasts, more strongly marked and vividly opposed than that of any other nation; and these contrasts are welded not seldom into as perfect harmony as is possible to human nature; for an Italian is melodious even in his discord, and is symmetrical even in his contrariety.

See the country in a time of flood, of pestilence, of fire—she is heroic, and the woe of one is the woe of all, with an unanimity of action and a strength of emotion that can alone arise out of a national character at once tender and full of force. Northern nations have nothing, for example, comparable for self-sacrifice to the Misericordia. For consolidation, for devotion to duty, for all the deepest and purest forms of charity, the Order has no equal in Europe.

Where else will you see, as you can see all through

Tuscany, the nobleman leaving his masked ball, the lover his mistress, the craftsman his labour, the foeman his vengeance, to go at the sound of the tocsin, and aid the poor and the sick and the dying?

Superficial commentators wonder that the disciples of Savonarola could come from the same people as the debauchees of the Decamerone, but the wonder is very idle.

A passionate sadness underlies in silence the gay and amorous temperament of the Italian; and not only in metaphor, but in fact, will the hair shirt of a silent sorrow be worn by him under the ribboned domino that he carries so airily in his life of intrigue.

No one will ever see it except one woman out of his many loves who is near enough to him to touch his heart as well as stir his passions;—no one else will ever see it, but there it is—and his sword is there too.

This earnestness was in Pascarèl beneath all the vivacity and lightness of his temperament; and it produced in him that mingled strength and tenderness which endeared him to the people.

Often when we have been in the city he has left my side as we laughed at some winestall in the market or played dominoes before some sunshiny trattoria, and has vanished in obedience to the bell of the Misericordia.

Often when we have gone through some village in which pestilence was raging, or where some sudden flood of water had washed away the little wealth of the contadini, he has taken his place by the sick beds or beside the bereaved and homeless peasantry, with a skilful gentleness and brotherliness that was more balm to the sufferer than herbs or gold.

I think that his laughter was all the richer over the cards and the wines in the little vine-hung loggia of the bettolini, because his eyes were dim many a time over a suffering and penniless stranger who would have died unaided and unshriven but for the pity of the player of the Arte. And I am sure that the salterello and the stornello were all the gayer and the sweeter on his mandoline, because he could touch the strings of it into melody that would soothe the death-bed of a child with visions of the angels.

CHAPTER V.
Fumo di Gloria.

THIS wandering life was to me perfect. I wished for nothing better than all that laughter at the wine fairs; than all that merriment at the village festivals; than all those stories told in the great threshing barns; than all that gay chit-chat with the women laying their straw to bleach on the shores, or the men spreading their river nets where the leaves thrilled in the wind; it was all perfect to me, as it would have been to any other creature young and of healthy body, and a soul not spoiled by the world and its ways.

And as for the people;—the dear people!—the more I dwelt amongst them the more I loved them. There is no other people on the face of the earth so entirely loveable even with their many faults as the Italians. But what is known of them by other nations?—hardly anything at all.

That the Italian patrician may be little understood outside the pale of his own immediate associates, it is not difficult to conceive. His confidence is rarely bestowed: and the pride which fences him in is at once the most delicate and the most impenetrable that a man can place betwixt himself and the outer world.

But it is passing strange that the Italian popolano, open to whosoever will to study him at their leisure, the Italian of the people, as seen in his streets and fields, by his hearth, and his market stall, is as little understood and as invariably misrepresented.

French vivacity and ease have passed into a proverb; yet, in reality, the French people are studied and conscious compared to the Italian, who is the most absolutely unstudied and unself-conscious of all God's creatures.

True, the Italian, even in the lowest strata of social life, has a repose and a dignity in him which befit his physiognomy and evince themselves in his calm and poetical attitudes. See a stone-breaker, or a mason, or a boatman asleep in the noonday sun, and you will surely see attitudes which no sculptor could wish bettered for his marble.

True, too, you will do ill to make a mock of him; high or low, it is the one unpardonable sin which no Italian will pardon; he is given also to the immoveable obstinacy of that animal which he will never name save under the delicate euphuism of "the little black gentleman;" and he has a lightning-like passion in him which may smite his neighbour to the earth in a trice about a cherry-stone, or a broken broom, or any other *casus belli* of the hour.

But, then, lo! how bright he is, how gregarious, how neighbourly, how instant and graceful in courtesy, how eager and kindly in willingness; how poetic his glee in song and dance, and holy day and pageant; how absolute his content upon the most meagre fare that ever held body and soul together; how certain his invariable selection of a pleasure for the eye and the ear rather than one for the mouth and the stomach.

See the gay, elastic grace of him; the mirth that ripples all day long about him like the sunlight, the laughter that shows his white teeth, the tumultuous shouts in which his lungs delight, the cheery sociability that brings him with a knot of his own kind at the street corners and under the house archways to talk the hours away with tireless tongue and shrewdest wit, and say, is there a creature kindlier or more mirthful anywhere in the width of the world?

And he will always have some delicate touch of the artist in him too, and always some fine instinct of the gentleman—let him be poor as he will, ill clad, half-starved, and ignorant even of the letters that make his name, let him feel the summer dust with bare feet, and the mountain wind through a ragged shirt, nay, let him be the veriest scamp and sinner in the world —but he will wear his tatters with a grace; he will bring a flower to a woman with the bow of a king; and he will resent an insolence with an air to which no purples and fine linen could lend dignity.

With the people I was happy all through that sweet season of the spring and the summer; and to pleasure Pascarèl, there was nothing they would not do to smooth the hardness of their modes of life to the donzella.

Not that such hardships counted for much with me.

From my infancy I had known what hunger meant to the full as well as any beggar child, and my years in old Verona had been bare of all save the sternest necessities of existence.

Pascarèl was true to his word.

It was always well with me. I never saw or heard anything that dear old dead Mariuccia would have deemed unfit for me had she been living then to shield me. Full of mirth indeed we were; mirth, endless and unstrained, babbling like a brook amongst the flowers and weeds of daily acts and words; but amongst it all there was not so much as a coarse word which could have harmed me; and when we were with the populace, who were apt to be coarse enough themselves in their jests and songs, Brunótta, at a sign from him, would slide her hand in mine and draw me gently away up to some little attic in the roof, or aside under some leafy pergola, and keep me there talking, always, as my habit was, of the miracles and the perfections of the life and ways of Pascarèl.

I was always to her the donzella; she was always a little shy with me and a little humble.

"Tanta bellina, tanta bellina!" she would murmur often, looking at me with a soft puzzled wistfulness in her bird-like eyes: and all that I could do availed nothing to induce her to set herself upon an equality with me. Day by day, instead of growing more familiar with me, she seemed to feel the difference that was between us with a clearer perception, and treated me with a wondering homage, of which my natural vanity was well contented to avail itself.

Nothing in the way of worship came much amiss to me at that time.

I had ceased to be troubled about the tinker's pot; I was consoled by the memories of the great race whence he came.

I had got in my mind a little picture of him as he must needs have been in those days: a slender, lithe brown child with beautiful eyes; full of mischief and of tenderness; of odd fancies and of loyal impulses; running along the white sun-baked roads of his beloved country with a little clattering burden of kettles, and flagons, and stewpans slung behind his shoulders.

And his father, too; I pictured him also, a man of much humour, as he said, telling strange, marvellous stories as he sat in the dust of the wayside tinkering his pots; a man who never could utterly forget that his people in old remote times had been great in the land, and who was always a little grave, with a little touch of the old arrogance, though a good kindly soul and a boon companion when the wine went round after the village games.

For those vanished grandeurs and powers of his race, which were almost mythical to him, Pascarèl himself never once cast a sigh down the wind. What his father had told him in childhood many an evening sitting under a wayside crucifix mending the copper pots and pans of the countryfolk might be true or might not.

The perished nobility of his forefathers woke no envy from him.

"It had been certainly a great race once; yes," he was wont to say, while half sceptical of the fact himself, "at least, so my father would have it; and Malespini, if that old liar may be believed about anything, which is doubtful. Traces of it crop up here and there in quaint old places; here a tomb, there a fortress, here a bronze knight that the children aim at in their games; there a manuscript, that some old monk unearths from his chapter rolls for want of something to do.

"Oh, I believe it was all true enough.

"There were mighty Pascarèlli in the olden days. But I am very glad that I was not of them; except, indeed, that I should have liked to strike a blow or two for Guido Calvacanti and have hindered the merry-making of those precious rascals who sent him out to die of the marsh fever.

"Great?

"No; certainly I would not be great. To be a great man is endlessly to crave something that you have not; to kiss the hands of monarchs and lick the feet of peoples. To be great? Who was ever more great than Dante, and what was his experience?—the bitterness of begged bread, and the steepness of palace stairs.

"Besides, given the genius to deserve it, the upshot of a life spent for greatness is absolutely uncertain. Look at Machiavelli.

"After having laid infallible rules for social and public success with such unapproachable astuteness that his name has become a synonym for unerring policy, Machiavelli passed his existence in obedience and submission to Rome, to Florence, to Charles, to Cosmo, to Leo, to Clement.

"He was born into a time favourable beyond every other to sudden changes of fortune—a time in which any fearless audacity might easily become the stepping-stone to a supreme authority; and yet Machiavelli, whom the world still holds as its ablest statesman—in principle—never, in practice rose above the level of a servant of civil and papal tyrannies, and, when his end came, died in obscurity and almost in penury.

"Theoretically, Machiavelli could rule the universe; but practically he never attained to anything finer than a more or less advantageous change of masters. To reign doctrinally may be all very well, but when it only results in serving actually, it seems very much better to be obscure and content without any trouble.

' Fumo di gloria non vale fumo di pipa."

"I, for one, at any rate, am thoroughly convinced of that truth of truths."

I hearkened to him sorrowful; for to my ignorant eyes the witch candle of fame seemed a pure and perfect planet; and I felt that the planet might have ruled his horoscope had he chosen.

"Is there no glory at all worth having, then?" I murmured.

He stretched himself where he rested amongst the arum-whitened grass, and took his cigaretto from his mouth:

"Well, there is one, perhaps. But it is to be had about once in five centuries.

"You know Or San Michele? It would have been a world's wonder had it stood alone, and not been companioned with such wondrous rivals that its own exceeding beauty scarce ever receives full justice.

"Where the jaspèr of Giotto and the marble of Brunelleschi, where the bronze of Ghiberti and the granite of Arnolfo rise everywhere in the sunlit air to challenge vision and adoration, Or San Michele fails of its full meed from men. Yet, perchance, in all the width of Florence there is not a nobler thing.

"It is like some massive casket of silver oxydised by time; such a casket as might have been made to hold the Tables of the Law by men to whose faith Sinai was a holy and imperishable truth.

"I know nothing of the rule or phrase of Architecture, but it seems to me surely that that square set strength, as of a fortress, towering against the clouds, and catching the last light always on its fretted parapet, and everywhere embossed and enriched with foliage, and tracery, and the figures of saints, and the shadows of vast arches, and the light of niches gold-starred and filled with divine forms, is a gift so perfect to the whole world, that, passing it, one should need say a prayer for great Taddeo's soul.

"Surely, nowhere is the rugged, changeless, mountain force of hewn stone piled against the sky, and the luxuriant, dreamlike, poetic delicacy of stone carven and shaped into leafage and loveliness more perfectly blended and made one than where Or San Michele rises out of the dim, many-coloured, twisting streets, in its mass of ebon darkness and of silvery light.

"Well, the other day, under the walls of it I stood, and looked at its Saint George where he leans upon his shield, so calm, so young, with his bared head and his quiet eyes.

"'That is our Donatello's,' said a Florentine beside me—a man of the people, who drove a horse for hire in the public ways, and who paused, cracking his whip, to tell this tale to me. 'Donatello did that, and it killed him. Do you not know? When he had done that Saint George, he showed it to his master. And the master said, "It wants one thing only." Now this saying our Donatello took gravely to heart, chiefly of all because his master would never explain where the fault lay; and so much did it hurt him, that he fell ill of it, and came nigh to death. Then he called his master to him. "Dear and great one, do tell me before I die," he said, "what is the one thing my statue lacks." The master smiled, and said, "Only—speech."

"Then I die happy," said our Donatello. And he—died—indeed, that hour.'

"Now, I cannot say that the pretty story is true; it is not in the least true; Donato died when he was eighty-three, in the Street of the Melon; and it was he himself who cried, 'Speak then—speak!' to his statue, as it was carried through the city. But whether true or false the tale, this fact is surely true, that it is well—nobly and purely well—with a people when the men amongst it who ply for hire on its public ways think caressingly of a sculptor dead five hundred years ago, and tell such a tale standing idly in the noonday sun, feeling the beauty and the pathos of it all.

"'Our Donatello' still to the people of Florence. 'Our own little Donato' still, our pet and pride, even as though he were living and working in their midst to-day, here in the shadows of the Stocking-maker's Street, where his Saint George keeps watch and ward.

"'Our little Donato' still, though dead so many hundred years ago.

"That is glory, if you will. And something more beautiful than any glory—Love."

He was silent a long while, gathering lazily with his left hand the arum lilies to bind them together for me.

Perhaps the wish for the moment passed over him that he had chosen to set his life up in stone, like to Donato's, in the face of Florence, rather than to weave its light and tangled skein out from the breaths of the wandering winds and the sands of the shifting shore.

END OF VOL. I.

www.ingramcontent.com/pod-product-compliance
Lightning Source LLC
Chambersburg PA
CBHW030733230426
43667CB00007B/697